Praise for *Game Wars*

"A colorful, action-packed account of three elaborate U.S. Fish and Wildlife Service undercover operations. There are stories of undercover stings, massive corruption and wild drives across the country."

—*Publishers Weekly*

"*Game Wars* points out the extent to which poaching menaces what wildlife we have left. It is something to be grateful for that the marshes of Louisiana still exist. A reader can feel grateful that a writer of Reisner's abilities found them before they were gone."

—*The Washington Post*

"A compelling account of wildlife killing in America, seen through the lens and heard through the tape recorders of dedicated undercover wildlife cops and turncoat poachers."

—*The Animals' Agenda*

"Reisner is a first-rate environmental journalist; his account of Hall's exploits is as thrilling as any movie chase scene—and infinitely more satisfying on those rare occasions when the hero wins."

—*Outside*

"Funny, fascinating and chilling—and it has a wonderful protagonist in Hall, a fearless game warden with strong opinions. An insightful look at a rare breed of cop and the crimes against nature he is trying to halt."

—*The Philadelphia Inquirer*

"Like *Cadillac Desert, Game Wars* is a splendid and frightening work. It has the additional advantage of reading like a first-rate detective novel. Reisner has a strong place in the upper echelon of those defending the environment with conscience, intelligence and energy."

—Jim Harrison

"An ecological morality tale with as much action and drama as a good thriller. An exciting narrative of intricate intrigues . . . filled with quick wit and hilarious character sketches. The book can be read as a true-life adventure tale."

—*Chicago Sun-Times*

PENGUIN BOOKS

GAME WARS

Marc Reisner is the author of *Cadillac Desert*, which was nominated for a National Book Critics Award in 1986. For many years a staff writer at the Natural Resources Defense Council, he lives in San Francisco with his wife and daughter.

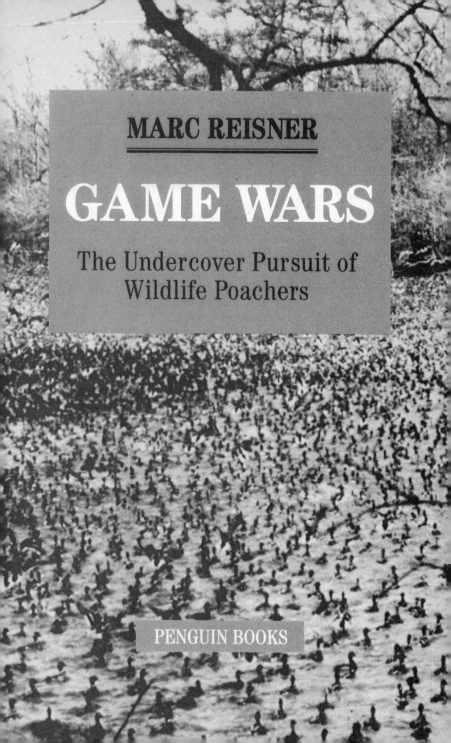

MARC REISNER

GAME WARS

The Undercover Pursuit of Wildlife Poachers

PENGUIN BOOKS

PENGUIN BOOKS
Published by the Penguin Group
Viking Penguin, a division of Penguin Books USA Inc.,
375 Hudson Street, New York, New York 10014, U.S.A.
Penguin Books Ltd, 27 Wrights Lane,
London W8 5TZ, England
Penguin Books Australia Ltd, Ringwood,
Victoria, Australia
Penguin Books Canada Ltd, 10 Alcorn Avenue, Suite 300,
Toronto, Ontario, Canada M4V 3B2
Penguin Books (N.Z.) Ltd, 182–190 Wairau Road,
Auckland 10, New Zealand

Penguin Books Ltd, Registered Offices:
Harmondsworth, Middlesex, England

First published in the United States of America by
Viking Penguin, a division of
Penguin Books USA Inc., 1991
Published in Penguin Books 1992

1 3 5 7 9 10 8 6 4 2

Author's Note:
Real names have been used throughout this book, with the following exceptions where
the names and identifying attributes are fictitious: Wayne Gans, Moses Feingold, Junior
Feingold, Donald Clayton, Dellard Watney, and John Haase. A few place names and loca-
tions have also been altered in order to protect the personal safety and legal rights of
certain individuals. Otherwise, all the characters are real and all the events described
are, to the best of my knowledge, true.

Photograph on pages iv-v of George Wilcox Lake,
near Stuttgart, Arkansas, circa 1934.

THE LIBRARY OF CONGRESS HAS CATALOGUED THE HARDCOVER AS FOLLOWS:
Reisner, Marc.
Game wars: the adventures of an undercover wildlife agent / Marc
Reisner.
ISBN 0-670-81486-5 (hc.)
ISBN 0 14 00.8768 0 (pbk.)
p. cm.
1. Hall, Dave. 2. Undercover wildlife agents—United States—
Biography. 3. U.S. Fish and Wildlife—Officials and employees—
Biography. 4. Wildlife conservation—United States. I. Title.
SK354.H33R45 1991
363.2'8—dc20 90–50517

Printed in the United States of America
Set in Century Book

For Lawrie and Ruthie

◆ ◆ ◆

Contents

Part I

ALLIGATORS

DAVE HALL'S office:

It's on the north shore of Lake Pontchartrain, in Slidell, Louisiana, a swamp cypress, longleaf pine, and tupelo gum forest that became a French trading post that became a lumber and fishing town that became a formless sprawl of warring hamburger joints and replicating mini-malls and metastasizing video outlets, interspersed with huge lots of unsold American cars. Car dealers, bank vice-presidents, sundry members of New Orleans' commuting upper-middle class live here, in brick split-level homes hidden amid monotonous second-growth pines. But driving through Slidell you see neither homes nor history, just a town that the consumer culture overran and, in the process of consuming, consumed.

Halfway down Gause Boulevard, the main drag, something out of place: a high chain-link fence enclosing ten acres of parking lots and buildings and a lawn with a pair of giant radar dishes off to the rear. The compound is NASA's. The radar dishes track missiles and satellites and keep them from knocking out Wichita Falls by mistake. The rear-most building, which looks like a giant-size house trailer built of cinder blocks, is leased to NASA's tenant, and that is where, from time to time, you can find Dave Hall.

Dave Hall's desk is in deep, hopeless disarray, as if it had snowed documents nonstop for several months. Stacks of cardboard filing boxes surround it on all sides, and these, too, are piled with great windblown drifts of file folders, clippings, and reports. Were it not for the pirogue and the crocodile skull, you'd guess the office belonged to some manic Labor Department statistician who finally went off the deep end. The skull gloats at you grinningly from atop a pine table at the back wall. It measures the length of an arm and the thickness of a linebacker's thigh and has a circumambient row of interlocking teeth the size of machine-gun shells. The pirogue, mounted on a gimballed frame, is off to one side of the room and reaches nearly from wall to wall. It was hollowed out of a single cypress log, long ago—for the great cypresses of the old South are gone—and probably belonged to some Cajun market hunter who used it to carry wild ducks or furs to the French markets at New Orleans.

Next to the table displaying the crocodile skull is a floor-to-ceiling bookcase that appears to be shedding books, as a dam spills floodwaters during a storm. *Endangered Species Recovery Plans*—multiple volumes in multicolored binders. *Code of Federal Regulations*—many volumes also. *Special Agent Basic School. Chesapeake Bay Submerged Vegetation. Defense Strategies in Undercover Operations.* The bookshelf is adorned with a sculpture made of antique fishing lures, the kind that look like weird winged mice or giant Pleistocene grubs and would scare the daylights out of anything but a barracuda or trophy bass. Next to Dave Hall's swivel chair is a massive accordion-style briefcase made of elephant hide. Duck decoys occupy every available space. Videocassettes lie around in piles. A tape recorder sits by the telephone, and another—a five-thousand-dollar, Swedish-made Nagra miniature stereo recorder commonly used in espionage work—peeps out of a half-open drawer. (I once asked Dave Hall why a Nagra recorder costs so much, and he said it can pick up a buzzing gnat from fifteen feet away, with enough audio-integrity to let you know it wasn't a fly.) Hanging on a wall is a blown-up photograph of a group of market hunters earlier in the century, standing in front of hundreds, perhaps thousands, of fresh-killed ducks hanging from racks. There are diplomas (B.S. and M.S. in wildlife biology from Mississippi State) and framed citations everywhere. A bottle of Joe Dugas's Miracle Remedy for Mangy Dogs, Sore Heads on Chickens, or Animals of Any Kind. An assortment of wooden duck and goose callers. A songbird trap. A certificate of honor from the

World Championship Goose-Calling Contest. The skin of a python about eighteen feet long. Audubon prints of birds. A wolverine pelt. More skulls—a nutria, perhaps, and a duck. In a desk drawer, a small silver snub-nosed .38. A shotgun in a gun case.

Who is this guy?

He is Charles Strickland, alligator poacher, alligator and reptile tanner, and all-purpose journeyman hoodlum.

He is Dave Hayes, a small-time New Orleans gangster with an apartment in the French Quarter and an oil-leasing business that launders a lucrative sideline in illegal furs, ivory, scrimshaw, marijuana, and cocaine.

He is Big Jim Pridgen, a Mississippi good old boy who runs a catering business specializing in illegal wild game—ducks, geese, sacalait, redfish, deer, your choice—out of a knotty-pine restaurant and no-tell motel in the red-light row south of Jackson. Big Jim has no permanent address or even a telephone because he's on the lam from a fang-toothed wife and has a gaggle of detectives and lawyers chasing him through four southern states.

And then, some of the time, he is Dave Hall, an absent father and husband with a nice cypress ranch house on a bayou of the Pearl River near Slidell.

But not much of the time.

For the better part of the past twenty-six years, he has lived his life on the road—in Acadian Louisiana, backwater Carolina, Alaska, Tennessee, Mexico, Mississippi, Arkansas, Florida, Kentucky, California. You could have found him in Seattle or Klamath Glen or Talkeetna or Larto Lake or Nogales or Nome, drinking in roadhouses and staying in motels, inhabiting a netherworld of booze, crank, tobacco haze, and spectral crime.

Or you could have found him hiding in a bayou or on a Brooklyn wharf, at two or three in the morning, with two concealed firearms on his person and a military-issue night scope.

He has infiltrated, undercover, alone, gangs of good old boy outlaws in the rural South who had the sheriffs and D.A.s working for them.

He was the first nonmember ever invited inside the secret chalet of the Brothers, the Alaskan branch of the Hell's Angels, who keep the skulls of their murdered enemies on display (and he certainly would have qualified as one of *them*).

He once walked in the front door of a New York gangster's home after the gangster—who had two armed Mexicans prominently on display—had told him he had detection equipment as good as you'd find at the White House, and if he was bugged he would be killed. He was bugged.

Who *is* this guy?

He was named Louisiana Conservationist of the Year in 1978.

He was named Louisiana Conservationist of the Year again in 1981, the first time anyone had won the title twice.

He won the Chevron National Conservation Award in 1987.

He won the National Wildlife Federation's Special Achievement Award in 1988. No one like him had ever won it before.

He was cited by the attorney general for the southern District of New York for performing "some of the most brilliant undercover detective work I have ever seen."

All of which is quite enough to feather anyone's cap, especially when all you are is a game warden.

To get to Jennings, Louisiana, you head out Airline Highway, past the scurvyish day-rate motels where Brother Jimmy Swaggart indulged his fascination with the female anatomy, until you pass the New Orleans Airport and U.S. 61—and the parallel Interstate 10, if you care to drive it—both rise up on concrete trestles and let you skim across the largest stretch of drowned land in the coterminous U.S.A. Two centuries ago, or less, Jennings would have been fifteen days, at least, from New Orleans. Since the route was more or less underwater, the way to go was in a boat (a semiportable boat like a pirogue). The pirogue was to uncivilized Louisiana what the horse was to the unplowed plains, the only means of locomotion that made sense. Even so, to go from New Orleans to Jennings was to endure a torture-training course. You would have had to shoulder your way against the Mississippi's languorous but insistent current for about a hundred miles until you reached Bayou Plaquemine, which connects the Mississippi with its sometime escape channel, the Atchafalaya. In those days, Bayou Plaquemine was navigable only three or four months of the year, when the Mississippi was running high and spilling its overflow into the Atchafalaya. Even though its gradient was only inches per mile, Bayou Plaquemine was a snarl of logjams and a disaster course of cutbanks, and with the engorged Mississippi worrying the current south you were in for a ride. Early sketches of the Atchafalaya and Bayou Plaquemine show small steamboats half keeled over or spinning around in whirlpools as bug-eyed passengers caterwaul on the decks.

When you reached the Atchafalaya basin itself, you had twenty miles of drowned bottomland forest to cross. Much of the time there was no dry land at all—none. The giant oaks and cypresses rocketed up to a hundred fifty, a hundred eighty feet. The place was filled with skulking alligators and black bears. Very early reports tell of huge spotted cats that almost *have* to have been jaguars, but we leveled this vast cathedral of gloom so fast we have no natural history on which we can rely. At noon it was dusk under a bright sun. Under cloud cover you had near-night. During a cloudburst, when the swamp drank the provenance of the sky and exhaled it as a hot asphyxiating vapor, and the mosquitoes and chiggers swarmed and multiplied, and the lightning flashes lit the morbid columns and crab-limbed branches of the encroaching trees, you wondered what on God's earth you were doing there. That you were there at all meant, almost assuredly, that you were a French-Acadian—a Cajun—because the Atchafalaya wilderness scared the rest of mankind to death.

After you managed to pick a route across the Atchafalaya's huge forested floodplain—*if* you managed, for a lot of people, even Cajuns, gave up in confusion or terror—you could stash your pirogue and go forth on foot along the modern route of Interstate 10, which pretty much demarcates the two types of Louisiana terrain—chronically wet and usually dry. But if you were a real Cajun and your boat was like your Siamese twin, you had to veer south, follow Grand Lake to the hurricane-haunted coast and paddle across West Blanche and Vermillion bays and then plow across twenty more miles of swamp to White Lake, which would lead you into the other Grand Lake (these are big lakes, fifteen miles across) and back north into Lake Arthur, at which point Jennings was a mere day's walk.

No early account of such a trip was ever published that does not dwell in excruciating detail on its miseries. Virgin Louisiana was much more difficult to cross than Nevada, where all you had to do was haul water along and keep from frying or freezing to death. Louisiana's most famous governor, Huey Long, was a thief, a charlatan, a tinhorn despot, a plunderer, a liar. But Huey built roads and drained swamps, and for this he is fondly remembered throughout the state.

Anyway. You make Jennings from New Orleans in four hours today, rising up on great trestles whenever you encounter a rimless swamp. For seemingly endless miles you are over shallow water. A northerner's first reaction is disbelief that such a vast piece of Louisiana is still so wet and uninhabitable. It isn't that no effort has been made to drain this place—to "reclaim and improve" it, as the introductory passages of billion-dollar federal appropriations bills always say. Louisiana has long been a nemesis and an endless opportunity for the Corps of Engineers, which has fought here a drowned-land version of the Bureau of Reclamation's holy war against western deserts. "It gives me great pleazhuh, Mister Chayh-man, to introduce Senate Bill 1466, the Bayou Chien-Boeuf-Black Drainage and Channelization Project. Mister Chayh-man, as the members of this great, most *ven*-erable, most distinguished body know, the people of Louisiana have been tyrannized—I say *des*-potized—by nate-tshuh from the moment our earliest ancestors settled our glorious but overflowing state. . . ." Buoyed by a hundred years of appropriations that have run into the many billions of dollars in modern money—for Louisiana alone—the Corps of Engineers has come at these marshes with draglines and dredges, with battalions and regiments of scrapers, skidders, and Caterpillar tractors; it has built up thousands of miles of serpentine levees along the Mississippi and Atchafalaya and the larger bayous, levees so massive that each linear inch may outweigh an elephant; it has sliced channels, rip-rapped banks, straightened bayous and creeks, and built huge dams upriver that have robbed the Mississippi Delta of its land-nourishing, Gulf-repelling silt (the bottom third of the state is built of sediment from the Middle West). But the

Corps has four hundred million annual acre-feet of runoff on its hands, and hurricanes that can dump twenty inches of rain in a day, and land so level those twenty inches may take a month to run off to sea, so the Corps's success has been limited—enough so, anyway, to let Dave Hall feel a rare measure of satisfaction. "This part of the state wasn't designed for humans to inhabit," he once fussed to me. "The only type of civilization that makes sense here is a floating civilization, like the early Cajuns had. Do anything else and you're ruining an unbelievable resource. I mean, we've gone to all this damned trouble to create a bunch of dry acreage for sugarcane and rice, and soybeans. Who the hell decided that soybeans are worth more than waterfowl?"

This particular trip—an impromptu, frantic, four-hundred-mile side excursion to Jennings and back—was chapter-and-verse Dave Hall. It was March of 1985. I had called him a few days earlier, saying I planned to be in Florida and wanted to stop by on my way back home to California. "Come on down!" he said. Then he disappeared. When I called again on the day I was to leave, I was told he was "in the field." That meant he was anywhere from the Mississippi Delta to the middle of Alaska. Often, when Dave Hall is in the field, no one has any idea where he is for several days, and during his intense undercover years, the possibility existed that wherever he was, he was dead. I left my flight information with his secretary and landed in New Orleans at seven in the evening. It was pouring, of course. When the pilot reversed the engines, sheets of spray went skyward, a waterfall in reverse.

I called Dave Hall's home.

"He wants you to meet him at the Lacassine Wildlife Refuge at eight o'clock tomorrow," said his son.

"A.M. or P.M.?"

"In the morning."

"Where's the Lacassine Wildlife Refuge?"

"It's over by Jennings."

"What state is Jennings in?"

"Louisiana."

"How far is Jennings from New Orleans?"

"About two hundred miles. It's right off the Interstate. He says to stay at the Holiday Inn."

I made the Holiday Inn by two in the morning. Dave Hall's dark blue Ford LTD, with its fat police tires and oversized exhaust, was parked outside.

"How long has he been here?" I asked the night clerk.

"About twenty minutes," he said,

He was already asleep.

I awoke about six. I stepped outside my door just as the sun hit the Florida coast. The eastern horizon was a thin band of purplish pink, fading quickly to black. Dave Hall was already up and out. He was standing on the parking lot, binoculars in hand, watching a low-flying wedge of geese beautifully silhouetted against the widening margin of light.

"Ho!" he said. "We got speckle-bellies moving out."

I hadn't seen him in months, but we might as well have had cocktails the night before. Dave Hall hasn't much use for hellos and goodbyes, and zero tolerance for small talk.

"Moving out where? To feed? Or . . . *back* from the fields?"

"They may be moving out for good, back to Canada."

"How do you know they're migrating back?"

"When you've watched geese as long as I have, you can sort of read their minds. Let's get some breakfast."

"How can you tell they're white-fronted geese?"

"That isn't hard. Speckle-bellies are darker than snow geese. We hardly have any Canada geese left—they're either hunted out or they're ending their migration farther north. But mainly you tell them apart by their call."

"What am I doing here in Jennings, Dave?"

"You told me you wanted to meet some Cajun outlaws. I'm gonna introduce you to a legend. One of the toughest bastards I ever ran into. The state game wardens chased him right into a swamp once and he hid out for about six months. Dove right out of his truck. He hid under some floating marsh mats for about two days while they turned that place upside down."

"What's his name?"

"A. J. Caro. Old A.J.'s killed as many alligators illegally as you've drunk cups of coffee."

Like much superb waterfowl habitat, the Lacassine National Wildlife Refuge is scenically nothing much. The landscape around it is unrelievedly flat and nearly devoid of trees. On cold March mornings, and this was one, there is often a viscous, cloying mist, which brings to mind a very dank and wet Kansas or an even gloomier Egdon Heath. Wherever swamps have been drained and turned into farmland in southern Louisiana, you see mostly sugarcane, cow pastures, or rice. As far as waterfowl are concerned, a sugarcane field is of almost no value. A pasture is of some worth to geese, which eat grass. Rice fields, however, aren't a bad swap—they are gleaned by both geese and ducks. Mechanical rice harvesters are inefficient at their work, and there is usually quite some edible residue left for the birds to eat when they migrate down. In fact, if it weren't for meals of rice scrounged in neighboring farm fields, the Lacassine Refuge could not begin to support the numbers of waterfowl that winter there.

"That there is really nothing," said Dave Hall, "compared to what we used to have here."

It took me a moment to see what he was referring to. Clustered in the middle of a field we were passing, just beyond rifle range, were four or five thousand geese. Four or five *thousand* geese. The density of birds—a thousand on a tennis court was a passable guess—was such as I had never seen. Most were blue-snow geese, which summer above the Arctic Circle on giant islands in the Beaufort Sea, some of the last real land before permanent ice cover begins—and here they were, huddled defiantly in their last little winter redoubt, a rice field on the edge of a wildlife refuge.

As we came closer to the Lacassine Refuge, we saw more flocks, as if we had been driving through suburbs and outer boroughs until we finally reached some teeming outdoor metropolis peopled by geese. They were everywhere. We saw them sweep off the ground in the far distance, great circling gyres of geese, dust devils of geese; they always flew in spirals as they rose, chorusing wildly, until some leader's cry or some mass consensus brought them back down to earth. Geese often mate for life, but how a goose could remain with its mate in such an aerial maelstrom was beyond me. As if to confirm such doubts, a lone goose suddenly flapped right over the car, low enough so we could watch it turn its head anxiously from left to right. Dave Hall's former boss, a legendary game warden named Willie J. Parker, once watched a pair of Canada geese flying over the Ohio River when a hunter shot one dead. The goose plummeted into shallow water, right by the riverbank, and was followed down by its mate, which circled it disconsolately. The goose got its bill under its dying mate and managed to push it a few feet up the bank. It stayed with its mate for some time, then took to the air, flying back and forth over the dead goose, clamoring into the night.

A pair of geese make a racket. A few thousand geese make a very loud racket. We pulled over, rolled down the windows, and the cacophony was electrifying. The landscape was boringly flat—a bleak panorama of lone trees and marshes and stubbly fields—but the geese in their numbers made it mesmerizingly wild. There were ducks, too, hundreds of them, swimming and dabbling in the irrigation canals. Most were pintails, which are beautiful, elegant ducks; the males have a long pointed tail and a mottled feather pattern like walnut burl. But they were reduced to nonentity status by the crowds of shrieking, braying geese.

Dave Hall began to drive again. He was hunched forward, steering with his elbow, peering through the upper windshield at a swarm of geese that had just funneled like smoke out of a nearby field. Then he was driving with a pair of binoculars trained on the geese. "More speckle-bellies," he said. "We got quite a few this year."

"Dave, do you still hunt geese?"

"Yup."

"Do you eat them?"

"Sure."

"Is a white-fronted goose good to eat?"

"It's the best. A speckle-belly tastes like a great big pintail."

"You love waterfowl more than anything in the out-of-doors."

"Sure. That's right. I am a duck and goose freak."

"But you eat them."

"Sure I do."

"Isn't it like eating your kids?"

"What do *you* eat?"

"Many animals are executed for my dining pleasure. I just have a hard time eating ducks and geese anymore."

"If it wasn't for waterfowl hunters, we'd hardly have any ducks *or* geese anymore. It's the users of the resource who have done the most to protect them. How many anti-hunters do you see buying up a couple million acres of Canadian marshland for nesting refuges? Does Ducks Unlimited do that, or do the Friends of Animals do that?"

"I've talked to some game wardens who won't hunt anymore. Or at least some have told me they won't hunt waterfowl until the populations go back up."

"I've heard that kind of bullbleep from a lot of game wardens, too. If I quit hunting, man, I'd probably turn into one of these antis who want to close it all down, too. But you wouldn't stop *poaching*. And if I quit, I'd be no good at my job. If you're a game warden, you've got to hunt to understand how a goose thinks. Then when you've got goose hunters around, you know what they're doing because you know what the geese are doing. Then you can get to the right place at the right time, and if the hunters have got overlimits you can nail their ass. You show me a game warden who's so correct he won't hunt and fish anymore, and I'll show you he ain't worth a damn at the job. Those are the same kind who're ineffective as undercover wardens. They hate the outlaws so much they can't even associate with them. You can't be an undercover agent if you aren't willing to associate with a lot of riffraff. Ivory poachers, goose creepers, drug pushers—they're all alike. Riffraff."

We passed a sign announcing that we had entered the Lacassine Refuge. The rice fields reverted instantly to marsh. We were still hearing geese, but now most of them were hidden by the tall water grasses that blanketed the refuge. The road became dirt, then rolled up onto a levee and rolled off again, at a small cluster of wooden buildings on a couple acres of lawn, overshadowed by huge willows. One of the buildings said REFUGE HEADQUARTERS.

The three people inside seemed relieved to see us. Two were employed by the Fish and Wildlife Service, graduate-level Eagle Scouts dressed in government brown with bronze name tags pinned to their chests. The third man was older, perhaps thirty-five or forty, with a walnut-oil complexion and thick, curly black hair. He was wearing new Levi's, a checkered flannel shirt, and a brown cotton jacket. He was handsome, with an air of quiet dignity in repose, but there was something sinister underneath—it was a brutally handsome face. The body was formed to match—five feet eight, close to two hundred pounds, a small running back with explosive speed.

Dave Hall had become prickly and a little gloomy in the car. Now he was suddenly animated.

"Hey, A.J.!" he said to the older man.

"How you doon, Dave?"

Dave Hall turned to the two wardens. "How you fellows today?"

"We're fine," said one.

"You been talking to old A.J. about his outlawin days?"

A.J. shuffled and stared at the floor. The wardens smiled faintly but said nothing.

"My friend's a writer," said Dave Hall. "He's gonna interview A.J. about alligator huntin. How many gators do you suppose you killed on the Lacassine Wildlife Refuge, A.J.?"

A.J. looked curiously at me, then back at his feet. "I doan believe I ever did outlaw on the Lacassine Refuge."

Even the Eagle Scouts had to laugh. A smile flickered across A.J.'s solemn face and disappeared. "Ask me no questions and I'll tell you no lies."

"How many, really?" persisted Dave Hall.

A.J. shrugged.

"A.J., then, dammit, what is the *most* alligators you ever killed in one night?"

"Hundred fourteen."

"Hundred fourteen," echoed Dave Hall. "Figure it. Back then you're gettin . . . what? . . ."

"Bout eight dollars a foot."

"Eight dollars a linear foot. Say the average gator is five feet. Forty dollars a gator times a hundred fourteen is . . ."

The two young refuge wardens were wide-eyed.

". . . is four thousand five hundred–plus dollars for one night's outlawin."

"Maybe that's high," said A.J. "I doan recall puttin that kinda money in the bank."

"The *bank!*" Dave Hall laughed. He turned to the wardens, then to me. "You see now why we had such a hellacious time shutting these old gator poachers down? It was the best money on the bayou. It was a whole hell of a lot better than working some old oil rig, don't deny that, A.J. A hunter who was good and diligent could make more money than the president of the local bank!"

"Unless he embezzles or somethin, a bank president doan go to jail," said A.J.

Dave Hall grinned. "A.J., you know I never put you in jail, though I'd have loved to. I took you *out* of the Cameron Parish jail."

"You done that. You know I'm grateful for it."

The Eagle Scouts seemed more puzzled than ever. Here was perhaps the best-known game warden in the United States swapping stories with one of the most audacious alligator poachers in Louisiana history. What was this about Dave Hall getting Caro *out* of jail?

"A.J. used to wade chest-high through the marshes with a .22 rifle on his back and his arms flat by his side so they didn't end up in some gator's mouth," said Dave Hall. "He'd zonk them gators and skin them in the marsh. *You* try skinning a gator in the middle of a swamp at night. Then he'd drag a thousand dollars in hides back to camp. Isn't that right, A.J.?"

"Right," said A.J. "Always keep your arms by your sides."

Dave Hall then got into a conversation with the wardens about conditions on the refuge. He wanted to know about species, numbers, food, weather, legal take, illegal kill, visitation—any conceivable question one could ask, he asked. A.J. and I leaned uncomfortably on the counter, not knowing whether to listen or talk to each other or what. Finally, Dave Hall said we should get some lunch, and he and A.J. and I strolled out the door. I could feel the wardens' eyes drilling into our backs. When we got outside, Dave Hall gave us both a sly grin. "They don't know what the hell to make of this," he said. "A game warden taking a notorious alligator poacher out to lunch."

"Former alligator poacher."

"I hope that's true."

We drove to Lake Arthur, taking a circumlocutory route so Dave Hall and A.J. could have a private conversation in the front seat. I caught snippets of it. A.J. was doing free-lance undercover work for federal law-enforcement agencies and had gotten into some kind of minor mess, from which Dave Hall said he would try to extricate him. When we got to the town of Lake Arthur, we parked in front of a café a couple of blocks from the lake. Dave Hall wanted to walk to the waterfront before we ate. Nearly everyone we passed gave a nod to A.J. "I'm a bouncer in a couple of local bars," he explained. "That's my sideline. Maybe I'm not popular, but I'm known."

Lake Arthur was once known as the duck-market-hunting capital of the world, a distinction which, at various times in our natural history, was also claimed by other towns: Newark, New Jersey (in the 1700s, when Manhattan markets were hung with wild ducks); Chincoteague, Virginia (in the 1800s); Colusa and Petaluma, California (one market hunter killed 6,200 canvasbacks near Petaluma in a single year, 1892); Greenville, Mississippi; Belle Glade, Florida. In the market-hunting era these places had one thing in common: a proximity to enormous reaches of wetlands, which brought in square miles of migratory ducks and geese, herons and egrets, teal and coots. Lake Arthur has changed perhaps the least of the former market-hunting capitals of the world. The lake still stretches southward for fifteen miles, then empties into the giant rimless bowl of Grand Lake, which empties into White Lake, near the Gulf. The same thunderheads rise over the same huge reaches of surrounding coastal marsh. But where you once had tens of millions of wintering waterfowl, you now have mere millions, and they are disappearing fast. "The habitat here, even though it's declining, is still pretty good," said Dave Hall. "Especially compared to California. We got some habitat that's underused. The biologists say we lost so much habitat along the flyway and that's the reason we get fewer birds. I say overhunting is probably as important a cause. What do you think, A.J.?"

"I doan know. I never was much for hunting canards."

"By the First World War overhunting had taken an awful toll in Chesapeake Bay and eastern Louisiana, but this here was still almost virgin," continued Dave Hall. "There was a railroad line to New Orleans, up where the Interstate is, and they built a spur line from Lake Charles down to Lake Arthur, mainly because of market hunting. Man, in the migration season those trains were carrying carloads of ducks. They didn't even bother with geese because they were too much trouble, and they got almost as much money for ducks. Thirty-five cents a pair. The Fred Dudley camp was delivering two thousand ducks a day, week after week. The hunters built houseboats and towed em out in the marshes and moved the whole family in—kids, wives, Grandma. The men hunted and the women and kids gutted the birds. They put them on ice in barrels and shipped them to New Orleans. If everything went right, they got there in eight hours. The freshest-killed ducks, they shipped them on as far away as Chicago! New York, too. They went to Nashville, Memphis, Mobile, Atlanta, Saint Louis. If you took a steamboat up or down the Mississippi, you ate nothing but crab and crawfish and viande de chevreuil and venison and wild duck. The steamships going out of New Orleans and Mobile were famous for their menus of wild game. Man, they must have thought it would never end."

We watched a pair of mallards going like hell across the lake, the only pair we saw. Then we walked back to the café and sat down to lunch. I ordered Cajun popcorn—deep-fried crawfish tails—and a mound appeared the size of an igloo. I ate most of it, and a washtub of coleslaw, while A.J. methodically consumed two five-story hamburgers and a fallen forest of French fries, which he washed down with a tank car of milk, followed by a quarter-section of pie. Dave Hall picked at a steak sandwich. One of his favorite expressions is "I'd rather . . . than eat," which is an inverted way of proclaiming the pleasures of food, but when I have eaten with him he has usually seemed indifferent to what's on his plate. He typically spends fifteen seconds with the menu, orders the first thing he sees—a steak and a salad—fidgets for a while with the expensive gadgetry he drags all over the place—video cameras, tape recorders, electronic goose callers, night scopes, all of which seem to break down more often than an Austin-Healey or he wouldn't fidget with them so much—then lapses into a spell of brooding thought or takes a catnap (if he didn't, he would long since have died of exhaustion, but he is said to have mild narcolepsy, too, though he won't admit it), then jerks back to life and begins doing what he loves best: talking a blue streak. On the occasion I am telling you about, he began at lunch, kept it up all afternoon with some help from A.J.—back in the car, back on the refuge, back at Lake Arthur again—kept going over dinner, and resumed a couple of days later, in his office in Slidell, talking about alligators and how he and A. J. Caro met.

In 1969, when he was a thirty-one-year-old game management agent with the United States Fish and Wildlife Service, Dave Hall was transferred to New Orleans, where—after he was promoted to Special Agent in Charge—his territory became a three-state domain that includes Arkansas, Mississippi, and Louisiana. His job there was no different from what it had been in Chincoteague, Virginia, where he had been based for three years: to prevent the illegal slaughter of fish and wildlife and try to control the unlawful trade in wild animals and exotic animal parts, mainly at the port of New Orleans. But that is like saying an agent of the Drug Enforcement Administration transferred to Miami has the same job he held in Fargo. Certain places in America have their signature kinds of crime. In south Florida, you have drugs. In New Jersey, you have racketeering. In Boston, you have car theft and chop shops. In Louisiana, you have poaching.

Louisiana has long been reputed to contain more lawless hunters and fishermen, per capita, than any of the other United States. There are several reasons. Southern Louisiana, in particular, is the last place in America, outside of Alaska, where significant numbers of people still earn some of their livelihood or gain much of their sustenance—"meat on the table"—from the land. They do it because their ancestors did it; because a lot of them are Cajun, and with Cajuns it is a matter of pride and tradition; because they have too little education to do anything else; because the region's major employer—the oil and gas industry—hires and fires in rhythm with the world price of oil. But mainly they do it because Louisiana remains one of the few places on earth where you *can*. It is, or was, the best habitat for wildlife in the entire world. At least a third of the state's once endless marshes have been lost; those that remain have been mined for food and furs and skins for two hundred–odd years; but southern Louisiana still raises fish and wildlife as if it were an important crop. The crawfish industry alone is worth one hundred fifty million dollars a year. You can seine one of the Mississippi's great oxbow lakes from end to end, drag out thousands of pounds of fish, do it week after week and year after year, and the fish keep coming back: sacalait, which Yankees call crappie, and catfish, and bream. (Commercial freshwater fishing for most species is illegal now, but plenty of people do it anyway.) Louisiana produces more wild furs and hides than all of Canada: nutria, an exotic, large aquatic rodent which outnumbered humans in the state until a few years ago, otter, mink, muskrat, beaver, alligators. The Louisiana Department of Wildlife and Fisheries may be the only state game agency with a fur division. Gastronomical exotica served at nouvelles brasseries from Boston to Beverly Hills come out of here: alligator steak, frogs, turtles. And then, off the coast, a spectacular haul of fish and shrimp and oysters and crabs keeps welling up, year after year, a bounty that seems to know no end.

Now, compared to what one used to find, these are dregs. There was a time when bear oil was one of the more lucrative exports leaving the French port of New Orleans. Black bears were several to the square mile, gorging on wild pecans and acorns and whatever swam in the marshes. There was a time when wild venison and bison meat were more common in Louisiana markets than domestic beef. (A lot of western Louisiana used to be a wild tall-grass prairie, growing bison as efficiently as it now raises soybeans and cotton.) There was a time when wild waterfowl kept a lot of southern Louisiana housed and clothed and fed. During the heyday of the market-hunting era—from 1880 to about 1915—the surface of Catahoula Lake, in late November, was covered by three, four, or five million ducks. Another million or two were on Lake Arthur. The two Grand lakes and White Lake, with a combined surface area larger than Tahoe but depths more accurately measured in inches than feet—an explosively productive habitat for ducks—held millions more. The marshes in between held millions. There were more ducks wintering in southern Louisiana than survive on the continent today. The birds funneled in, blackening the sky, dropping down in dazzling numbers. Except for the buffalo herds and the great sun-obscuring flocks of passenger pigeons, there was no other wild spectacle like it in America. A few very old people are still around who saw it near the end—World War I being the demarcation between incredible, stupefying abundance and mere plenitude—and they all say you cannot imagine what you did not see.

Little by little at first, then with an accelerating rush, this phenomenal smorgasbord of fish and fur and fowl began to disappear from the state (or, more accurately, from the Deep South, for the whole lower Mississippi basin, from Arkansas down, swarmed with wildlife in pioneer times). By the late nineteenth century most of the bears were hunted out. The bison were already gone. Canals were sliced through impenetrable marshes, fires flamed off a lot of surface cover in drought years, and the market massacre of waterfowl began, continuing for some decades until it was stopped—until it was declared illegal, in any case—at the close of the First World War.

As the requiem for wild abundance played on and on, a dirge was sounding, too, for the people who earned a livelihood from it. In Illinois, in Nebraska, the pioneers who had fed themselves on game could quickly substitute cows and crops. But southern Louisiana, the sump down which half of America's surface runoff swirls, resisted the most indefatigable efforts to reclaim it, and the Cajun folk were not particularly inclined to try. Cajun culture was sunny, easy, somnolent—not lazy, really, but that fearsome Yankee industriousness was simply never there. Cajuns were wedded to the wilderness, to the swampy forests and bayous and lakes to which they had been banished. And now—we are in the 1950s and 1960s—their own breezy excesses had stolen its plenitude away. All they had left in abundance, and all that was still legal to trap and hunt, were crawfish, the small mammals they call varmints, and alligators.

For a creature that can grow to fourteen feet, that has a special gustatory fondness for pigs and dogs, that bellows and snorts clouds of vapor and is armored with bone-snapping teeth, alligators managed to slip under the crushing wave of civilization for a long time—long after the wave had washed past them, rolling west. They were killed out quickly at the fringes of their range—southern Illinois, northern North Carolina, Galveston Bay—but in their territorial heartland they hung on in great numbers until after the First World War. Americans, being mostly of European ancestry, were rarely inclined to eat reptiles, as they devoured the bison and elk and antelope they found grazing the continent. It was difficult and expensive to cure the tough, crinkly, foul-smelling hides. Alligators were, in a word, useless. They were also nocturnal, elusive, hard to kill (even with a rifle—a bullet moving at a shallow angle will bounce right off a big alligator's snout), and usually reclusive enough to keep out of harm's way. As the cattle industry was being established in northern Florida in the late 1800s, cowboys began making alligator hides into saddles and boots, but they could hardly extirpate an alligator population which, at the time, numbered more than two million in Florida alone. There were millions more in the other Deep South states, especially in Louisiana, whose primordial alligator habitat was more extensive even than Florida's. The creatures began to decline somewhat through the missionary work of the Corps of Engineers, which until very recently was hell-bent on draining America's wetlands down to the very last acre. Humans became a more impressive threat with the invention of the airboat, a swamp skiff with an airplane motor mounted at the rear—the only craft that can run down an alligator in a marsh. But alligators were never really threatened until the fashion industry decided their skins were chic.

Species that had disappeared earlier—Carolina parakeets, bison, wolves, bears—were done in because they got in the way of settlement, of farmers and crops and cattle. Others—passenger pigeons are the famous example—were slaughtered for sport, so-called, and food. The alligator was a peculiar lesson in how vanity and urban wealth can ruin the wild. Tanning alligator hides is difficult, and only the softer pieces of skin can be used, so alligator leather has never been cheap. When America was a relatively underdeveloped land of subsistence farmers and small towns, there was never a market for alligator hides. No yeoman farmer could afford to go through a pair or two of expensive alligator boots every year, not when cow leather was much cheaper. But alligator leather is wonderfully well suited for streetwear, and for the accoutrements of a wealthy and acquisitive urban society when it runs out of other things to have. It is also what fashion loves best: a novelty. By the 1920s, the Jazz Age, close to two hundred thousand

Florida alligators annually became boots, shoes, wallets, purses, luggage, curios, belts, even clocks—you can pay through the nose for such stuff at any Deco antique show. Florida's huge marshes, still mostly intact, were crawling with market hunters in fast skiffs and airboats; some were even using spotter planes to locate alligator holes during the dry season. By the late 1930s, the kill was down by half. What biologists call the resource base had been kicked apart in about two decades, and by the 1940s, with the larger animals—the breeding population—hunted out, the whole population collapsed. Fewer than ten thousand Florida alligators were taken in 1943, although the season was still open and prices were high. It was no different in any of the other alligator states. Louisiana lost 90 percent of its alligators between 1938 and 1958. Alabama's were almost gone by 1941, when it became the first state to give the creatures complete protection. Arkansas, Florida, Louisiana, Georgia, and Mississippi followed suit in the 1960s, Texas in 1970. Alligators were also protected by Congress under the Endangered Species Act of 1973.

One result of the American alligator's demise was a sudden, enormous increase in the "harvest" overseas, followed by a sudden, awe-inspiring population collapse. Four million nine hundred twenty-six thousand nine hundred and eight legal caiman hides went through the port of Manaus, Brazil, in 1950 alone. It was a slaughter that could not possibly be sustained—did anyone wonder how the fashion industry could use so many hides?—and it lasted only a few years. By the 1960s, caiman shipments through Manaus had declined by 98 percent. Malaysian crocodile exports were down 90 percent from one year to the next. All of this was, of course, predictable. But it was also predictable that, with complete protection, a creature as opportunistic and adaptable as the American alligator would rebound fairly soon, despite ongoing habitat loss. It didn't. Outside a few well-policed refuges, it didn't recover at all.

What ensued, according to Dave Hall, was "the first great overhunting-versus-habitat debate in the history of wildlife conservation in the United States." In the early twentieth century, no one doubted that market hunting—not habitat loss—had blown North American waterfowl a long way toward oblivion. Their summer habitat, in the continent's far northern latitudes, was still intact, and only in California and parts of the Middle West had their winter habitat been seriously disturbed. How could you blame anything but overhunting when one California market hunter murdered six thousand two hundred canvasback ducks in a single year? The same applied to wolves and bison, to grizzly bears and passenger pigeons. They had all disappeared, or nearly disappeared, long before their habitat was destroyed; we had simply shot out their lights. But in the case of the alligator, opinion hunkered into two camps: those who thought an enormous amount of illegal hunting was going on, and those who blamed the creature's continuing slide toward extinction on habitat loss. One of the few proponents of theory one—and it was a troublesome theory, for what it really implied was a mass breakdown in law enforcement at fish and game departments throughout the South—was Dave Hall. The most notable exponent of the second point of view was the Louisiana Department of Wildlife and Fisheries.

In the fall of 1966, two years after Louisiana banned all alligator hunting and three years before Dave Hall got to New Orleans, Dr. Leslie Glasgow, the director of the state's Department of Wildlife and Fisheries—it was then known as the Louisiana Wildlife and Fisheries Commission—received a confidential report on corruption within his department.

To put this whole story in some kind of context, I suppose it would help to distinguish between petty corruption and real corruption in the realm of fish and game. In states where the power elite—the judges and state senators and corporate CEOs—all belong to the huntnfishn crowd, petty corruption at the state fish and game agency is something you accept. In a state like Connecticut, hardly anyone in the power elite belongs to the huntnfishn crowd; in southern and western states, damn near everyone does. And the press is always ready to leap on some big shot who is arrested for, say, five times the legal limit of ducks. This sort of petty, silly violation can also snowball: an overlimit of ducks serves as an excuse for newspapers to reach their grimy tentacles all over the place—lobbyists' luncheons and Kiwanis Club romps, minority nonhiring policy and factory wastes—any ethical transgression they can find, they will, once someone is regarded as fair game and is in the public eye. And it can all begin with an overlimit of ducks! So you have to nip this kind of thing in the bud. That is why governors—and this was particularly true twenty or thirty years ago, when a much larger proportion of the male population hunted and fished—like to appoint some crony as head of the fish and game agency, someone whom an important campaign contributor can call when a game warden nabs him in an old-fashioned killing frenzy . . . someone who can *fix the damn thing.*

In Louisiana, where rural people have always supplemented their larders with food from the wild, a get-tough policy on game law violations could make a governor universally unpopular. Huey Long used to bring the adoring masses to their feet with tirades against his own "coon-servation officers." It was a brave game warden who brought in armloads of violators in an atmosphere such as this. And because the game wardens, who were notoriously underpaid, could earn a few dollars or some wild ducks and rabbits by looking the other way, many of them learned to tolerate the system, too—or get fired or promoted to a desk job.

Any truthful Louisiana game warden will admit that a lot of small-scale graft still goes on today. But the report Leslie Glasgow held in his hand spoke of things more ominous. It had come to him from one of his wardens and was a synopsis of the warden's conversation with a recently arrested small-time alligator poacher who felt he had been double-crossed. "He complained that it was unfair for the big dealers to operate openly, on a large scale, while the little dealers were forced out of business," the warden recounted. "He told me that the Mares brothers and Ralph Sagrera in Abbeville, Louisiana, were known through the South for their dealings in illegal alligator skins but that because of their connections they were untouchable."

The Mares brothers, Joseph and René, who were then among the largest fur dealers in the world, had their headquarters in the French Quarter—a few blocks from the riverfront markets that had once sold millions of wild ducks and geese, and, coincidentally, a block away from the old rococo New Orleans courthouse, where Leslie Glasgow's office was. If what the poacher had told the warden was true, then tens of thousands of alligator hides were being traded right under Wildlife and Fisheries' nose.

As for Leslie Glasgow, he was an anomaly running a department like Wildlife and Fisheries. It was an open question how much corruption from the Huey era had carried over into the 1960s, but LDWF's reputation was odoriferous enough to prompt Governor John McKeithan to appoint Leslie Glasgow to run it. A well-known professor of wildlife management at Louisiana State University, Glasgow, according to Dave Hall (who used to bus down to LSU from Mississippi State to attend his seminars), was "the Aldo Leopold of the South—a scholar, an outdoorsman, a philosopher, and a naturalist. He was greatly respected. Everyone called him Prof Glasgow. To have him running Wildlife and Fisheries was a hell of a public relations coup. What they didn't expect was his determination to enforce the law."

Enforcing the law wasn't as easy as it might seem. First of all, the poacher who had tipped Glasgow's warden adamantly refused to cooperate. He seemed scared to death. That left Glasgow the option of putting the Mares brothers' warehouse under surveillance. But Wildlife and Fisheries already had the warehouse under routine surveillance, and nothing amiss had ever been reported. Either the Mares brothers were very cautious, or every warden assigned to watch their operation was either afraid to buck the system or was bought off.

An undercover sting was a possibility. The federals had used undercover wardens successfully in the past. But Glasgow had no one really trained in covert operations. Besides, the Mares brothers probably bought only from people they knew. He needed someone they knew to try to sell them some alligator skins, and that brought him around full circle. The only alligator hunter even willing to finger Joe and René had just said he wouldn't cooperate. What could he do, Glasgow wondered, *raid* the warehouse? But to do that you needed a warrant, and for a warrant you needed probable cause, and he had none. A raggedy-ass old poacher's word against two millionaire fur dealers, two of the upstanding citizens of New Orleans, wouldn't work.

Some weeks before Glasgow received the report on Joe and René Mares, an LDWF game warden named Gamble had been approached by a suspected alligator hunter named Rigsby and was openly offered a bribe—twenty dollars a night, an open-ended deal—if he would stay away from Clear Lake, up near Natchitoches, one of the last places where alligators were still reasonably common. Aside from the generous nature of the bribe—twenty dollars was then a game warden's daily wage—the offer was nothing unusual; wardens were offered bribes all the time. What was unusual—other than, perhaps, the fact that Gamble spurned the bribe—was that Rigsby followed it up with a threat. He was so *mad* that his bribe had been refused, he told Gamble, that he was going to have him fired or at least transferred. When Gamble laughed, Rigsby—or so Gamble testified later on—told him, "Watch—I got connections at Wildlife and Fisheries that are better than your own."

Rigsby's threat, bluff or not, had made Ira Gamble laugh, but it made one of his partners, a warden whose name was Burgess, livid. "I'm gonna get that sonofabitch," he told Gamble, and began stalking him day and night. Rigsby evidently hadn't counted on someone like Burgess. A few nights later, as he was hauling a seven-foot reptile out of Clear Lake, he suddenly found himself handcuffed to the warden's arm.

In custody, Rigsby became meek as a lamb. When you threaten an officer of the law—especially one whose partner is as fierce as Burgess evidently was—you have reason to be scared. He would do *anything*, Rigsby pleaded with Gamble and Burgess, if they would just go easy on him.

Someone who evidenced such a conversion was a person of considerable interest to Leslie Glasgow, and perhaps even more so to Preston Mauboules, the senior officer who was overseeing the Mares case. Mauboules was an authentic Cajun—dark, somewhat slight, with a mysterious Gaelic air—whom Glasgow had made into his internal-affairs investigator and confidant. It was his job to get to the bottom of this Mares business, and Rigsby was probably the best opportunity he would get. So he worked him.

Dave Hall has videoed himself "working" poachers he has put in jail, and when I saw one of those tapes I understood why he lectures at the Federal Law Enforcement Training Center in Glynco, Georgia, every year—a *game warden* instructing the federal, state and Canadian undercover-agent corps in the fine points of surveillance, subterfuge, and criminal psychology. You would not guess that he has anything but the poacher's dearest interest at heart. He believes people ought to be able to make a living from the land. He doesn't care if this is the twentieth century: this country we live in is called *America*, by God, where hunting and fishing are a privilege that should have been put in the *Constitution*. He admires the old market hunters more than anyone else in the world. He draws the line when people begin shooting at game wardens, and when they violate the law (which, he fails to mention, is drawing the line pretty early). But the law can change. No one could hunt wood ducks in the 1920s because they had become so scarce; now they are one of our most common ducks. In Massachusetts, deer hunting was banned as early as 1700; now there may be more deer in Massachusetts than when the *Mayflower* arrived. If you practice game *management*, there is no upper limit on the amount of wildlife you can have. Even today. He isn't in this business just to hunt down violators of the law (there, again, he is wandering a bit from the truth; every game warden, particularly Dave Hall, *loves* to hunt down violators of the law). If he were king, he would crank this country back a hundred eighty years to where we aren't all fast-food managers and accountants and lawn-mower salesmen and goddamned public-relations men. He'd take America and make it *wild* again. When we lost our wilderness, our right to fish and hunt freely, we lost something American at the core. We lost our ties to nature and the land. We lost a freedom as essential as democracy. But we will never regain it so long as we have greedy fools cleaning out wildlife as if there were no tomorrow. This lecture goes on and on, offering poachers with seven teeth and second-grade educations and moonshine stills in their awful backyards *enlightenment*— on species recovery and propagation, habitat, the passenger pigeon and the buffalo. He has turned some of them, in the end, into the world's most improbable . . . *conservationists*. You see why game wardens are an utterly different breed, because there is a bond between them and those they hunt down. In a cop's ideal world, robbing a bank would never be legal. In a game warden's ideal world, making your living by hunting waterfowl would. Cops acquire informants and undercover collaborators from the ranks of criminals for reasons of revenge or lucre or because they want to avoid jail; rarely does a cop turn a criminal into a born-again law-enforcement *evangelist.* Dave Hall turns notorious poachers into born-again conservationists all the time.

Preston Mauboules must have been good at this game, too. By the third or fourth visit to Rigsby's house, he reported later to Glasgow, he had finally made some headway. Rigsby had at least accepted the *idea* of cooperating in an undercover investigation. The problem was that Rigsby was even more frightened of Joe Mares than of jail. Wildlife and Fisheries had no real witness- or informant-protection program, but Mauboules persuaded Rigsby that if he cooperated, he would be safe. With a mournful, doubting look, Rigsby picked up the phone and dialed Mares's number. Sure, Mares told him, business was open: he would buy as many alligators as Rigsby could bring in.

The delivery was arranged for June 11, late at night, at the Mares brothers' French Quarter warehouse. On June 10, Mares called Rigsby back and told him the deal was off. He had just gotten word that an undercover game warden would try to sell him some alligator skins the next day.

Mauboules and Glasgow were thunderstruck. Whether they suspected each other, no one can say, but there weren't many people inside Wildlife and Fisheries who had been told the department was trying to lure Joe and René Mares into a trap. Did someone have their phone bugged? Could Burgess and Gamble be crooked? Had Rigsby thought better of it and confessed to Mares? It was hardly likely, for he seemed to be trembling in fear's jaws. Mares had told Rigsby on the phone that he knew *he* was "solid"—that someone else would try to make the undercover sale—but Rigsby didn't seem convinced. If anything, he seemed convinced he was going to be badly hurt. On the other hand, he was stuck. If he didn't reschedule the delivery, or try to, Mares would suspect him for sure. They rescheduled on June 19, a week later; then Rigsby called Mauboules and read him the riot act.

Mauboules didn't know what to say. He promised Rigsby that a trusted game warden would make the delivery with him, undercover. He would of course be armed. He would not let Rigsby out of his sight. Then Mauboules settled in his chair and breathed a loud sigh. Someone had tipped off Mares—someone in the department. Someone, obviously, with a very big stake in Mares's continued operation. Someone who probably had no business even knowing an undercover sting was planned. Of course, if Mares were caught, he might say exactly whom at Wildlife and Fisheries he had bribed, in order to cop a plea.

The sting still went as planned. Rigsby and his protector, LDWF warden Lester Hebert, arrived, unloaded the skins, and had Joe Mares hand them an envelope full of money on the street. The whole thing was filmed from an office window a couple of doors away. Mauboules was there, seeing it for himself. For Rigsby's sake, they didn't take down Mares right away. On the following night, two more large deliveries of alligator skins arrived. Glasgow and Mauboules still elected to do nothing. Then, on the next day, a panel truck drove up and Mares's men loaded some large cardboard drums inside. Sooner or later they had to make their move. They pulled the truck over a few blocks down the street. The cardboard drums were filled with hundreds of salted-down alligator skins. Some of the drums were tagged with official Wildlife and Fisheries permits. Mauboules's men commandeered the truck and drove it back to the Mares warehouse, where they served Joe and René Mares with warrants for their arrest. That night Rigsby got a call from Joe Mares, telling him what he was going to do to him.

Several weeks later—nothing had yet happened to Rigsby—Joe and René Mares requested a meeting with Leslie Glasgow in his office. No more than ninety seconds had gone by when Joe Mares, who had just sat down, got back up again, went to the window, and, with his back to Glasgow, said, "Mr. Glasgow, you either drop this case on us or we'll see that your head rolls." An exact quote. Glasgow immediately kicked them out of his office.

I'm going to give you facts here, not speculation, because no one really knows how what happened next was arranged. The governor, senators and congressmen, state legislators, the district attorney himself—whom exactly did the Mares brothers get to and how? A lot of suspicion—well, here I go with some speculation—fell on the district attorney, simply because of who he was. His name was Garrison, Big Jim Garrison, and he was quite well known around the world then because he was the same Jim Garrison who was saying that the Warren

Commission report on the Kennedy assassination was a perfidious cover-up. Some people thought Garrison was a modern Zola; others thought he was simply mad. Whatever he was, he wasn't your run-of-the-mill D.A. in a charcoal pin-striped suit and boat-size wing tips. He was a carnival-barker sort of D.A., someone who might have been a Las Vegas promoter if he hadn't gone into law, which immediately suggested to some that he must be a crook, even though his reputation as a prosecutor was clean.

To Leslie Glasgow, at any rate—and to Dave Hall, who was watching this indictment with keen interest from afar—the Mares brothers case was one that you couldn't lose. The Mareses might be able to tinker with the sentencing so they'd avoid jail, but how could any district attorney *lose* this kind of case? He couldn't; the assistant D.A. himself had told him and Mauboules that. They had photographs of money changing hands on the street. As hard evidence, they had big barrels full of alligator skins. They had the driver's testimony that he had picked them up at the Mares brothers warehouse. They had several LDWF agents willing to testify. The case was so fundamentally sound that Mauboules wouldn't even have to ask Rigsby to jeopardize himself by appearing in court. On the day the case came to trial, he and Maboules already had their celebratory lunch planned. After a long string of inconsequential arrests of poachers like Rigsby—gyppo outlaws—they were finally going to land a big fish.

They had overlooked one possibility, one so farfetched it hadn't even occurred to them. It is always the district attorney's prerogative to nol-pros a case—simply not to bring it to trial. And that, without a word of explanation, is what the assistant D.A. did on the morning the Mares indictment was called. Dave Hall says, "The case was openly, blatantly, and unapologetically thrown."

Some months later, Louisiana Governor John McKeithan fired Leslie Glasgow as director of the Louisiana Wildlife and Fisheries commission. Walter J. Hickel, who was serving as Richard Nixon's secretary of the interior, immediately appointed him as his assistant secretary for Fish, Wildlife, and Parks. In that position, Glasgow was in charge of the Fish and Wildlife Service and its hundred-eighty-odd special agents—the whole corps of federal game wardens. And one of the first things the still-seething Glasgow did was transfer an up-and-coming young law-enforcement agent from Memphis, who had already shown a special talent at undercover work, into the effulgent, steaming bayous south and west of New Orleans. His assignment was to save the American alligator from what was beginning to look like possible extinction.

According to A. J. Caro, there were twenty thousand people poaching alligators when Dave Hall was sent down in 1969. When he ventured that statistic, Dave Hall snorted in disbelief.

"There weren't nearly that many."

"There was."

"A.J., you're out of your mind."

"I doan mean they were doin it for a living like some of us were makin most of our money from alligators. We were professionals. I mean you had that many people in the parishes between New Orleans and Texas who were gettin table meat and makin some income off the land, and if they saw a cocodrie, they was gonna pop it."

"There were two or three thousand, maybe. At the most."

I asked, "How did they know how to sell the skins?"

"Everybody knew," said A.J. "You had middlemen selling to middle-men. There was Wildlife and Fisheries people who'd sell them to you and buy them from you. The New Orleans Mafia was in on it."

"You'll never prove that," Dave Hall admonished me.

"It's true. You know it's true," said A.J. "They used to deal them on Carlos Marcello's estate, down by his pumphouse. I saw Wildlife and Fisheries people over there. I sat with them at dinner at Jack Kelly's in New York."

"Who's Carlos Marcello?"

"He is the head—excuse me—he is *reputed* to be the head of the New Orleans mob," said Dave Hall. "But we never found any evidence he was dealing alligators himself. He probably just let the local outlaws use his estate. It was good P.R. in them bayous, a rich man opening his land to the public."

A.J. nodded. "That was before coke and all this shit. The Mafia types wouldn't bother with alligators today. Even then gators were never more than a sideline to these people."

"Were there any murders you could link to this alligator business?"

"Probably three," said Dave Hall. "Although one of those could have been over something else."

A.J. nodded. "Five, when you count the two who might as well be dead."

Word about the Mares case was soon all over Louisiana and the South. Rigsby's pathetic example—even though Joe Mares never made a lesson of him through violence—meant it didn't pay to collaborate with the authorities, at least not in the Banana Republic of Louisiana. Mares's example was not lost on the other big alligator skin buyers either. "The Mares case did two things," Dave Hall would recall. "It made everyone a lot more careful. We started seeing thousands and thousands of alligator skins that we suspected were laundered the way they launder drug money. Jefferson County in Texas still had a legal season—don't ask me why—so a big bogus operation got set up where skins from Louisiana alligators, Georgia alligators, alligators from all over the South were shipped over there and certified as Texas alligators. The number of alligators that were supposed to come out of that county would have covered it about three feet deep, but they got away with that for a while. The other thing it did was cause other dealers to step in and fill the Mareses' shoes. Even though they got this case nol-prosed, they decided they'd better lay low for a while. But then all of a sudden these other dealers are taking over, and we don't know for sure who they are. We had to start from scratch again. Informants were tough to find, we had a whole new hierarchy of buyers and exporters . . . man, it was flustrating. For a while all we could do was go after the actual hunters, which meant we were chasing some of the wiliest damn outlaws in creation all over the swamps."

Dave Hall loves to tell stories about backwoods types he has run into in his life. Some offer themselves more vividly to story-telling than others. There was Boyd Abrams, up in Flat Lick, Kentucky, a self-described mountain man who ran a filthy roadside menagerie called the Dogpatch Zoo. Letters and calls came in from all over complaining about the Dogpatch Zoo, so game wardens had to stop by now and then to see if old Boyd hadn't trapped some poor beaver to stick in one of his cramped dank cells or if he hadn't somehow managed to get hold of something really illegal, like a wolf or grizzly bear. Boyd's habit was to buy old horses—he said he bought them; others complained that he rustled them—and have a couple of crazed hillbillies slit their throats and chop them to pieces on his front lawn, so he could feed them to his carnivores. The first time Dave Hall went up to the Dogpatch Zoo with his boss, agent Willie J. Parker, Boyd invited them in for a cup of coffee. Dave Hall made it as far as the kitchen, then turned around and ran out the door, throwing up. "If he took two baths a year, that was plenty. He chewed tobacco—chaw, they call it in those hillbilly holes—and spit it all over the floor. He was the stinkingest bastard in the stinkingest house I ever encountered, and I tell you, boy, I seen a few. Willie J. Parker said, 'If you threw a handful of millet seed on Boyd, it'd germinate instantly.' Goddamn, I'd like to find that Boyd Abrams. He disappeared up in Michigan someplace."

There was Romulus Scalf, a revivalist preacher who migrated from Tennessee to Florida, saw that poaching alligators was more profitable (in his case) than preaching, and began cleaning out the Everglades. Romulus fancied himself a mountain man like Boyd, so he wrestled alligators for fun, keeping them chained live in his attic until he got a purchase order. "Romulus Scalf kind of identified with the alligator," said Dave Hall, smiling fondly. "He sure smelled like one."

But in the Louisiana bayous, where poaching was not "table meat" but an underground economy—where, in Dave Hall's words, "game laws were violated more than the speed limit"—down there, the backwoods types you ran into could be of a different breed: implacable, unflinching, and ornery beyond belief. Down there, you ran into Ranzell and Clinton Dufrene.

In the Acadian triangle, Dufrenes are as omnipresent as Boudreauxs and Nunezes and Heberts, so Ranzell and Clinton were at most distantly related. What they had in common was an unmitigated streak of violence, a contempt for all laws, and an almost suicidal defiance of authority. "Most Cajuns are sweet-natured people," says Dave Hall. "But there's some that are just . . . *crazy.*"

Ranzell was the crazier of the two. Around Point au Chien, where he lived with an Indian wife and ragamuffin brood, he was king of the bayou. Since the age of ten he had hauled crawfish and crab traps and two-hundred-pound alligators into boats, and dragged his boats up and down levees, and poached cypress trees. For sport, he fought. His list of convictions and arrest warrants—aggravated assault, attempted murder, reckless endangerment—filled a file folder at the Terrebonne Parish sheriff's office. When Dave Hall went down there and learned the deputies hadn't arrested Ranzell on several outstanding warrants, he asked why, and they just shrugged. He was only beating up on his own kind, they said. "What they meant," he says, "was that they were too afraid of him to bring him in. He also had too many relatives who voted."

It was winter, not the season poachers normally hunted alligators. But Dave Hall had received numerous reports that Ranzell was killing anything in the marshes that could be sold on the black market—muskrat, deer, squirrels, ducks, rabbits, you name it. Selling migratory waterfowl was a serious game-law offense, and the one that roused Dave Hall's ire most; he and some other state and federal wardens decided to stake out Ranzell's hunting domain to see if they could catch him with a market-size bag. On the first day they caught him with thirty-five ducks over limit. They cited him, but Ranzell remained cool; thus far, it was a routine case.

A few days later, the telephone rang in Dave Hall's home. The caller, who had a strong Cajun accent, was one of many volunteer informants Dave Hall had come to rely on, but he was too scared to say who he was.

"Mister Dave, I jus want you to know, dat Ranzell, he back at it. He still killen dem ducks and deer and sellin em too. And he mad! He think somebody round Point au Chien reported him to you other day, and he sayin he gonna kill whoever call. Please be careful, Mister Dave. Dat homme is crazy!"

Dave Hall contacted J. J. Guidry, a Cajun warden familiar with Ranzell's turf, who was probably as fearless as he. They went down and staked out the area for days. They waited, ate, and went to sleep; they waited, ate, and went to sleep. On the fourth or fifth day, they saw Ranzell in his pirogue, carefully hiding two burlap sacks full of poached ducks. This time Ranzell was totally uncooperative, and that was putting it mildly. He raved and cursed, denied killing the ducks—he had found them somewhere—and refused to show any identification. They were miles from a road. Dave Hall decided that it was pointless to arrest Ranzell then and there. He was coming back, he told him, with a federal arrest warrant in his hand.

Dave Hall has a college master's degree, he has won conservation awards, he has rubbed shoulders with nature-loving café society in New Orleans and Washington and New York, but he is still a barroom brawler at heart, and he will take machismo to all kinds of extremes. He was not going to be intimidated by a roughneck like Ranzell Dufrene. He knew, however, that Ranzell's explosive nature would likely set his own formidable temper off, so he called Perry White, the federal wildlife agent working out of Baton Rouge, and asked him to come along. Perry was older and wiser, and, most important, absolutely refused to carry a gun. His defensive weapon was sweet reason—which, at times, was insured by the blackjack he carried in the right rear pocket of his pants.

With a warrant issued by a United States magistrate, Dave Hall and Perry White drove to Point au Chien a couple of days later. They knocked on Ranzell's door just after dark. The timbre of his voice as he screamed "WHO IS IT?" told them that the case was no longer routine. Ranzell came out the door stomping his feet like a crazy man, punching air and cursing nonstop.

"Ranzell—"

"Communist motherfuckers!"

"Ranzell—"

"Fuckin sissy duck cops!"

"Ranzell—"

"GET THE FUCK OFF MY PROPERTY!"

"Ranzell, we got to take you in. It's our job. You ain't necessarily gonna have to stay in jail, but we got to book you."

"I been fetchin food for my kids. You want to take food out of my babies' mouths? There ain't enough of you Communist fuckers to take me in!"

"Ranzell, you are coming with us."

Ranzell's eyes blazed like lasers. Dave Hall decided he had better cuff him fast. "A show of force was in order. Just like with Qaddafi." He stalked up to the porch and grabbed Ranzell by the arm. Ranzell coiled his other arm and backhanded his fist into Dave Hall's jaw. The blow was enough to knock him down, but he had a clenched mitt on Ranzell's shirt, and with a trip-kick he had him on the floor. Then they were in a gnashing dogfight, crashing inside the trailer, heaving over furniture, smashing into walls, ripping each other's ears and clothes. Ranzell's wife was screaming. His children were under the beds, wailing in terror. Perry had his blackjack out and had it poised to give Ranzell a whack, but Ranzell saw it coming and jerked his head away. The blackjack hit Dave Hall's hand and broke a couple of bones. Ranzell broke free as Dave Hall howled in pain, but he grabbed him again and maneuvered him into a one-armed headlock. Perry was still dancing around the two, looking for a clear shot at Ranzell's head. When he got one, the sound was like the crash of a watermelon dropped off a roof. Ranzell collapsed like an emptied sack and just lay there. Blood began oozing out of his thick black hair and pooling on the floor.

By then Ranzell's father had run over from next door. "You kilt him!" he screamed. "You fuckin bastards kilt him!"

"You kilt him!" shrieked his wife.

Ranzell wasn't dead. He still lay there gurgling expletives. "Fucking motherfuckin fuckers . . ." After Dave Hall and Perry surveyed the damage the blackjack had done, they decided he needed immediate medical attention. Ignoring his family's screams and shrieks and threats—it was a miracle, Dave Hall mused later, that one of them hadn't grabbed a shotgun and let them have it—they lugged him to the car and raced to Houma, twenty miles away. Dave Hall's hand was too badly hurt to let him drive, so he ministered to Ranzell. The doctors at the Houma hospital shaved Ranzell bald as a billiard ball, stitched him up, and loaded him full of narcotics. Dave Hall and Perry then raced to New Orleans, where the jailers took one look at him—he seemed done up for the electric chair, handcuffed and shaved bald—and sent him back to the hospital. Dave Hall waited up all night before Ranzell, his head now bandaged like a mummy's, was behind bars.

Ranzell's wound looked worse than it was. He lived. In fact, he lived another couple of years. He got six months of jail time for assaulting an officer of the law, then lost the police-brutality suit he filed against

Dave Hall. Then, to vent his rage, he waylaid a trapper whom he suspected of informing on him and nearly killed him; all that stopped him
was the presence of the man's son. That got him another six months
in prison. Then, shortly after returning home, he stuck a shotgun in his
mouth and ended his life, all because of an overlimit of ducks.

When Dave Hall drove me down to Des Allemands to meet Clinton
Dufrene in 1987, he had just turned forty-eight. He looked thirty-six. He
was stocky, about five feet nine, and powerful, but whatever menace
he projected with his build and sinister Gaelic features and icewater
eyes was diluted by his manner and his clothes. Clinton was very soft-
spoken. He was also a dandy. When he came out to greet us he was
dressed like a tennis player, in neat white shorts, ribbed crew socks, a
Lacoste shirt, and a plain white Caterpillar hat. He was enormously tan.
Of course, Claude Dallas was soft-spoken and very polite and always
dressed like a dandy, too, in his ornamental cowboy clothes, and Claude
had emptied a Magnum into two Idaho wardens and finished them off
with a .22 slug behind the ear.

Clinton had a lot in common with Dallas. He was hardworking, a
professional—braving the suffocating marsh-country nights and mos-
quito swarms, enduring drenching downpours, forswearing sleep, jumping out of his airboat to wrestle frenzied alligators off baited hooks.
Like Dallas, Clinton had a lot of local sympathy. He came by it cleverly,
living up to his reputation as a bully but distributing a lot of free wild
food. Clinton's geese, crabs, and fish graced many impoverished tables
around Des Allemands. He had lookouts everywhere who called his
house if they saw a game warden's truck, boat, or aircraft passing by.
And—the mark of a real professional—he had the local justice system
fixed. When Dave Hall and some Louisiana wardens finally caught him
red-handed, with a fish-shocking device, a bin full of illegal furs, and a
freezer full of alligator hides, he walked.

But Clinton's success, both at poaching wildlife and evading the law,
was owed mainly to his airboats. He built them himself. They were light
pontoon craft that weighed next to nothing and had 220-horsepower
engines mounted at the rear. On flat water, with a top end of just under
seventy miles per hour, a Clinton Dufrene airboat could run circles
around the game wardens' 50-horsepower bass barges. Wildlife and

Fisheries agents were once so frustrated by their inability to catch him that they borrowed a helicopter and chased him through a marsh, but Clinton darted around like a water strider, taking cover under trees, cutting his motor and suddenly reversing course, until the helicopter ran low on fuel and had to give up.

Clinton usually worked alone, sometimes with help from his one-legged son. Clinton said his son's leg got mangled when he was working on a boat motor; Dave Hall says it got wrapped in a boat mooring line as they were escaping a posse of game wardens and that the boy nearly bled to death before Clinton shook the wardens off and got him to a hospital. "Clinton's not quite like he used to be, but he's still fearless. And you're talking about a guy with an explosive temper! I remember one time, after I finally put him away and he'd gotten a little religion and begun to go straight, we met down there by Bayou Gauche and he invited me into his house for coffee. He was as personable and mild-mannered as anyone could be. When I got inside the house I saw that all but one door had been torn off its hinges. I mean they were *torn* off. Great big strips of doorjamb wood still hanging on the hinges. There were holes the size of a fist all through the walls of the house."

During his first couple of years in New Orleans, Dave Hall would wake up early, have his breakfast and coffee, then drive into the marshes to run all-day-and-all-night game patrols that were like search-and-engage missions in Vietnam. The poachers were fish swimming in a welcoming sea. His fight was not with them but with a culture. These were descendants of people who had been reviled and, in many cases, were virtual slaves; who had inherited no decent land for industry or farms; they lived in places unreachable by road; their children had at most a year or two of schooling; they felt they *had no choice* but to live off the land. That it had become illegal was of no concern at all. One just had to avoid being caught.

"These were people who were taking something different from the land every month of the year," says Dave Hall. "In the fall and winter there were ducks. Geese. Oysters. Rabbits. Squirrels. In the spring they trapped crawfish. In June there were frogs. Alligators. Shrimp. I mean, this is how these people *lived*. There was practically no cash economy here in the nineteenth century, except closer to the Mississippi where the rice plantations were. They just went out day by day and hauled in wild food. Then when the cities were growing in the South and there was a demand for products of the land, a lot of these folks became market hunters. They went from subsistence living to making pretty good cash income from ducks and furs and alligator skins. Now, I've seen this happen with the Eskimos: when you introduce a subsistence people to a cash economy, it's like giving them drugs. They just beat the hell out of their wild resource and don't really realize or even care whether it's going to last. That's what they were doing with the alligator. The idea of *game* management is something they ain't even gonna think twice about. To them it's just a plot by rich people to give them less of the spoils. I remember one poacher saying, 'No one left me no buffalo, so I ain't gonna leave anyone no ducks.' You can't have a lot of people thinking like that and expect the wildlife to last. But you can sympathize with them somewhat because they feel like they're on the losing end of a feudal system. They see some rich duck club buy some island in the Mississippi where their grandfathers used to hunt a lot of ducks— not for amusement but for table food—and all of a sudden there are posted guards warning them off. They feel like romantic Robin Hood types who're leading a dying way of life. The trouble is it ain't so romantic anymore when they've killed everything off. That's what we were dealing with. When I got to Louisiana, the price of alligator skins was higher than ever. It was like the good old days of market hunting had started over again. There was so much money in it that they had the game wardens and sheriffs fixed. There were local judges who were fixed, though I can't prove that. What judge is gonna send an alligator poacher with the same last name to jail when he's probably blood kin in some way and he's just trying to make an honest Cajun living off the land. They had everything going their way. Not *everything*. There were always honest state wardens, and we had good people in the department like Alan Ensminger, the chief of the refuge division, and Richard Yancey, the assistant director under Glasgow, and Ted Joanen—he's the top biologist at the Rockefeller Refuge now—who were trying to run Wildlife and Fisheries the way it should have been run. But they were overwhelmed. The Louisiana system—the outlawin tradition, the widespread corruption . . . how do you fight *that?* It was like drugs are today. Then in come us hard-core, no-nonsense federal game wardens telling these people that we're gonna shut down this outlawin for their own good. I won em over little by little. I got A.J. to recognize I was right, and probably Clinton. But at first, son, they just went wild down here when they saw we meant *business.* We damn near had to shoot our way in and out of these bayous."

It was in April of 1971 that the Plott case broke. Right afterward, the murders began.

The original Endangered Species Conservation Act, which became fully effective in June of 1970, had made a federal crime of the interstate shipment of reptiles and amphibians taken contrary to state law. As soon as the act was passed, the Fish and Wildlife Service put every potential alligator skin dealer in the country under close watch.

The international fur and reptile hide business is a much bigger industry than one might think—yearly sales of raw and finished products are in the many billions—but it is dominated by a handful of big tanneries and distributors, and only a few of those are in the United States. One of the largest, besides the Mares brothers, was the Q. C. Plott Raw Fur and Ginseng Company, whose offices were on Peachtree Street in Atlanta, Georgia. All through 1970, shipments leaving the Plott warehouse were inspected at New Orleans—which was where Plott shipped out most of his goods—and nothing illegal was found. On a hunch, the USFWS began checking other ports and, finally, in April of 1971, discovered a huge shipment of carefully camouflaged alligator hides about to be loaded in Savannah for Japan. The shipping manifest said they originated from the firm of Q. C. Plott.

The service's agents burst into Plott's offices and boxed his files before any of them could be destroyed. It was pure dumb luck that Plott had an anal-compulsive bookkeeper; every transaction, legal and illegal, had been meticulously transcribed. Plott's records revealed that, during the previous three years, he had sent out more than one hundred twenty-seven thousand American alligator skins, most of them overseas. That figure represented nearly half the estimated number of alligators surviving in the United States. Fifty firms in seventeen countries were regularly buying from Plott. But of far greater interest, at least to Dave Hall, was a fat folder of receipts indicating who had sold him hides. There were more than two hundred names; it was a Who's Who of alligator poaching in the United States. Dozens of potential indictments were sitting in Plott's files. The odds were also high that some of the indicted, when offered immunity, would turn state's evidence and reveal how they had managed to poach alligators with relative impunity all those years.

One name on the list was Pappy Wellborn, who had supplied Plott with masses of hides from Texas. Pappy lived in Beaumont, the seat of Jefferson County, the last county in the United States where commercial alligator hunting was still legal. Pappy had long been suspected as the mastermind of the operation that laundered alligator skins from other states, mainly Louisiana. Rumors were rife that Wildlife and Fisheries people were in business with him. Not long after the Plott operation unraveled, two men broke into Pappy's home at two-thirty in the morning, beat him and his wife mercilessly, and left them for dead. His business records were the only things the assailants took as they left.

Hank McGee, a convicted alligator poacher who lived near Morgan City, was also on the list. A couple of weeks after Pappy Wellborn and his wife were beaten comatose, McGee and his Indian buddy Billiot were found floating in a Louisiana marsh. They had been shot, respectively, sixteen and fifteen times.

About a month later, Dave Hall got a call from James Nunez, the resident game warden on the Rockefeller Refuge, near Avery Island, on the southwestern Louisiana coast. James said he had visited the best friend of another convicted alligator poacher, Johnny Boudreaux—who had allegedly hanged himself in the Lafayette, Louisiana, jail—in the Cameron Parish prison, and because of Johnny's untimely and suspicious death, his friend desperately wanted out.

Boudreaux's friend, A. J. Caro, was someone Dave Hall knew by reputation only. Most of the South's alligator habitat had by then been hunted out; the state and federal refuges were the only places where one still found concentrations of the creatures. The refuges—and Everglades National Park, another last alligator redoubt—were much more heavily patrolled, and anyone caught hunting on one was looking at a certain jail term, so most poachers weren't up to the risk. Caro was one of the few. He had been the scourge of the Lacassine and Rockefeller refuges for years.

Caro was an escape artist. Caught several times, he had also been the object of at least a dozen mad-dog chases. During one of them, Caro was in his pickup, going hell-for-leather down a public road with two carloads of game wardens breathing his exhaust. The wardens radioed a bridge tender up ahead to raise his drawbridge. Caro didn't blink. He flung open the door, threw himself out, somersaulted into the marsh, and instantly disappeared. A couple of infuriated wardens stayed around all night, patrolling with spotlights, and reinforcements arrived the next day in swamp boats and a spotter plane. Caro was gone. Actually, he wasn't gone. He was probably within spitting distance of one of the search boats, dangling from a buoyant mass of surface vegetation and breathing through a cane reed, like John Colter hiding from the Blackfeet in an icy stream. The game wardens finally gave up, but Caro figured his home would be staked out for days, so he remained in the marshes for nearly three weeks. He killed muskrats, frogs, and snakes for food; he lived in empty trapper and hunting camps. Then he crossed into Texas, on foot, and stayed there for several months. He never told anyone where he had hidden, but everyone assumed he went to Pappy Wellborn's. That was the reason James Nunez called Dave Hall: with Pappy lying comatose, Boudreaux suspiciously hanged in jail, and Caro a personal friend of both, there was no telling who might be after him, what kind of danger he might be in, and what he might do or say in exchange for an early release.

"A.J. was of no help to us at first," remembers Dave Hall. "Everything he told us was an evasion or a flat-out lie. I didn't trust him an inch, and I guess he didn't trust me either. All he would tell me was that there were a lot of big people involved in Louisiana alligator poaching on both sides of the fence and he was scared for his life. He wasn't scared to the point where he was crying, but he seemed plenty scared. I could have told him, 'Give me names and dates and places or I ain't gonna help you.' But to be honest with you, if I'd have taken on Wildlife and Fisheries I'm not sure who was gonna win. I would have gotten in a hellacious battle, maybe put a few people on the spot, and the poaching would have gone on like before. I wanted to shut down the dealers. It's easier to fight crime than corruption. Besides Mares and Plott, we still didn't know who the really big ones were. A.J. was an investment in the future—that's how I saw him. That's always been my style. You got to be patient. You got to be a good judge of character. I thought maybe there was an off chance that A.J. would return a favor someday if I asked him to. But back then I never trusted him at all."

Dave Hall grinned at Caro after he said this. "The amount of risk I took with A.J. probably never was justified by the trust I had in him then."

A.J. was listening soberly to this assessment of himself. "Like Dave said, you got to be a good judge of character. Now I admit I was outside the law and all this. There are people you call outlaws who got as strong a sense of morals as anyone. Dave done me a big favor I knew I had to repay. I was hopin he'd never call me, doncha know, cause I figured he'd be askin me to do some undercover thing and I might get hurt or somethin. Anyways, later on, after what them guys did, he didn even have to call me. I end up callin Dave."

It is utterly at odds with standard procedure in Louisiana to have a prisoner removed from a parish jail when he is up on state or parish charges. Dave Hall was never one for standard procedure. Two days later, U.S. marshals were taking A. J. Caro to the federal penitentiary in Atlanta, for his own protection. Unable to make bail, he would ultimately serve six months there.

A. J. Caro was not the most colorful outlaw who was offered up by Plott's files, nor was he potentially the most useful to the Fish and Wildlife Service and Dave Hall. Honors in both categories had to go to Woodrow Dufrene. Woody Dufrene had been Plott's main supplier of raw Louisiana hides. During a ten-month period, from June of 1970 to April of 1971, Plott had paid him $44,929.74 for 3,451 alligator skins. In modern money, circa 1989, that was $150,000 a year for selling alligator skins, and since Woody sold to others besides Plott, he made a good deal more. Woody was proof that an enterprising alligator poacher could make almost as much money, tax-free, as the president of the United States.

Before making all that money, Woody, to use Dave Hall's phrase, "was the kind of guy that just flat-ass couldn't do right." After shucking around at fishing, trapping, farm labor, and petty crime through his twenties, he had decided to become an entrepreneur. A Cajun entrepreneur is going to have something to do with meat, fish, skins, furs, or bait, unless he gets into drugs or moonshine. Woody picked pet food. He had his own little rendering plant in Kenner, a few miles outside New Orleans. The source of Woody's dog and kitty chow was of uncertain origin, but a lot of horse trailers were seen backing into his loading dock. In Cajun Louisiana, just about any four-legged creature, wild or tame, is regarded as legitimate food for man or man's best friend, but Woody's pet-food plant was a little too close to New Orleans; urban sensibilities and animal-rights activists shut him down. Unfazed, Woody began using nutria meat—trappers would otherwise have tossed the carcasses away—but a few months later his plant burned down. He scraped together his remaining savings and got into turtle farming at about the same time the Department of Agriculture discovered that turtles carry salmonella and banned turtle meat.

So there he was, fifty years old, a little brown Cajun capitalist without two nickels to rub together and pray for a dollar. Alligator skins were his last, best hope. He had been poaching and selling them for just a few years, however, when he decided to try one last semilegitimate career: hair. One of the people to whom Woody sold alligators—all this came out later—was Thomas D'Amato, one of the princes of the Louisiana fur and hide trade. One day, when Woody was delivering D'Amato a load of skins, he met D'Amato's son-in-law, a hijacker and journeyman thug named Kelly, who had an import-export front near the Brooklyn wharves. Kelly stole and sold anything that came his way—hijacked clothes, counterfeit money, art, alligator skins, dope. He got into hair in the sixties, when there was a thankfully short-lived wig craze. The Hong Kong manufacturers were paying premium prices for authentic Indian hair, which makes the best wigs. The nearest place where you could find Indian hair in large quantities, on unsuspecting heads, was among the remnant tribes of Central America. Kelly gave Woody a passport, a plane ticket, an envelope stuffed with cash, and several duffels full of hijacked clothes. Woody flew to Belize, rented a jeep, and went into the hinterland looking for hair. The female population of whole villages was soon sporting shaved heads and gaudy Hawaiian shirts. (Woody claimed that he found some missionaries who, in return for a large contribution to their church, convinced the women that cutting their hair was an offering to God.) The village menfolk, however, soon had enough of bald-headed daughters and wives, and Woody had to flee for his life. He flew back to the States, his new career nipped in the bud. "I hated to give it up," he told Dave Hall. "I was gettin that hayr fer nuthin." By then, however, the price of alligator skins had gone way up, so Woody made his killing for another two years, until the Plott evidence dumped him in jail in 1972. He got one of the longest sentences ever meted out for wildlife poaching, a year and a half in the federal penitentiary in Texas. Dave Hall went to his sentencing and consoled his poor family, who were all wailing away.

"Woody," he said, "I hope your friends take care of your family while you're in prison. But in case they don't, you ought to see me when you get out. I might have a job for you."

Woody came to see Dave Hall two days after he got out.

By then Dave Hall was no longer Dave Hall. He was Charles Strickland, the co-owner of a covert alligator-tanning operation in the French Quarter, at 2756 Toulouse Street.

One of the Plott indictees whom Dave Hall had decided to "work" was Wenzell Zimmerman, a big, shambling German who owned one of the handful of tanneries still operating in the United States. His feeling that Zimmerman might cooperate was, he says, mostly a hunch, but it was undoubtedly more. Dave Hall is a history buff—historical fiction is about all he reads for pleasure—and he knew that the same people who were capable of roasting babies and horsewhipping naked women to death were also—among the Europeans who settled America—the culture that had treated the Indians with greater sympathy and tolerance than any other. In faraway wilderness, one ran into Germans all the time. There was some gene imprint in German culture that inculcated an appreciation of wild nature. For whatever motive, Zimmerman was ready to cooperate right away. "I'd have to call Big Zim one of the most honorable men I've ever met. He came from three or four generations of tanners. His granddaddy was one of the early Germans in Louisiana. He settled down there with most of them at Des Allemands and started a tannery right about the time of the Civil War. Zim got into some financial trouble and started tanning alligator skins from Plott. I really don't think he felt good about it cause he wasn't a chronic violator or anything. He was just desperate for a time. Even Plott wasn't that bad a guy. We had both of them cooperating with us pretty quick."

At Zimmerman's tannery, for just over a year, Dave Hall had the best of worlds: he was hunting outlaws, but they were coming to him. He was running a roach motel. Only rarely did he have to go to some trouble to lure them inside. An informant's tip came in one day, conveyed through a friendly FBI agent, that a man in North Carolina named Pruitt was trying to take over from Plott. Pruitt, according to his FBI profile, was a racketeer and big-time gambler. His partner, Monroe Jackson, had connections in the high ranks of organized crime and thought he could make some safe money dealing expensive reptile skins. Dave Hall got Pruitt's number through the informant (even though he was endangering the FBI agent's job) and rang him up. Pruitt was a little hincky, so Dave Hall said he would like to come up and see him the following week.

HALL (STRICKLAND): I can tell you . . . I carry quite a bit of cash . . .

PRUITT: Yeah, well, we do too, you know . . .

HALL: I don't . . . you know there has been some deals where . . . when people know that someone's carrying a lot of cash they get kinda rambunctious.

PRUITT: Yes, yes, well . . .

HALL: I been through that before too . . .

PRUITT: There you go . . . we have to . . . we know exactly what you're talking about . . .

HALL: I carry plenty, but I'll protect it . . .

PRUITT: Yeah, there ain't going to be nothing like that from this end at all cause we . . .

HALL: Un-hunh . . .
PRUITT: I'll guarantee everything . . .

They had dinner in Raleigh. A little crook talk, a couple more paranoid little outbursts for effect—"a lot of outlaws don't trust you unless they think you've killed someone"—and three weeks later, on August 18, 1974, Pruitt and his two partners were driving down to Zimmerman's tannery with a shipment of alligator hides. It was a shipment so large— a linear half mile of skins—that they carried it in a huge, refrigerated semitrailer rig. Pruitt was telling Strickland and his buddy Tommy Candies, a Wildlife and Fisheries warden, that he had the alligator business in the Southeast all sewed up, that as long as any were left they would be sold by him, when a mob of federal and state game wardens came in the door.

This was the first big take-down at Big Zim's tannery, so it had to be played for maximum effect. As USFWS agent James Bartee was putting cuffs on Tommy Candies, he became a whirligig of obscenities and began resisting arrest, to the point where Bartee was still nursing his aches several days later. In court, U.S. Magistrate Harry Lee, who was a personal friend of Dave Hall, asked subject Strickland whether he had any cash on hand to make bail, and Strickland leaped up, venting his fury on the federal and state officers who had confiscated it. The transcript did not note that Magistrate Lee, about to burst into laughter, had to pretend he had dropped his pen so he could climb under his desk and frantically suppress the urge. The court record did not note that suspect Pruitt, who was very much impressed by Strickland's defiance of police and court authority, told him later in their holding cell that he had a good lawyer who would keep him out of jail for sure.

By late 1974, however, when Woody Dufrene was finally released from the penitentiary, Zimmerman's tannery had outlived its usefulness. They had made bust after bust, and Charles Strickland had become a familiar figure in the New Orleans courthouse, where district attorneys and police were under strict orders not to recognize him, but most of the outlaws they were busting were pretty minor characters. Which isn't to say that the alligator business was shut down—anything but. In fact, a fascinating little lesson in the ecology of poaching was being learned in the southern wilds. After Mares and then Plott were pinched off, annual alligator censuses taken in the southern states showed that the creatures were on the rebound. Habitat loss, it seemed, was not that great a problem; it was commercial hunting that had been doing the animals in. Then, in some states, or at least in certain parts of those states, the situation appeared to reverse. Alligators were again in decline—or at least not multiplying nearly as much as they should have been. No one could figure out why. Habitat loss? Drought? Poaching? As far as the Fish and Wildlife Service was concerned, every major alligator dealer in the country had been shut down. Plott and Zimmerman were collaborating. Mares was constantly watched. Pappy Wellborn was on a respirator in a hospital bed, a human vegetable for life. Woody Dufrene had spent the past eighteen months in jail. There might be thousands of erstwhile alligator poachers living in the swamps, but there was no point in killing alligators if you had no one to sell to. Alligator hides are different from feathers or furs or other wild contraband: they don't keep or freeze well. You can't really keep them live around the house, as you can with exotic parrots, until buyers show up. The beasts have to be killed on demand, skinned, salted down, and shipped fast for curing. As far as Dave Hall and his fellow agents were concerned, they had closed down all the big buyers, all the important sources of demand.

In Dave Hall's pantheon of criminals, there are bad dudes, bad-ass dudes, outlaws, raggedy-ass outlaws, gangsters, no-goods, scumbags, lowlifes, dirtbags, dirtballs, hoodlums, gyppo hoodlums, fucking hoodlums, and bikers. Jack Kelly was, interchangeably, any of these at once, but more often he was a plain, ordinary lowlife. A lowlife is just a rung above a biker in Dave Hall's estimation. "Kelly," he says, "he was the sort of lowlife who'd swagger down the street with a .38 and just as soon blow you away as look at you. It's so corrupt up there in New York I don't know what-all he got away with, but if we hadn't socked him for alligator hides someone'd have got him sooner or later for extortion, hijacking, or something a hell of a lot worse."

Kelly had been a shadowy figure since the Plott investigation, along with his suspected partner, Jacques Klapisch, one of the largest fur traders in the world. Plott's files showed he had done business with both of them. The FBI profile on Kelly made him out to be a buyer of hijacked goods, if not a major hijacker himself. He had a store in Brooklyn that sold clothes—presumably a front. Why would someone like this traffic in alligator hides, with so much easy money to be made heisting goods from trucks, trains, and ships? All the other big alligator dealers operated out of the South. New York City was not where one would expect to find big business in *alligator hides.*

That was conventional wisdom until Woody Dufrene showed up at Dave Hall's receptionist's desk two days after he was released from jail. The receptionist ran into Dave Hall's office with a frightened look. Woody, she was convinced, was packing a heater and was going to kill everyone in sight before sticking it in his own mouth. Dave Hall contemplated the silver .38 he keeps in his desk, then scoffed. A revenge murder wasn't Woody Dufrene's style.

Woody had come to unburden himself. He had had a lot of time to think in prison, and at first he could think only of how much he hated Dave Hall. He had hated him especially when his wife came to visit, looking thinner and more haggard as the months passed. Woody's tax-free boodle from alligators had been squandered God knows how, and the dregs that remained had run out about halfway through his prison term. His family had been reduced to subsistence, to charity and food stamps.

That was over now, but Woody was busted and had no job and needed money. His "gangster" friends had offered him some work, but he didn't want to do it.

"Why not?" asked Dave Hall. He didn't want to press him about who his gangster friends were.

"I want you to get em," said Woody.

"How come?"

"They didn do nothin for my family. They would of let em starve. I hepped em make millions and they would of let em starve. Dave, this cocodrie business, doncha know, it's all I ever made money at. I can't do nothin else. Like you say, I want it to be legal once more. It ain't ever gonna be legal if these guys keep killin em out. We got to get em."

Well, now he might as well make the plunge. "Who are they?"

"Kelly and Klapisch. I never told you, but they runnin the whole business now. They're as big as Plott was. They buyin from all over the South."

"How are you gonna help us?"

"They plannin on pickin up a big load next week."

All Woody knew was that Kelly and one of his partners intended to come to New Orleans sometime on September 12, that they were going to stay at the Airport Hilton, and that they were going to haul a load of hides back to New York. He wasn't sure how and wasn't even sure the hides would go to New York, but since Kelly's people ruled the wharves, that was where they would probably go. That was where they had always gone. Dave Hall reasoned that they could grab Kelly as soon as he took possession of the hides, but they wanted to get him in a federal violation, so they needed to let him cross a state line. Then they might as well let him reach his final destination, wherever it was, so they could jump his shipping operation. Perhaps they could capture a foreign buyer or two as well; Woody had said that nearly all his hides went overseas, chiefly to Japan. "Drift your net more, and you catch more fish. But you risk losing your net." What this meant was they would have to tail Kelly, conceivably all the way to New York. He would be watching for a tail, so they would have to shift cars quite a bit. They could lose him in traffic. They would have to watch for a decoy run to New York while the shipment was actually going out through Galveston or Houston or somewhere else.

What resulted was a hastily conjured, seriocomic chase out of the moonshine era and the Keystone Kops: thirty federal game wardens and troopers, in about ten cars and a spotter plane, trying to keep up with two evasive and paranoid drivers running a load of alligator skins for nearly two thousand miles.

When Kelly arrived at the Hilton, he was driving a rented sedan. His partner—who was later identified as Martin Dara, a small-time hoodlum whom Kelly often employed as a mule—was driving a station wagon. This had to be a trick. You didn't haul alligator skins in *station wagons*. On the other hand, if you used a truck, you would have to stop at weigh stations, and your contents might be inspected there. A station wagon was the least suspicious-looking vehicle on the road, with everything inside visible through the windows. You could stuff one with boxed or bagged hides and rate just a quick casual glance. What driver, what game warden even, would pass you by and say to himself, "Oh, there goes a big load of alligator skins"? This Kelly was not dumb. He was no violet either. These hides would *stink*. After three days cooped up in cars stuffed with alligator skins, Kelly and Dara would smell like dead alligators for about a month. As for the cars, Hertz might do well to render them into scrap.

Within two hours of Kelly and Dara's arrival at the Hilton, a pilgrimage of poachers began arriving at their suite. Mike Macalusa, a long-suspected alligator poacher, drove up from Des Allemands. Then Clinton Dufrene. Then Edwin Tregle, a former deputy sheriff and Louisiana game warden who had twice been convicted of poaching alligators. Then Manu Rodriguez, another suspected big-time poacher. Then Alton Dufrene, another one. When Kelly and Dara finally drove out of the garage the next morning, their vehicles were filled to the roofs with boxes and burlap bags. Even a large alligator's skin rolls up into a tight little drum, so they were hauling four or five hundred hides, a hundred thousand dollars' worth of stinking loot. It wasn't enough for Kelly, who stayed behind to pick up more skins. Dara went ahead with two carloads of agents on his tail.

Every two or three hundred miles the cars that had been following Dara had to drop away; since he was speeding up to ninety-five at times, there was no way they could get in front of him, and he must have had his eyes glued to the tail-view mirror. Two or three hundred miles was long enough. Somewhere in North Carolina it dawned on everyone that no one had actually *seen* an alligator skin in the car. What if this was some intricate ruse, and Dara was driving a load of rolled-up rags in sacks to New York? What if this expensive, taxpayer-financed pursuit was a red herring, and Kelly was unloading the real hides in Savannah?

The question was answered when Dara made a long stop and three or four cats gathered on the roof of his car, sniffing furiously at the window seals.

While Dara was roaring along at nearly twice the speed limit, then wheeling off at an exit and waiting before getting back on; when he was suddenly slowing to forty and then doubling his speed, he never got a ticket—not once in eighteen hundred miles. The agents were stopped three times by state police. One agent was so afraid of losing Dara that he burst out of his car when the first trooper pulled him over, and found himself looking at a drawn revolver. At Richmond, Virginia, Dara stopped at a motel just before three in the morning. The exhausted agents couldn't afford to sleep; Dara might be playing a sneak-out game. He emerged from his room at five. He ate a quick breakfast and got on Interstate 95 again. By then he had a spotter plane circling over his head at two thousand feet, but he was now driving as if his suspicions were finally at rest. At two-twenty in the afternoon, he drove past the gate guards and into Kelly's estate on the inner south shore of Long Island, at Breezy Point. The locus of the biggest alligator-poaching operation in the United States was a gangster's six-bedroom home in an exclusive suburb on Long Island. The smell neighbors must have thought was from a school of fish rotting in the Sound was one source of Jack Kelly's livelihood.

The guarded gate presented a problem. There was a marina right by Kelly's house, and he might try to sneak the skins out by water. He could take them straight to Kennedy Airport, which was right across Jamaica Bay. He could run them through the Narrows and to the wharves at Gowanus Bay in Brooklyn. To make sure he didn't, they had to have a lookout nearby. But no one could get in without the guard's calling Kelly's house first. An undercover state trooper named Peter Silvaine found his inspiration with a little girl on a bicycle. As she rode by, Silvaine jumped out of the car. "Police business, miss," he said brusquely, seizing the bicycle as the wide-eyed girl ran away. Silvaine rolled up his pants and sleeves and waved cheerfully to the guards at the gate as he pedaled by. He knocked on a neighbor's door and asked the man if he knew Kelly. The man did. He asked the man what he thought of Kelly. "I hate the son of a bitch," the man said, "and so does everyone else."

As the other agents sat half-reclining in their cars a couple of blocks from the main Breezy Point gate, eating a dinner of sandwiches and pizza, Silvaine was eating a steak and a salad and drinking a nice bottle of red wine. He watched Kelly's car enter his driveway at just past nine.

At eight-thirty the next morning both station wagons left Breezy Point. Silvaine followed at a discreet distance on his bicycle, then jumped into one of the waiting cars. Kelly and Dara did not seem to notice them as they went by. They drove directly into New York on the Queensborough Bridge, skirted the Plaza Hotel—where some of the alligators might well reappear later, as five-hundred-dollar shoes—and took the Lincoln Tunnel to Newark. They ended up in a warehouse district near Elizabeth, New Jersey. A steel garage door went up and they drove into a low, white-painted brick warehouse. MEG IMPORTS was written over the door. It was from here, Jacques Klapisch's front, that the equivalent—it was learned later—of a quarter of America's surviving alligators had left the United States in the past three years. Most were doused with fragrant oil to camouflage the smell and packed in wooden boxes labeled "machine parts."

Silvaine, whose relish for character acting could not be quelled, found an empty Thunderbird bottle in the street and staggered up to the warehouse, where he collapsed outside the fence so he could see what was going on within. Kelly, Klapisch, Dara, and several other men were standing in an open interior courtyard. The floor was covered with skins.

Some of the suspects scattered when the raid began. Others froze. Martin Dara, the mule, took off in a car. He was run down five or six blocks away by Dave Hall and agent Jerry Smith—on foot. "Pigs!" people screamed from the windows above. "You dirty rotten pigs."

Kelly and Klapisch both received jail time—suspended to probation in each case—and fines totaling ninety-five hundred dollars. That had been enough of a lesson for Quince Plott, who got a similar sentence, but Dave Hall was sure that Kelly and Klapisch would be tempted to get back in business again. Kelly's access to the mob-controlled Brooklyn wharves was an invaluable asset; once he got skins as far as New York they were gone unless USFWS agents followed him around day and night. The service was so short on manpower (the Nixon administration had sharply reduced its enforcement ranks, from more than two hundred thirty agents to a hundred and eighty) that neither he nor Klapisch was being watched at all. Besides, jail wasn't likely to faze Kelly in the slightest. "Kelly," says Dave Hall, "was a career criminal. He never made a legal dollar in his life. Plott was a basically legitimate businessman who'd gone wrong. When you're dedicated to a life of crime and you're making the money Kelly was with hides, a couple months' sentence, even if they make you serve it, is just downtime."

Meanwhile, in the wilds of the South, no one really knew what the alligator's status was—whether it was recovering or still sliding downhill. Dave Hall has a fat sheaf of clippings on the alligator "problem," dating mostly from the late 1960s to the mid-1970s, and what is most striking about them is the sense of ambivalence: it is unclear whether the "problem" was too few alligators or too many. According to an article from the New Orleans *Times Picayune*, which appeared on June 18, 1972, "Louisiana game officials claim the alligator population in the state now numbers a minimum of 250,000 and has reached the point where a controlled harvest is necessary." Just two years later, however, an outdoors columnist, Ed Riciutti, wrote that during an extensive tour of Cameron Parish he had seen alligators only in protected refuges; everywhere else, they were gone. An article from the *Christian Science Monitor*, dated April 5, 1972, quoted Everglades Park officials as saying that 90 to 95 percent of the alligators in the park itself had been illegally hunted out; Dr. Frank Craighead, a well-known wildlife ecologist, offered a figure of 98 to 99 percent for the state at large. Since Craighead estimated that there were once two million alligators in the state, then, by his yardstick, only forty thousand or so remained. Just four years later, however, an article in the *Times Picayune* estimated Florida's population of alligators at half a million. The numbers were apparently jumping all over the place: down in Louisiana, up in Florida.

Nathaniel Reed, who replaced Leslie Glasgow as assistant secretary of the interior for Fish, Wildlife, and Parks, thought he had an answer to the confusion: when a big poaching ring got established—Mares, Plott, Klapisch and Kelly, or someone else—alligator numbers went down. When they were nailed, the numbers went up. Reed, a wealthy Republican from Jupiter Island, on Florida's Gold Coast, who somehow managed to become a fierce-natured conservationist, says he found the relationship difficult to believe at first (and there are many who still do). "I thought it was absurd at first. It sounded like a joke. My biologists, some of them, were telling me it was a joke. But every time the alligator seemed to be in trouble we busted up another ring. After Plott, the numbers went up. Then they seemed to be in trouble again. That was Klapisch and Kelly taking over from Plott. Everyone knows a big drug haul can affect the street supply. If someone like the Hunts make a run on silver, they can affect the supply and the price. No one could believe it could be the same way with alligators."

What Reed did not know, as his brief reign at Interior was about to end, was that Kelly and Klapisch, in the two years since their sentencing, had, according to strong circumstantial evidence, shipped out ten to thirty thousand alligator hides to the insatiable markets in France, Italy, and Japan—especially Japan. He might never have known had not A. J. Caro called Dave Hall in 1976, saying that if he did not deputize him as a free-lance undercover agent he was going to kill Kelly himself.

By then A. J. Caro had been out of jail for nearly three years. Dave Hall had had little contact with him—he didn't want to push him too hard. He had tried to put out some feelers to learn what A.J. was up to, but he didn't know whom to believe. James Nunez at the Rockefeller Refuge thought he was poaching alligators again and would be caught any day. State game wardens said he was a bouncer at a local bar and seemed to be clean, at least as far as alligators were concerned. Someone else said he had gotten in with a biker crowd; he might be dealing drugs or making methamphetamines. A.J. was working part-time as a bouncer—an occupation where a criminal record helps—but otherwise they were all wrong. Caro was no longer killing alligators. He was buying hides by the thousands from others and driving them to New York, then moving them to Japan-bound ships in a mailman's uniform, driving a surplus postal service truck.

When Caro called Dave Hall he was in Lake Arthur, nearly two hundred miles away. "I want you to come out here and I'll tell you the whole story," he said.

"I ain't comin all the way out there, A.J. Tell me on the phone."

"I can't tell it on the phone. I shouldn't even be on the phone to you. There's still a lot of worried folks around here. They might have it tapped."

A.J. said he would come in by bus if Dave Hall paid the fare. He didn't want anyone to see him at Dave Hall's office, which was then in downtown New Orleans. He should come to the Greyhound station.

Dave Hall found Caro there at three in the afternoon the next day. By dribs and drabs—Caro was being extraordinarily evasive—the story finally came out. Kelly and Klapisch had barely been bothered by the bust Woody Dufrene had set up. They had surrogates arranging big alligator-hide buys as they sat in the courtroom dock. How did Dave Hall think he, Caro, had made a living over the past couple of years? Kelly was advancing him hundreds of thousands of dollars to buy hides from the local hunters, then paying him for each trip to Breezy Point and Newark. He had spent a lot of the past year in a van enduring turnpike trance. With the price of hides constantly going up—it was now forty dollars the linear foot—Klapisch and Kelly were making too much money to quit. They were paying him more money than he had ever seen in his life, and were still getting rich. On his last trip, to help him over his freeway blues, Caro had taken his girlfriend with him. She was a Cajun girl, small, pretty, black-haired, and nut-brown. He should have noticed that Kelly was ogling her the moment they walked in his door. The hides Caro had brought were fresh, not even salted, and Kelly said he could earn a couple hundred more dollars by taking them to Klapisch's warehouse and salting them down. His girlfriend had remained behind, at Kelly's invitation; she could go shopping with his wife. There was no wife, at least not that day. Caro never told Dave Hall exactly what had happened to his girlfriend. Apparently she wasn't sure herself; Caro was convinced she had been drugged. All Dave Hall would tell me is that Caro was sure something "bad, bad, bad" had happened to her, and he was enraged—so enraged that Kelly might not be long for this world.

"What are you gonna do about Kelly, A.J.?"

"If I can't put Jack in jail, I'm gonna kill him. No one can stop me."

"How do you propose we put his ass in jail?"

"He's bein real careful now. I doan even know who's supplying him other than me. You ain't gonna tail him to New York again unless you tail me, and I don't want that. I want to get him for you."

"A.J., I can't let you go up there if you're maybe gonna kill Kelly. I'll tell you what, though. I might let you do it if you go up there with one of my agents."

"I can't go up to Jack Kelly's with no undercover game warden. He could get us both killed. Kelly smells cops like a hound smells deer."

"It ain't a he I have in mind. It's a she."

"That's crazy."

"Look at it this way—"

"I didn even know there was such a thing as a female game warden. You mean *undercover?*"

"If you bring a girl along, first off, Kelly isn't going to suspect that you're mad enough at him to kill him. He'll probably think your girlfriend couldn't even remember what happened to her. Why would you bring *another* girl if you knew what happened to the last one?"

"Bein with a policewoman all the time could cramp my style with Jack."

"And second, I need an agent to make my evidence in this case. You got to admit, A.J., that you aren't the world's most credible witness if it comes out what they did to your girl. Their lawyers are just going to argue that you set them up. Pure revenge. Kelly will argue that the hide delivery is a total fabrication."

"What if Jack figures out who she is? You'd get us both killed."

"The last thing Jack Kelly thinks could exist is a female undercover game warden."

There were, at the time, only three or four female undercover game wardens in the country, all of them working for the Fish and Wildlife Service. Because of the affirmative-action laws, more and more women were applying to be game wardens. They were strongly motivated, nearly all of them, but if they were figuring that it would be easier than being a street cop, they were in for a rude shock. Big brawny male game wardens were often menaced when they told riffraff and roughnecks that they were under arrest. If a *woman* tried to collar a gang of poachers, even in the company of a male warden, all hell broke loose. Deer season! Duck season! That is pretty much what a significant minority of American males live for. Have a *woman* tell you you were under arrest . . . for a doe . . . for an overlimit of *ducks?* In 1984, one female game warden was shot to death. Many of the women who went to work for Fish and Wildlife didn't last two years, even if they did no undercover work.

There were, however, a couple who had worked out exceptionally well. One who showed considerable promise had been on the job less than a year and had never handled a case remotely like this. Dave Hall had a lot of confidence in her, anyway. She was small, pretty, smart, Italian, and tough as a wolverine. At twenty-six, she was young enough for A.J., and dark enough to pass for Cajun. If Kelly had any suspicions about her, he would probably forget about them soon enough. Kelly would take a shine to Marie Palladini. She was perfect.

"They talk about me being an unorthodox guy," said Dave Hall. "If anything had happened to Marie I might have been unorthodox enough to want to kill those scumbags."

Dave Hall's first problem, however, was not Marie, Kelly, Klapisch, or even Caro—for what would *he* be like as a free-lance undercover game warden?—but the institution that curdles his soul: bureaucracy. He asked Marie to fly down to New Orleans to see if she could stand working with Caro. He introduced them at a French Quarter café and left. Marie called later that night. She could not only work with A.J., she even liked him a little bit. She spent most of the next day with him to be sure and also to reinvent twenty-six years of her life. They left the next day in Caro's van for Patuxent, Maryland, carrying some of the same gator hides that had been seized from Kelly and Klapisch eighteen months earlier. All Marie remembers about the drive is that she endured fifteen straight hours of instruction in coon-ass talk. "Talking Pittsburgh ain't gonna cut it with Kelly," Caro had said.

Patuxent is the home of the USFWS Wildlife Research Center, and the place where Caro was to pick up more alligator skins; it contains, in addition to captive breeders and endangered species, a huge trove of confiscated wild animal parts. Caro took one brief look at the pile of alligator skins that had been requisitioned for him and waved them away. They had been frozen; there were telltale marks of freezer burn. There were also hornbacks—skins from the tough, armored alligator back.

The Patuxent biologists didn't see any freezer burn. Well, perhaps a little. Anyway, what difference would it make if he delivered frozen hides and a few hornbacks?

Caro said Kelly and Klapisch sold mainly to Japan, and the Japanese hide dealers were fanatics about quality. Besides, there was no market for hornbacks now; they were used mainly to make purses, and right now women for some reason didn't want to store their perfume and hankies in a dead reptile pouch. Hornbacks would immediately be suspect.

The biologists told Caro he was out of his mind.

Caro wasn't getting anywhere with these guys. He went to a telephone and called Dave Hall in New Orleans.

As a former alligator buyer and tanner, Dave Hall knew Caro was right. You didn't pay forty dollars a foot for freezer-burned hides. He was right about the hornbacks, too. There hadn't been a hornback market in years. Dave Hall called Washington and insisted that Caro needed fresh alligator hides.

The chief said he didn't have any fresh skins. And if Caro went back to Louisiana and killed some alligators, that would be highly illegal. That could not be countenanced. Alligators were a fully protected species.

The chief had mentioned killing alligators; he hadn't said anything about taking them on consignment from dealers who already had them in possession. Dave Hall got Caro back on the line and told him to pick up a prepaid ticket to New Orleans at the airport counter. When he arrived, Dave Hall met him in his personal truck and gave him the keys, along with credit cards, spending money, and some exquisitely detailed instructions.

"A.J., if you kill any gators, or solicit someone to kill any, I'm gonna bust your ass. You *buy* those suckers. I don't care from who. And if you wreck my truck we're both gonna have to take off for Mexico."

When Caro reappeared three days later, the pickup truck contained about three hundred alligator hides under a tarp. Dave Hall winced. Why did he have to buy so goddamned many? Caro said Kelly knew exactly how many were available, and if he brought fewer, Kelly would be suspicious. Dave Hall helped A.J. salt down the hides and stuff them in fiber barrels. He wasn't precisely sure if what he was doing was legal or not. They shipped them back to Maryland by air freight, without a hitch.

The next afternoon, Marie and A.J. were parked at a shopping center five miles from Breezy Point, where Caro was arguing stubbornly with a resistant and equally stubborn Marie that she would have to give up her badge and gun.

As far as Marie was concerned, accompanying a notorious poacher to the house of a notorious thug on an undercover sting was one thing. Having to speak coon-ass on about two days' practice in a potential life-or-death situation was one thing. Worrying that anything she drank would have a pair of Quaaludes dissolved in it and that she would wake up with Kelly's sperm in her was one thing. But giving up her badge and gun was something else. She absolutely refused.

"I think you got to," Caro said.

"I will not!"

"Kelly is gonna suspect you no matter who you are or how you look. He's gonna suspect me. In his business you suspect everyone twenty-four hours a day. He's gonna find a chance to go through your purse, and if he finds a gun and badge, I doan know what Jack would do. He could kill us."

The badge was one thing, Marie said. What about the gun? Lots of women carry pistols, especially going to New York.

Caro said they didn't carry police .38s. Besides, Kelly had contacts who could run a check on the gun.

Marie decided to call Dave Hall.

With extreme reluctance, Dave Hall sided with Caro. Kelly hadn't made millions by being a fool. A body wire, he had already decided, was out, and a gun and badge were ill advised, too.

Marie almost said she wanted to quit the job on the spot. But Dave Hall promised that there would be an agent on a bicycle pedaling around Breezy Point Peter Silvaine–style, another agent on a motorcycle no more than a few minutes away, and a helicopter making periodic overflights whenever she was at Kelly's house. He also said that Caro was extremely quick and lethal with his hands.

◆ ◆ ◆

A.J. had told Marie that he didn't know how Kelly would act, but at the beginning he would probably be "squirrelly." He was as squirrelly as a Bouvier. He wouldn't even see them the night they arrived; he told them to stay at a motel. The next day he told them to stay at a different motel. He still wouldn't see them. Marie began to worry. So did A.J. At Marie's insistence, they were sleeping in separate rooms. What if Kelly came over to spy on them and noticed that? What girlfriend of Caro's would sleep in a separate bed, let alone a different room?

On the morning of the third day, Kelly called and told them to be at his store in Brooklyn at noon.

Kelly's store was crammed to the rafters with hijacked clothes. "Jack would buy out these eighteen-wheeler trucks some dudes had hijacked," remembers Caro. "He'd go down to the gubmint wharves and hep hisself. I never see corruption as bad as it was there in New York. Jack just seemed to have everyone bought off." Kelly bought just about anything, from pornography to television sets, but most of that stuff he sold to fences and mob-owned shops. His specialty, besides alligator skins, was clothes. He ran the sort of low-rent discount emporium where you shielded your eyes as you walked in: multicolored platform shoes, hallucinatory polyester shirts, full-Cleveland leisure suits—anything a lip-smacking, gum-chewing secretary or upwardly mobile Flatbush street punk felt was hip in the 1970s, when the fashion business took leave of its senses, Kelly was sure to have in stock. Paint-splatter ties. Lapels a yard wide. Denim cowboy boots. Putrescent green Sansabelt slacks. Marie remembers him as thirty-five, of middle height, frumpily dressed in an expensive but tasteless jacket and zip-up jodhpur boots. He was also totally bald. He wore a toupee made of hair that Woody Dufrene had probably stolen from some Indian girl's head. "He looked like Robert Duvall," she says, "with snake eyes."

Kelly had a buddy named Billy Greenblatt, a skinny Jewish thug who packed a heater so big it looked like a tumor in his armpit. He gave Marie a wink as they were introduced; Jack gave her a stare. Kelly told them to get in the van and follow him home. But they didn't go to Breezy Point. They were headed north, toward Queens, and finally parked in front of some house off Woodhaven Boulevard in Rego Park. Kelly opened the garage door and told them to back the van in. Marie froze. A.J. looked nervous, too.

Kelly came up to the van. "My mother's house," he said. "Got to be more careful since the fucking federals got us last time."

"When do we get the van back?" Caro asked.

"You won't need it," Kelly said. "Billy'll drive you where you have to go. We'll leave the hides here until they're ready to go to the wharf."

Marie Palladini had no body wire, no gun, no radio, no badge (a flashed badge implies massive manhunts and the electric chair to a trigger-happy outlaw and can be a covert agent's last chance to stay alive). And now she and Caro lost their last means of emergency escape: the van. Everything depended on a Cajun alligator poacher's wits. And her own.

They got in Kelly's car, Marie shouldering up against Billy Greenblatt and his brutishly big .44, and went to Kelly's cottage in the Rockaways. It was a place that belonged in the Louisiana bayous rather than in a deteriorating beach suburb just outside New York. The cottage had no locks on the doors or windows, no running water or toilet inside, a pair of plastic-covered kitchen chairs, and a double bed. It was a place where Kelly took women, and the decor, Marie observed, was a perfect reflection of Jack's approach to sex. Marie could not shower. She could not even brush her teeth unless she went to the spigot outside. And she was going to have to sleep in the same bed as A.J., unless one of them felt like sleeping on a cracked and curled linoleum floor.

Marie remembers the first night as . . . awkward. She was not married, but still . . . did female undercover agents sleep with outlaws, even if they were now on the same side? Even if they didn't make love? A.J., of course, was in a lustful mood right away. They hadn't been in bed one minute before he began stroking Marie's arm. She rebuffed him with savage firmness. He took it well. Then they both lay there for half an hour, unable to sleep. Caro finally got up, went outside to the spigot, and carefully washed his shirt with a bar of soap. He hung it over a lampshade, turned on the lamp, and went soundly to sleep. At about three in the morning, Marie did, too.

It was a ritual they were to repeat for the next several days.

The Japanese buyers to whom Kelly sold most of his hides had worked out an intricate system of covering their tracks. From Kelly's the skins would go to a freight forwarder. The freight forwarder would take them to the ship just as it was about to leave, minimizing the risk of a leisurely customs inspection. Kelly would not be paid until the ship was on the high seas, beyond the two-hundred-mile limit; out there, the skins could no longer be seized. The money, all cash, came from a laundry account in some local bank. Only then, after Kelly was paid, would Caro get his share. The whole business kept the Japanese disassociated from Kelly and Klapisch, who they knew might be watched. With the conservationists getting as much press as they did in the United States, the revelation that Japanese tanners were annihilating America's alligator stocks could turn into an international brouhaha, profoundly embarrassing to Japan.

Until Caro was paid for the hides, the government didn't have much of a case. Dave Hall was also determined to get the foreign buyers this time. He had chased poachers around the marshes for a solid decade, and that hadn't stopped the alligator trade. He had arrested Klapisch and Kelly eighteen months earlier and that hadn't shut them down either. As long as there was demand from above and beyond, a lot of alligators were going to be illegally slaughtered. All of this meant that the operation would go on longer than expected.

For Marie, the wait was excruciating. She spent most of each day with Kelly's wife, Barbara—who was at least an Italian, a *paisana*—at his clothing store. Selling cheap clothing is not how a female undercover game warden ordinarily likes to spend her day. Marie was bored to tears, and exhausted, too, because she was constantly inventing a life, lying to Barbara about her parents, her upbringing, her career, her relationship with A.J.—almost everything she said she had just made up.

For A. J. Caro, on the other hand, the two weeks in New York on this trip were as far from boring as any he had ever spent.

What began as a simple alligator-hide case was turning into an accidental but far-reaching sting involving hijacking, prostitution, counterfeit money, official bribery—it was amazing how fast and far the net spread, and it was Caro, the curly-haired Cajun poacher from Lake Arthur, Louisiana, who was stringing it out all by himself. He told Kelly right away that he did not want to sit around the cottage waiting for his money to arrive. He wanted some action. He also needed money. Kelly asked him if he could drive a mail truck. "I think he's jokin, doncha know," Caro remembered. "But he'd bought hisself a gubmint-surplus mail truck with the official decals all washed off and he hired some guy to paint it back on. I tell you what, it was realistic. Then he got a mailman's uniform somehow. Maybe he kill the guy, I doan know." I believe Caro was being facetious; I don't know. Dave Hall said, "It was a stroke of genius, especially considering it came from a punk like Kelly, because everything the guy handled was illegal, but he delivered it like it was the U.S. mail. Don't kid yourself—the New York docks are watched, the fencing operations are watched, and after the first case in 1974 Kelly became a known hoodlum to law enforcement in New York. But he has these guys running around delivering all these hot goods in a goddamn mailman's uniform and a postal service truck. How many times have you seen a mailman in a mail truck go by and you said to yourself, 'Oh, there goes a gangster delivering stolen merchandise'? He slipped right through the law's legs."

It was soon obvious how Kelly could afford to live in a six-bedroom house in a guarded suburb, with Italian marble fireplaces and a ten-thousand-dollar stereo and alarm system. Klapisch was making most of his money from furs and alligator hides, but Kelly's lucre came mainly from goods that just fell off a truck: An eighteen-wheeler would be borrowed for a few hours by some hijackers. Kelly would be called. He and Billy Greenblatt would run out to look over the goods. Kelly would buy, say, fifty thousand dollars' worth of merchandise for ten thousand in cash. Caro would be reached by radio. He would come by in his postal service truck, load it up, and deliver to a series of discount joints and fences. The eighteen-wheeler would go back whence it came, and the shippers and sellers and buyers of the merchandise would write off the loss as a cost of doing business in New York. Kelly would pay Caro a few hundred dollars for delivering a load, then pocket the rest for himself.

Caro's delivery runs were the only opportunity he and Marie had to communicate with the task force of agents assigned to the Kelly-Klapisch operation. It was risky for Caro to meet anyone on the street, or even to make a daily telephone call, because no one was certain Kelly wasn't having him watched. Once or twice a day, he would make a bathroom stop, find a pay phone on the way, and make a very quick call. Half an hour later, the Fish and Wildlife Service agent who was running around New York on a motorcycle would follow his lead and find him somewhere in traffic. Then he would pull alongside at a stoplight and get the latest news on Kelly, Marie, and the hides. It seemed pretty foolproof until the day A.J. disappeared.

That he reappeared two days later, still alive, showed the righteous stuff of which Caro was made.

Kelly's penchant for hijacking and his inconsolable greed had both grown in lockstep since Caro had last seen him several months before. He had begun taking foolish chances, buying loads from people he had never met. They might be undercover police or types who would take his money and make him a pair of cement shoes, but Kelly's avariciousness had gotten the better of him. "Jack always wanted more," Caro says. "He couldn't make enough girls or have enough money. Greed worked on him just like coke or crystal—he'd make a big score and right away he wanted to do it again."

One morning, when Marie and Caro were with Kelly at his shop, he got a call from someone who said he had just gotten a truck and wanted to sell him the contents. Kelly evidently wanted them to take the truck someplace else, but an hour later the hijackers brought it by and parked it right outside, a huge semi on a crowded Brooklyn street. Kelly was so anxious to get rid of them that he took Caro and Greenblatt and followed them to an empty warehouse that fences often used. Caro says he didn't know what Kelly had promised to pay on the phone, but the hijackers seemed to think he had promised more.

"There was three of them. One was black, the other was some kind of Puerto Rican, and the third was a white-haired dude like Johnny Winter. I seen right away that they were junkies—they were all strung out and like this. I knew we were in trouble even before the guns came

out. They told us they'd shot the driver and dumped him off the road—
they didn't kill him or anything, just shot him—but they was gonna kill
us if Jack didn't come up with more money for the load. Two of em
had pistols and the white dude had a sawed-off shotgun under a raincoat.
Jack, he was pissing in his pants, he was so scared. Billy was set to
moan. Jack tells them he didn't have that kinda money around, but he'd
leave to go get it. The black dude, he say, 'There ain't nobody leavin.
We're gonna kill you all right here. Get down on your knees.' Kelly and
Greenblatt got right down, like they was right to go die just like a
whimperin dog. Jack is just crying about how they is crazy to do this
and they gonna be caught and all. I admit at that point it looked bad
for us. They was bad-looking people, and I almost thought it had all
caught up with me. But I says to them, 'Look. First, if you're gonna kill
me, you're gonna kill me standing up. I ain't gonna grovel like no dog.'
And I just stood there in this big shed, looking at the shotgun while
they talking among themselves. I'm thinking I bought us about a minute's
time, so I say on, 'Look. This ain't gonna get y'all no money. I'll tell you
what, I'll stay here and be a hostage while Jack goes and gets some
more money. Let's do our bidness the way you all make some money,
and we don't get killed. There ain't no reason for mayhem cause of a
deal that went a little bit sour and can be fixed up just like that. Where
I come from, man, we don't go killin people except as a last resort. Us
Cajuns like to work things out a little.' "

I have streamlined some of Caro's language here and there, but this
comes almost directly off the tape, and I wish you could hear it because
Caro's tone of voice is a finger stroking a frog's belly, a mother cooing
to her young. Here were three strung-out New York junkies to whom
killing people was like swatting flies, and they were facing a stolid little
curly-headed Cajun alligator hunter talking elementary logic and showing not a speck of fear, and he was talking in a tone of such surpassing
calm that you wouldn't have been surprised if one of the junkies had
walked over and given him a kiss. The junkies told Kelly he had twenty-
four hours to come up with twenty-four thousand dollars in cash. Then
they smoked some black heroin and mellowed quite a bit and took
A.J. to a diner nearby.

"Did you trust Jack?" I asked Caro.

"Not really," he said. "But I figured we were dead anyway, so something had to happen. Not that I was big, brave, or nothin . . . I was so scared I was about to shit in my pants. But then these junkies took me to this diner and we sat down until Kelly showed up with the money a lot of hours later, and I started telling em stories about alligator huntin and the Cajun way of life and all, and we had a few laughs and for some reason they seemed to like me a bit. We got sort of close. So I started thinkin about workin on them a little, too."

This is what had happened to Anthony J. Caro, an Italian-blooded Cajun from Lake Arthur, Louisiana: a small-time crook, a swamp poacher, who suddenly found himself among big-time crooks in New York City, he was learning that he was a tougher and better crook than any of them. "The one thing about outlaws," says Dave Hall's Outlaw Rule Number One, "is they're always trying to prove they're a better outlaw than the next outlaw." So Caro was just behaving as any outlaw would, talking crook talk, making deals, going for the brass ring . . . but, at the same time, he was an undercover agent, and he was downright brilliant in that role, too . . . so why not be both? Who said you couldn't be a criminal and an undercover agent at the same time? He could run around with Kelly doing deals and making thousands a week, penetrating one ring of crooks after another, and in the end he would take them all down. A criminal and an undercover cop! He was like a bluefish ripping through a school of bait. Opportunities like this didn't come every day to alligator poachers from Lake Arthur, Louisiana.

To Dave Hall, though, Caro's skill with these outlaws was becoming a nightmare. He was out of control, he was doing crash deals, and he was acting as his *deputy*. Dave Hall had deputized Woody Dufrene one time, sending him to the Smoky Mountains to look into some bad deer and bear poaching that was reportedly going on, and Woody had driven over there in his Okie truck and played such a convincing swamp rat that he learned who the outlaw hunters were and the agents had taken them down. But Woody had gone in there, done his job, and come back. Caro was a drunken driver in a runaway bus, picking up crooks left and right. He had almost gotten himself killed, he had been held hostage; and he wouldn't stop. He was doing a miraculous job—this alligator case had blossomed like a jungle orchid, and Caro was going to take a lot of people down. But the defense lawyers could have a field day with A.J., who was not a cop in any sense of the word and hadn't even been formally deputized. And besides, he was angling to get himself killed. Every new gang he got in with might smoke him out somehow, and then there was Marie, innocently sitting in Kelly's store ... Caro's lunatic escapades might get her killed, too.

But he wouldn't quit. The hides still hadn't moved—or Caro, in any event, hadn't been paid—so he kept running around with Kelly, doing the grand circuit of New York crime. He and Kelly bought a hundred thousand in counterfeit money for around twenty thousand dollars and sold it for twenty-five thousand. He and Kelly went to a fence with a big coin and stamp collection Kelly had somehow acquired, and sold it for a princely sum. They got a box of stolen requisition orders that let them walk into a warehouse and come out with thousands of dollars' worth of merchandise someone else had paid for. There were so many orders Kelly threw some of them away. "It was unbelievable, how many deals we were makin and how much we were runnin around. It got so that in the end everybody had to come in—Customs, the FBI—because the activity got so broad. Some of these people was big-time. Like one had three or four guys with him and when he got up to leave, those guys jumped like he was president or something. There was one guy with two whorehouses—he had sixty girls in one and about forty in the other, a whole floor in an eleven-story building. There was whips and chains and anything you wanted. When we come in to any of these places, these guys would say to Jack, 'Who's this?,' and they'd look me over close. I'd like to know how many times one of em said, 'Well, you *look* all right, but if you're not, dude, you're dead.' "

Dave Hall needed one more thing from Caro which entailed perhaps an even greater risk.

Ever since the hides had been dropped at Kelly's mother's house, their final destination had been a complete mystery. Kelly wouldn't say where they were going, and A.J. would invite trouble if he asked. Klapisch's warehouse was staked out twenty-four hours a day by Dave Hall's people, and they hadn't gone there. They evidently weren't going to Breezy Point. Somehow the USFWS had to find out who the buyers were.

Caro had a hunch. A criminal like Kelly didn't keep records, at least not for very long. And those he kept were probably not in his house. His house had been raided in 1974 and a lot of incriminating evidence was seized. Incriminating evidence was apt to put you in jail, and if it concerned big-time gangsters with a lot to lose—the sort of people Kelly dealt with all the time—it was apt to get you killed. A mobster who went to prison because of evidence seized at Jack Kelly's house was going to put out a contract on Jack Kelly's life.

The place to keep such records was in your car. If there was a raid, you at least had a chance to get away; you might not even be at your house when the raid occurred. If you kept your files in your car, you could scatter them to the wind or throw them in a dumpster.

Kelly kept his beneath the right front seat. It took Caro about ten seconds to find them when he went out after dinner one night to take a walk. The consignment of hides was to be shipped to "Croskin"—the code name for Inoue and Company in Tokyo. Caro didn't have any chance to make copies. He simply ripped the pages out of Kelly's records book and stuffed them in his pants. Tomorrow he and Marie were going to have to get out fast.

One of the agents who had been walking the street in front of Kelly's store gave Marie a sign at eleven the next morning. She went outside and found him at a phone booth. She was to get out of town right away. She never looked back. About an hour later, forty-odd federal agents were in Jack Kelly's front yard.

To everyone's disbelief, Caro stayed with the gang. At first Dave Hall thought he was subconsciously trying to commit suicide. But when Caro got on the phone to him a couple of days later, he told Dave Hall that he was reasonably sure Kelly, who was free on bail, didn't suspect him yet. Marie had finessed her way out of Barbara Kelly's clutches—she had said that a relative had suddenly gotten sick, or something—and the alibi had seemed to stick; they didn't seem to connect her with the raid. Because Kelly's record book had been seized, Jack hadn't had a chance to notice the missing pages. It was conceivable that Kelly suspected him, but he seemed to be convinced that the federals had found him out through the Japanese. In any event, he said, he had too much going on to get out yet. A.J. was being maddeningly evasive again. *What* did he have going on? He wouldn't say. At first Dave Hall felt Caro was simply trying to make as much money as he could while he was still in with Kelly's circle of crooks. It infuriated him, because Caro might be called as a material witness in the trial and his penchant for consorting with gangsters would give his moral character a sorry taint. Dave Hall was tempted to leave him to a deserved fate—until A.J. called again about ten days later, from Kennedy Airport, where he was crouched behind the Delta Airlines ticket counter.

Caro was very brief on the phone because he was very scared. He said only that he had managed to escape with his clothes, and if he didn't get the next flight out they were going to find him dead on the concourse. Dave Hall immediately wired him a ticket to New Orleans; then he alerted the airport police. If there was going to be a gunfight, he wanted to make sure the right people got shot.

Caro called from the New Orleans airport about four hours later. He said he was safe, but for the next month or so, he would need a place to live.

He ended up spending the month at Dave Hall's.

The reason Caro had stayed behind in New York, it came out, was that at the same time he was working freelance for Dave Hall, and delivering hijacked goods in a postal service truck, and buying goods from junkies with Kelly and Billy Greenblatt, and visiting mob-owned brothels on Manhattan's East Side, he had also been working undercover for the Drug Enforcement Administration—without telling Dave Hall. Making that case had taken some time, he said, and he didn't want a failure so early in his new career.

"He was the most elusive, evasive, out-of-control outlaw I ever turned," Dave Hall said, a mixture of exasperation and pure admiration in his voice. "And he may always be an outlaw to some degree. But my kids loved him when he lived with us. And as far as being an undercover operative, he was about the best I ever saw."

Since the late 1970s, the alligator population in Louisiana has rebounded so dramatically that a legal season now exists. No one knows for certain how many alligators there are, but half a million is a decent guess—

enough so that a legal cull of some thirty thousand a year doesn't dent the numbers. You couldn't say that Louisiana is up to its neck in alligators, as Florida appears to be—there they sun themselves on golf courses and are sometimes found in swimming pools—but you could say it is up to its knees. The recovery of the American alligator is probably the greatest success story in North American wildlife conservation, and Dave Hall was very much responsible for it. So was A. J. Caro, who, in the fall of 1987, had disappeared.

Finding Caro was one of the main items on Dave Hall's agenda in November of that year, when he took me on a tour of his alligator poacher friends. "He's gotten himself involved in such down-and-dirty stuff that I always fear for his life," he said. "Last I heard he was working some big drug case in Mexico. Before that he piloted a boat to Jamaica and made a huge undercover pot buy from some Rastafarians who were living in caves. Damn! You know what they did to Kiki Camarena, that DEA agent the Mexican drug mafia and their police friends kidnapped. It was horrible. There ain't many people I know who can take care of themselves like Caro, but these drug hoodlums are the worst. They'd kill Mother Teresa if she got in the way."

Another item on Dave Hall's agenda was simply to let himself be seen. Alligator hunters were now getting as much as thirty-five dollars per linear foot for hides, which meant that a midsize alligator was worth two hundred dollars—which meant that you couldn't rule out another poaching epidemic. (By 1989, the price was up to fifty dollars a linear foot.) "The thing I'm proudest of is that I've taught a lot of these people restraint," he said. "There are hundreds of people who make a substantial little legal income hunting gators now, and if they don't start wasting all those gators again, they can do it indefinitely. But I'm worried some of them may get greedy again, and when one does, the others might. So I go through here now and then to let em know they're still being watched and to learn who's killing too many. Now that they're learning the value of *management*"—Dave Hall hardly ever says that word without emphasis—"they're informin on each other all the time. Self-policing, I guess you could call it."

Woody Dufrene, who was now a fairly old man, had gotten himself trapped in some flimsy shack when a hurricane came through in 1984;

amid the screaming winds and flapping roofs and falling trees Woody had suffered a major stroke and was a while getting to a hospital, so he was in pretty bad shape. "We'd better pass Woody by this time," said Dave Hall. "I hope he improves because I really want you to meet him." He said it as if Woody were one of his most valued friends. We kept going, rattling down a bomb-cratered stretch of U.S. 90, the highway on which Dave Hall and Perry White had raced Ranzell Dufrene to the hospital nearly twenty years before. We turned off about forty minutes southwest of New Orleans, after crossing Lake Cataouatche, and took a rubbly back road to Kraemer, just below Lac Des Allemands. Next to the Florida Everglades, this was once the alligator-poaching capital of the United States.

The first ex-poacher we visited was Edwin Tregle, who at the height of his poaching career was a citizen special agent with Louisiana Wildlife and Fisheries and, later, a deputy sheriff in Jefferson Parish. "I keep hearing stories that old Treg is taking illegal gators again," said Dave Hall. "I'm told he's dealing drugs, too, now that they're pinching off the sea routes into Florida." (Some months later, Tregle was convicted and sent to the penitentiary for dealing cocaine.)

Tregle, whatever his source of income, was living well for a bayou man. He had a big white-brick ranch house, the longest Cadillac ever made, and several boats. One offered tourists rides around Bayou Chevreuil—alligator-roar-in-concealed-squawkbox, mechanical-pirate-in-woods, the whole nine yards. His daughter, who looked tough enough to be a linebacker for the Rams, was taking a load of gawkers out when we drove up; she gave a cheery wave to Dave Hall. Tregle himself did his best to appear cheerful, though he didn't quite pull it off; his eyes were asking what in hell we were doing there. Tregle was a large man, almost distinguished-looking, with a gravelly voice and courtly air. He reminded me of a mafia don. When he smiled, he showed several missing teeth. ("Teeth, waterfowl, alligators, illegitimate kids," Dave Hall groused to me later in the car when I mentioned Tregle's missing teeth, "it's all the same lack of a sense of *management*.")

"How you doin, Treg?"

"Just fine, Dave. Just fine. What brings you down?"

"Just a little tour of my old alligator-poaching turf. You all havin a good year with them gators?"

Tregle motioned to his backyard shed. There was a huge pile of rolled alligator hides inside, probably seven or eight hundred in all. "Got a lot of folks bringin em in," he said. "I just sell em these days."

"You ain't heard about any outlaw activity, have you, Treg?"

"Aw, no. It's all legal now. Everybody obeying the law."

"I'll bet my ass they're not."

"No, no," Tregle protested.

"You know if the outlawin starts up again, we're gonna come down on you hard," said Dave Hall.

"Yes, sir," agreed Tregle. "Yes, sir." What he probably meant was, You sons of bitches can't watch us night and day.

"I hear reports of people takin' tags from one area and using them in another," said Dave Hall. "You hear anything about that?"

"No, no," said Tregle.

We went back to Tregle's shed. Despite his obvious wealth, his backyard was full of chickens and ducks; Cajuns love to feed themselves. Skulls from some twelve- and thirteen-foot alligators, big as bombshells, were nailed to a tree outside. "Killin all the big ones now," Tregle said. "Don't got but a lot of little ones." We stood by the impressive pile of rolled-up hides. It was worth, probably, a hundred twenty thousand dollars. "Dave helped make all this legal again," Tregle said to me. "He worked hard to give us a season again, after them alligators come back."

"Treg, you haven't heard anything about A. J. Caro, have you?"

"No, no . . . cause he live over by Lake Arthur. I doan see much of him anyway."

"You hunters all knew each other, though . . ."

"I know, but I ain't seen A.J. in years."

We left Tregle's and went down the road to visit someone Dave Hall asked me not to mention by name. The odds that any of the outlaw characters in this book will ever read it are low, but Dave Hall is nothing if not careful. The news that we were in the neighborhood had already gotten around, for people began dropping in from all over. Some pleasantries would be exchanged, a little desultory talk about ducks or politics or the last flood, and then some gossip would quietly be offered about so-and-so's outlaw activities. Poaching, drugs, a robbery—it seemed as if Dave Hall got more information on every permutation of local crime than all the parish police and game wardens combined. When I mentioned this, he shrugged. "Some of these outlaws who went straight I've become friendly with. Like Caro and Woody and Clinton Dufrene. At least if they've gone mostly straight. In this business, in these close-knit Cajun parishes, you don't win without informants. I will go to some trouble to get informants. But I like a lot of the outlaws I've shut down. They were only doing what come natural. Besides, they're interesting people."

As we drove around, Dave Hall told me a little about Caro's life and career after the Kelly-Klapisch case. His testimony, along with Marie's, seemed certain to send Kelly to the penitentiary, so Kelly figured he might as well turn state's evidence. The trigger-happy junkies, the counterfeiter, the brothel owner, the drug figures Caro worked—all were taken down. Kelly talked his way out of a severe sentence, but still he wouldn't quit; he was convicted twice again of dealing in poached alligators, then seemed to disappear. Apparently, though, he'd just decided to lay low for a while, because Caro found out a few years later that the price Kelly had put on his head immediately after he escaped New York had not been removed. "Jack's still alive," he told Dave Hall, "and he still wants me dead." By then, Caro had performed so much successful undercover work for various law-enforcement agencies that several bounties had been put out on him. Even so, it was Kelly he seemed to fear most, so long as Kelly himself stayed alive.

The Fish and Wildlife Service used A. J. Caro one more time, in 1979. The Hoopa Indian reservation sits right at the mouth of the Klamath River in California, one of the last highly productive salmon rivers south of Oregon (most of the others have been wrecked by dams and logging and irrigation diversions). Like most West Coast Indians, the Hoopa are permitted to take as many salmon as they need for subsistence. In the late 1970s the Klamath salmon run began to decline dramatically. Part of the reason was California's intense drought in 1976 and 1977, which dried up many spawning tributaries. But rumors were rife that the Indians had organized into poaching gangs, and that, with the huge popularity of salmon in a society increasingly averse to red meat, plenty of restaurants and fish markets were buying on the black market. Both the California Department of Fish and Game and the Fish and Wildlife Service had tried to infiltrate the poachers, but their success was almost nil. No Indian was willing to work undercover, and for the average white game warden to try was almost suicide; these outlaw Indians were a well-armed, violent, and suspicious bunch, and beyond fear when drunk. The Pacific region of the USFWS finally did what other law-enforcement people have done under similar circumstances: they called Dave Hall. He sent them A. J. Caro.

Caro passed himself off as an itinerant, part-Indian Okie looking to make some money in the West. For cover, he had brought his girl-friend—he actually married her on the case. They parked their camper at the mouth of the river, right off U.S. 101, and lived there for three months. Caro was inside one of the gangs in about three weeks. He went out with Indians to garbage dumps, where they murdered bears; the galls were sold to Koreans from southern California, who resold the powdered organ in their native country, where its price recently hit five thousand dollars a pound. At night Caro helped string nets across the river to trap sturgeon. He was soon running tons of fresh illegal fish to markets all over Oregon and California. On one such trip—this is Caro's version—he helped a young woman whose truck had broken down, had intercourse with her that same night, and found himself charged with rape. "I believe his story," said Dave Hall, "but it's typical A.J.: nerves of steel and balls of brass, and just childlike judgment when it comes to something like a piece of ass." During the trial, Caro's real identity was exposed; he had to flee for his life and lost his new wife, but the experience didn't slow him down. "The stuff he was getting into afterward was heavier and heavier," Dave Hall told me. "This Mexican drug stuff . . . I know he took a bunch of Colombians down. He got addicted. If you've got the nerve for it, undercover work can be as addictive as narcotics."

We never found A.J. that day, nor did anyone seem to know where he was. On the way back to New Orleans, I asked Dave Hall whether he ever felt—now that alligators were skulking into southern suburbs and making off with dogs and even attacking swimmers now and then—

that the alligator's recovery has been so complete it might backfire on the species.

Dave Hall does not like to be drawn into arguments about the virtues and drawbacks of abundant alligators. "In the Everglades, their holes are important for other wildlife. In Louisiana, they eat a lot of nuisance animals. They eat egg-eaters like raccoons, which is good for waterfowl, but they eat waterfowl, too. I'm not saying alligators are the friendliest animals on this earth or the most important. I'm far, far more concerned that we save our waterfowl than that we save the alligator. But they deserve to survive as much as we do. And the alligator, dammit, is an example. South of Alaska and Canada, almost all the best wildlife habitat is being used for something else. We've got a few dozen little wildlife refuges and a huge amount of what was unbelievably good habitat that's growing crops or is loaded with people. In Louisiana, we've got a lot less alligator habitat than we did in 1966—a lot less. But we've got a lot *more* alligators. That proves that if you manage your habitat right, even if it's man-habitat now, and control overhunting . . . if you do that, wildlife has a chance. We ain't ever going to restore the wild habitat we've lost, so we've got to manage things so that wildlife can make it on compromised habitat. The biologists, a lot of them, are into pristine habitat. And they think overhunting is never as big a problem as it really is. I get in arguments with them all the time. These alligator cases were the *perfect example* of what I'm talking about, and a lot of them still don't believe me." He sounded disgusted.

I spoke with Dave Hall a number of times after our trip into southern Louisiana, through the now-quiet marshes where he once nearly had to shoot his way in and shoot his way back out. Each time I asked if he had heard anything about A.J. Each time the answer was no. "I'm almost certain he's been killed," he said. "He's been out of touch for way too long. In the past, when he knew I was looking for him, he'd always call me back in a few days. I just think he got in over his head. Man, I would really miss old A.J. He was a personal triumph for me, but he's also basically a good dude. How many people do you suppose there are who have his kind of guts?"

Late in the spring of 1988 Dave Hall gave me a call. His first words were "He's alive."

Part II

IVORY

O F THE many thousands of vertebrate species on the planet, only a handful yield ivory, and of these, only three have ever produced it in commercial quantities. One is the elephant—both the Asian and African species have tusks. Another is the sperm whale, the great-toothed carnivorous whale, which has molars the size of telephones. (Ivory is nothing more than enamel, whether it comes from teeth or tusks, but to work it into things people are willing to pay big money for—rendered landscapes or ships or polar bears, billiard balls, jewelry, the meticulously carved AK-47 assault rifles now popular with cocaine gangsters—you need a large workable piece.) The third source of ivory, and the only one native to North America, is the walrus.

Sperm whales were an important source only as long as they lasted. All the early North American whaling towns owed their existence mainly to that species, whose fine spermaceti oil brought extraordinary prices, and whose ambergris, a waxy substance still used as a perfume base, was worth even more. Peter Matthiessen has called the sperm whale the most significant animal, after the beaver, in the economic development of North America. But the species was nearly wiped out by the early part of the twentieth century—sperm whales and right whales were the first to go commercially extinct—and its ivory, though much in demand, has never been common since.

Elephants, which are more abundant and easier to kill and have tusks much larger than sperm whale teeth, have been commercially exploited for ivory and almost nothing else since early Roman times. Elephants used to be found around the southern fringe of the Mediterranean Sea, but the Romans and Carthaginians, who were good elephant handlers and major ivory traders, managed to hunt out the North African population by about the first century A.D. The Romans pushed far enough into Asia to begin plundering that continent's species—which is smaller and somewhat more docile than the African—but they were always rebuffed by the Sahara, so the vast majority of Africa's elephants lived relatively unperturbed until the Boers arrived, in the early seventeenth century, with guns. According to Ian Redmond, an elephant conservationist, the colonial Dutch, having barely settled into South Africa, exported fifty thousand pounds of ivory a year between 1608 and 1612— it was by far their most valuable commodity of trade. But only on the open veldt were elephants relatively easy to kill, and the millions of animals in Africa's yawning interior remained almost untouched until the slave trade began.

It was during the slave era that elephant ivory became an industry, with many importers in the richer countries and many thousands of people, mainly in Asia, who did nothing else but carve ivory for a living. No one has any idea how much ivory was shipped out of Africa between 1750 and 1850, when hundreds of slave ships left port every year, many of them loaded with tusks as well as chattel. Better records were kept later on, some of which have been examined by Ian Redmond; he believes that, in the 1880s, about two million pounds of ivory—sixty to a hundred thousand elephants' worth—were annually coming out of Africa alone. (The Asian elephant was, of course, being decimated at the same time.) Much as the beaver trappers pushed back America's western frontier, the Arab slavers and the ivory traders were primarily responsible for opening up the African continent; they built the roads and trails that led to coffee colonialism. Most of the South African elephant population was wiped out fairly early in the 1800s; the Angolan elephant was a rarity by the 1860s; the Ivory Coast was ivoryless by 1909. The Europeans who colonized Africa must have felt, as did their counterparts in America, that the continent was inexhaustible, for annual elephant quotas were almost unknown. Taxes and licenses did little to slow the kill rate; they simply made ivory a more important source of revenue for colonial governments. By the early 1900s big-game hunters were slaughtering elephants alongside commercial ivory traders, and the sport hunters weren't necessarily as selective about the specimens they shot; a lot of them killed anything that moved. (There are scores of books written by and about the white hunters, most of them good-humored, interminable diaries of slaughter: "Brought down a bull elephant, its two female mates, and, for good measure, a baby—all within half an hour.") The hunters and traders left plundered West Africa behind and moved into East Africa, which in the 1950s was the main source of ivory exports Redmond estimates at one million four hundred fifty thousand pounds a year.

Except during the two world wars, when the colonial white hunters were annihilating one another for a while, a very brief period, from about 1958 to 1970, was the only reprieve the African elephant has enjoyed in the past three hundred and seventy-five years. African wildlife conservationists have grown so used to wretched disappointment and defeat that they refer to this short hiatus between sanctioned and illegal killing as a golden age. By the 1960s, white hunters were being supplanted by tourists, who may have bought a few ivory trinkets in Nairobi shops but who, on the other hand, represented an economically important reason to ensure the elephant's survival. Largely for such reasons, a number of game reserves, in which legal hunting is prohibited or strictly controlled, were created in the transitional era between colonialism and independence.

No halfway reliable elephant census was ever conducted in Africa prior to the late 1960s, when the continental population is believed to have amounted to one and a quarter to one and a half million. But a conservative estimate, according to Ian Redmond and others who have studied the species carefully, is that ten million elephants could have been counted throughout all of Africa a century and a half earlier.

One can't say exactly what caused the ivory trade—more and more of it illegal—to boom in the early 1970s. No one has even figured out whether price escalation was the flame that heated demand or whether demand drove up the thermometer of price. All one can do is mention the factors that set the stage. After colonialism, which was bad enough, many African countries found themselves governed by buffoonery, which was worse. Savage, inefficient, and corrupt indigenous regimes unwittingly encouraged the growth of black markets—sometimes the only functioning sector of the national economy—where anything could be bought or sold. More and more people (and there *were* more and more people) turned to outlaw activities as their only hope of living halfway decently. An African who sold a dozen elephant tusks a year was the richest person in his village. (An African villager who sells a pair of rhino horns today earns more money than he would see in a lifetime of farming.)

Meanwhile, as Africa sank deeper and deeper into poverty, political chaos, and the population quagmire, several of the South and East Asian countries were experiencing, by comparison, a miracle of economic growth and stability. In Taiwan, per capita income in 1988 was fifteen times higher than in 1970. Japan's shattered postwar economy was rebuilt into the most formidable in the world. Hong Kong developed spectacularly, as did Singapore, Korea, and then Thailand. Most of these countries have much stronger economic ties to Africa than does the United States. They have become, in effect, benign—and sometimes not so benign—colonists.

In the midst of this rocketing economic growth, Asian society has remained a strange muddle of hypermodernism and atavism. Multimillionaire computer entrepreneurs in Korea still believe devoutly in the therapeutic properties of bear galls, a folk medicine reaching back four thousand years. Powdered rhinoceros horn, which is even more highly valued as a thaumaturgical cure-all, particularly in Taiwan, sells by weight at a price three times as high as cocaine's, about forty thousand dollars a kilogram for Sumatran rhino and fifteen thousand for the African variety. In Yemen, oil-rich males will pay almost as much for the whole horn, which is prized as the handle of the obligatory dagger many Yemenese men carry around. (A rhinoceros horn is nothing but a very large and fat fingernail, and a rhinoceros is basically a temperamental horned cow, but superstition has little to do with biology.)

By the amount of lucre it produces, however, no animal export in recent years has measured up against elephant ivory, most of which goes to Asia, too. That ivory trading is now almost universally illegal makes no difference; close to 95 percent of the ivory now in commerce has been poached. The rhinoceros has been protected for almost two decades, but since 1973 the African rhino population has declined from more than sixty-five thousand to fewer than thirty-eight hundred. The elephant is now racing down the same slippery slope. Between the end of the Second World War and 1969, the world price of ivory (which is carefully monitored, like the Dow-Jones index, in the countries involved in the trade) fluctuated between three and six dollars a pound. In 1970 it made a small ominous jump, lodging at seven dollars and forty-five cents by the end of the year. Then it rose like California real estate. In 1978 ivory was up to seventy-five dollars a kilogram. In 1988 it hit seventy-five dollars a pound. A very fine pair of antique tusks, six or seven feet long, can now bring seventy-five thousand dollars easily.

The impact of such prices on the African elephant population has been horrific. Between 1968 and 1989 the elephant count went from nearly one and a half million animals to somewhere between four hundred thousand and seven hundred thousand—depending on whether you believe official statistics or the far more pessimistic figures provided by some conservationists. In the Central African Republic, which is nearly the size of Texas, the elephant population has dwindled in two decades from one hundred sixty thousand to barely ten thousand. In Uganda's Murchison Falls National Park, all but about twenty of the nine thousand elephants that roamed the park in the 1960s had been slaughtered by 1982. (Most were apparently killed by Ugandan soldiers—hundreds, in all probability, by Idi Amin himself.) Poachers, most of them Somali *shiftas*, or bandits, have shrunk the herds in Kenya's Tsavo National Park from forty-five thousand animals in 1969 to five thousand today. East Africa has the continent's greatest concentration of national parks, it has some of the best-equipped game wardens, its governments are now among the least corrupt in Africa (which isn't saying much), and tourism is the region's most important money-earner. But East Africa was losing fourteen thousand five hundred elephants a year between 1977 and 1989. It is a textbook example of apparently limitless money chasing a finite and increasingly scarce good; people are now buying elephant ivory on the assumption that elephants will eventually go extinct. It was only a matter of time before two other laws governing supply and demand came into play: the involvement of world-level criminals such as cocaine kings, for some of whom wildlife dealing is a sideline (Pablo Escobar, the leader of the Medellín cartel, kept thousands of rare exotic animals on his various estates), and the shift to a somewhat inferior but increasingly valuable source, like the walrus.

It wasn't until the spring of 1980, when the Soviet Union cabled an angry diplomatic protest to the U.S. secretary of state, that anyone fathomed the seriousness of the walrus-poaching problem. That some walrus were being poached was beyond doubt, but the Russians intimated that thousands—many thousands—were being slaughtered each year. For proof, they could offer photographs—of Siberian beaches littered with dead walrus, and, in gruesome close-up, of walrus with their heads and ossiks (the penis, which has a bone) removed. The tone of anger—which is usual in a diplomatic protest but not in one of this kind—may have had much to do with the fact that the Russians had received a similar protest from the United States some years before. Conceivably, the whole business was a cynical little charade, a ruse to deflect attention from the Soviets' own culpability. But it would have to be investigated.

Like most marine mammals, walrus took a terrible drubbing in the last two or three centuries. John Cabot was impressed by the thousands he saw lolling around the mouth of the Saint Lawrence River, and the first New England settlers reported that a fairly large colony swam in Massachusetts Bay. By the 1800s, however, the walrus had already been wiped out in its southern range. It survives today only in the extreme North Atlantic and in the Bering Sea. Though its habitat is far less accessible than that of the elephant, its habits tend to make it an easier kill. Before evolutionary stability was given a rude shock by *Homo sapiens*, walrus had only polar bears and killer whales to fear; they are much bigger than cows, have three-foot tusks to defend themselves with, and spend much of their time on drift ice. One of the things that made the Soviet cable believable, in fact, is that a hauled-out walrus, like an elephant seal, has too little fear of man; if you can find a colony, you can walk up with a machine gun and blast every member away.

With rare exceptions, the only modern people who kill walrus are Eskimos. The Marine Mammal Protection Act of 1972, which outlawed all walrus hunting in the United States, made an exception for the Alaskan Eskimos. They can kill as many as they want, at any time of year, so long as they do it "nonwastefully" and for "subsistence"—terms that have never been clearly defined and never will be. In the case of walrus, the meaning generally accepted by the courts is that everything is legal—killing for meat, killing for ivory, killing for ritual—except killing for the purpose of selling raw ivory to non-Eskimos.

To Eskimos, the importance of fishing and hunting is beyond question: it was the only life their ancestors knew, and today, granting indigenous people permission to hunt for subsistence is a most important means of preserving their cultural heritage. To outlaw the hunting of marine mammals among Eskimos would have the same effect on them as the annihilation of the bison had on the Plains tribes, who have wandered lost in the white man's world ever since he destroyed theirs. When the subsistence clause was being debated before Congress—and it was, extensively and passionately—its opponents argued that the cultural issue was moot: alcohol, technology, and the white man's cash economy had already corrupted Eskimo society beyond redemption. Some conservationists who sympathized in principle doubted that subsistence hunting could ever be controlled; endangered or threatened species like the elephant seal and bowhead whale, and even the walrus—which was not officially threatened but was becoming rare—might be driven to extinction before a workable definition of "subsistence" and a method of enforcing it were ever found. Particularly in the case of the walrus, they said, pressure on the elephant stocks might soon be felt, like a rolling seismic wave, all the way up to the Bering Sea; if Eskimos could kill walrus legally, they would end up selling tusks on the world ivory market, and if that happened, the species was done for.

Congress essentially ducked the issue. The selling of raw ivory to non-Eskimos would be illegal, and that was all. For once, though, this particular ban-with-exemptions-and-stipulations-attached was based on something more than Congress's habitual impulse to be all things to all people at once. The fact is that most Eskimos are not good ivory carvers. The very best are concentrated in Hong Kong; most of the rest are in Japan, mainland China, and Taiwan—the traditional Asian ivory markets—and in a few old U.S. whaling ports like Lahaina and Bellingham and Provincetown. A large walrus tusk carved by a reasonably proficient Eskimo artisan might be worth, in today's market, about fifteen hundred dollars; in the hands of an expert Hong Kong carver, it would be worth three or four times more. The whole idea, then, was to keep raw ivory out of the hands of the top carvers and scrimshaw artists because their skill commands vastly greater prices, and those prices were likely to exert greater pressure on the walrus herds. Besides, if Eskimos carved all the ivory they hunted, many more of them would be gainfully employed, and an ancient cultural tradition would be saved.

It was an idea that, in theory, made some sense until economics intervened. Had the price of ivory remained at six or seven dollars a pound, that would have been one thing; hunting walrus amid treacherous drift ice is too dangerous for a thirty-dollar tusk. But a world market price climbing past forty dollars a pound in 1980—six hundred dollars for the ivory of just one walrus—made such a risk worthwhile.

On top of this, you had the fact that, for a brief period in the 1970s, Alaska took over intrastate enforcement of the Marine Mammal Protection Act and elected to open a season on walrus for everyone, Eskimos or whites, with sales of raw ivory permitted if it was "tagged." All that did, of course, was create a lot of official, interchangeable tags that were priced and hoarded like taxicab medallions, because if you were clever you could use one many times over.

And on top of the "certified" walrus ivory—an enforcement nightmare—you had the great unmentionable: drugs. The drug that society has chosen to legalize—alcohol—has done even more damage to Eskimo culture than it has caused among the Indians. (It has been theorized that Eskimos lack an enzyme that in whites quickly metabolizes alcohol, but whether or not that is true, many Eskimos drink like Irishmen.) Unlike most Indians, however, Eskimos in Alaska have also exhibited a weakness for—which may merely reflect the availability of—narcotics and other mind-altering drugs. Marijuana is the drug of choice, but cocaine is gaining ground, perhaps because it produces a raving, ecstatic high in the most niveous surroundings; and in an environment as bleak and impoverished as the Eskimos', that is exactly what one wants. It is also an expensive drug, but a pair of walrus tusks can keep you supplied, if you are fairly moderate, for at least a couple of weeks.

In other words, the situation in the early 1980s was absolutely right for a mass epidemic of walrus poaching—and there was no easy way to control it or even define it. Eskimos slaughtering hundreds of walrus with automatic weapons were not technically violating the law. Eskimos with walrus ivory stacked like cordwood in their backyards were not violating the law. Eskimos selling and trading raw ivory were not violating the law unless they were caught trading it for drugs or selling it to whites. And the only person in the enforcement branch of the United States Fish and Wildlife Service who seemed to realize the impossibility of its position was its agent-in-charge from—of all places—Louisiana.

Throughout his career, Dave Hall has recruited, as he puts it, some "unusual-type people" to help him with undercover operations. He drafted A. J. Caro and Woody Dufrene, a stolid Cajun pair of outlaw alligator hunters, to help him shut down the most lucrative U.S. wildlife poaching conspiracy since the plume- and market-hunting era. He has used a grade-school friend, Lonnie "Buck" Pridgen, who owns a bar, restaurant, and no-tell motel in Jackson, Mississippi, on so many occasions that southern game wardens call it the Roach Motel. His network of informants and collaborators has included car dealers (who will lend him a Cadillac Seville or a Range Rover or whatever set of wheels might impress someone he is attempting to sting), a bank vice-president (who vouches that his phony account has millions in it), state troopers (who, for fear of giving up his identity, always pretend not to know him, though the whole Louisiana force seems to), commercial fishermen, raccoon and nutria trappers, oil drillers and wildcatters, and tour-boat guides in the bayous (in Louisiana, things of interest to Dave Hall often can be seen only from boats). But nothing he has ever done was quite so irregular as running an undercover operation, so far away from home, on a fellow SAC's turf, and no accomplice of his was ever so unusual as William Vaughn Doak.

I met Doak for the first time on a fall day in 1985, when Dave Hall drove me across Lake Pontchartrain to interview him at his shop on Conti Street in the French Quarter. Dave Hall was, as usual, utterly preoccupied with a mountain of work he had taken on, so he had told me next to nothing about Doak or his shop. It was somewhat startling, therefore, to see a gigantic pair of elephant tusks in the window and a sign hanging overhead that said: ENDANGERED SPECIES. I could see more wildlife artifacts inside, along with many display cases and shelves full of native crafts—it looked like a place in which you could drop a lot of money.

"Is this stuff legal?" I asked as he parked the car outside.

"All of it," he said. "As far as I know. As far as Doak knows, too. When he opened up here a few years ago, we were watching him constantly. I went in there a bunch of times to try to get him to show me something illegal, but he has papers for everything. Those tusks there, they were probably taken from an elephant fifty or sixty years ago, when there were hardly any laws about ivory hunting and collecting. They're certified legal. I don't know if there's an elephant left with those kind of tusks anyway. They've all been killed. We checked him out, Wildlife and Fisheries checked him out, and we never came up with anything on him.

"He calls the place 'Endangered Species' cause he believes wildlife and ancient human cultures that have managed to survive into the modern age are both endangered. His philosophy is to sell these artifacts and whatnot so people will appreciate how wildlife and native culture go together. They use the resource, and that's why they value it. Like the Indians and the buffalo. Like with duck hunters—man, if it weren't for duck hunters trying to protect the resource *they use*, we'd've been out of ducks a long time ago. But Doak swears that if anything's banned, he won't sell it. People see this place, I mean conservationist types who are walking through the Quarter, they get indignant, they might walk in and want to chew old Doak out for selling stuff like this, and he says, 'Look, if you want people like the Dinka in the Sudan to survive, we can help them survive by buying their native wildlife crafts. That way they aren't gonna go work on an oil rig or chop down their rain forest or whatever. We're not robbing them; we're helping them. You want wildlife to survive in this age, it's got to have some economic value, too—that's just realistic. But I'll support any national or international ban on any species that's in trouble, and I will never knowingly sell something that's illegal.' People hear that, and they think, Hey, this old boy has got a point, and they walk out of here with their wallets a few pounds lighter, thinking they've just helped some tribe in the Amazon survive, which may be true, but they've also made Vaughn Doak a bundle of money. This guy Doak is a hustler, a con artist, and a supersalesman *supreme*."

Doak turned out to be a big man, friendly in a laconic way, and younger-looking than his forty-five years. He looked to me like a much more filled-out Jon Voight, with the same blue eyes and flared nose and mop of blond hair cascading down his forehead. We chatted in the shop for a while, surrounded by what seemed to be a million dollars' worth of antique elephant tusks, African tribal weapons, Tibetan jewelry, New Guinean penis gourds, Indonesian spirit sculptures, Indian statuaries, Mexican silver, bearskins, scrimshaw, jade—the prices on some of it were astronomical. Two thousand for the mask. Thirty-five thousand for the pair of tusks. Eleven hundred for the totem. "You should see the trouble he goes to to get some of it," said Dave Hall. "He's been shot at, roadblocked, got malaria—he'll go upriver into the heart of New Guinea for this stuff, three hundred miles from the nearest gas."

In his office, Doak told me that his family had settled in the Middle West and later in Florida, leading fairly conventional lives—his father was in the motel business. A strong young athlete, he had been a football star in high school. Although he came of age in the fifties, he was far more in tune with the sixties, and, like so many of the flower children, he ended up in California after college, having absolutely no idea what he wanted to do. Actually, he wanted to make movies—he had done some acting and taken some film courses—but found the film business hard to get into unless you were willing to start out in pornography— which he did. "I was on the leading edge of the sex wave. I mean, the curler. I came up with the Mitchell brothers and Alex de Renzy and the whole pioneer group that was making the first neighborhood-movie-house sex films. Most of my stuff was R-rated—one of the reasons I got out was because it was getting too raunchy for me." (Dave Hall had told me that one of Doak's films was the raunchiest he had ever seen, but he is a complete Puritan on matters sexual.) "I don't know if the stuff I made was all that good, but I wasn't making much money at it, so I got some investors together and we opened a bar down in San Jose. We called it the Ore House. I had this idea for an aqua show, where girls would be modeling bikinis, except they'd wear only the bottom piece, and instead of walking around the bar they'd model it in a pool, and instead of an ordinary pool this one would be right in the bar, with big glass sides like an aquarium that you could see right through."

Dave Hall was right about Doak's instinct for salesmanship. There may never have been a pool-size aquarium full of half-naked women in the middle of a bar before Doak opened the Ore House in San Jose, and there may never be one again. The novelty of the place was such that, by the measure of alcohol sales, the Ore House quickly became the record-setting bar in a high-consumption state. In a typical month, its clientele went through four hundred kegs of beer. Now that he was making money, Doak, who suffers the curse of intelligence—he is very easily bored—let the place run itself and kept trying to make films. The one that nearly got him killed, if someone could ever find a copy, might serve as the perfect icon of that trashiest of American eras, the Nixon decade.

"One of my girls ran with a gang of bikers called the Gypsy Jokers," he said. "They used to hang out at a bar down the street. Most of them were renegades from the Hell's Angels. I was told that the Angels were under orders from Sonny Barger, their leader, to shoot these guys off their Harleys if they got the chance, because they were giving bikers a bad name. And, he was right, because these guys were *vicious*. But I got along with a couple of them all right, and I thought, Who could be more realistic playing frontier outlaws than the most wildest outlaw types we've got around today? The bikers probably aren't all that different from what the mountain men and those guys were like. So I wrote a script for a western, a sex western with bikers playing both the outlaws and Indians and me playing the sheriff. It was an off-the-wall idea, sort of like *The Texas Chainsaw Massacre*, but that movie made a lot of money and it also was a cult classic.

"The problem is you can't rely on bikers for anything. These guys never showed up when we were scheduled to shoot. I figured I'd never get them to stay on a production schedule, so I gave up on that idea . . . but then I thought, why not just make a movie of bikers being themselves? Just being, you know, crazy lunatics?

"They got into that when I told them about it. I got a bunch of them organized in a parking lot in some godforsaken part of San Jose, and they really went at it. They were flat-ass drunk and high on speed, and they were eating glass and doing wheelies and smashing bottles over each other's heads and doing all the things bikers do. I was running through film like crazy, but they made such an ungodly racket that somebody got half the police force down on us. It was like a huge SWAT raid. These cops couldn't believe what we were doing. I had to finish filming way up in the mountains, which was a little scary because you don't want to be in the middle of nowhere with a bunch of people like that. Anyway, it was a good film, but it had a lot of violence in it. When I started showing it in my bar, it was a scene. All these Silicon Valley types watching half-naked girls swim in a pool and looking at a film of bikers going berserk. It was great for business. The bikers saw that, and I guess they wanted to make the profits themselves. They told me to give them back the film, and I said I wouldn't because we had an agreement and all that. Well, you know how bikers feel about agreements. They came in one night and pretty much broke my place in half. They smashed my skull with a beer stein and sent my manager to the hospital for weeks." Doak showed me the scar on his head, under his thatch of hair. It resembled a zipper. "I was surprised they didn't kill us cause they were *mad*. Between that and the vice squad always coming down on us, it was too much for me, so I sold out and took off. I didn't know where I was going.

"I ended up in London. That was where my life changed. I was walking down by the Blackwall Tunnel one day and looked into a warehouse and saw a huge pile of ivory lying around. There must have been a hundred and fifty gunnysacks. The guy in charge said he had people making it into *netsuke*, which is a Japanese amulet, and other things—jewelry—and he said he was making a lot of money. Well, I looked at the stuff they were producing, and I thought I could carve at least as well as that—I had some talent at art—so I started doing the same thing. Buying ivory wholesale, carving it and selling it. I lived over there for a year and a half or two doing that—in London and way out at Land's End. I got to know the ivory business backwards and forwards, which led me into artifacts, native crafts—everything you see in this store. I opened my own shop in New Orleans in 1975. I came here because we get a lot of convention traffic and Texas is next door. I don't know about native crafts, but southerners appreciate animal crafts more than people in the rest of the country. And in Texas they have lots of money. It's bad for profits to handle only legal stuff because a lot of people in this business will sell anything, and I don't make as much money as I could. But my conscience is clear, and I won't go to jail. And if I hadn't been all aboveboard, Dave probably wouldn't have given me the chance to get involved in the ivory case. I hadn't been traveling or having any wild times in a while back at that time, and I was really bored."

Dave Hall said, "After about a year of watching him and seeing that he always dealt straight, I thought to myself, Man, if we ever get onto a big wildlife-poaching ring, we could really use this place. Not just the place, which we couldn't duplicate for a million dollars, but *Doak* here. If we could get him to work with us and some bad guys decided to check him out, you know, run a background check, they were gonna be told, 'Yeah, Doak, I remember him, he was this dude who made porno films and had this bar with topless mermaids swimming around, and one time he made a movie about a motorcycle gang in a parking lot that brought out the whole damned SWAT unit. Sure, I remember Vaughn Doak. He was a *crazy* mother.' To an outlaw, a background like that is like getting a reference from the pope. Man, I wanted to use this Endangered Species *bad.* I just didn't know how I could do it until this walrus business came down on us."

Among his colleagues in the law-enforcement branch of the Fish and Wildlife Service, Dave Hall is widely admired for his abilities, but also regarded by some—even by some who admire him—as an arrogant, holier-than-thou, willful, opinionated, pathologically driven, and hopelessly egotistical son of a bitch. He has had that reputation for a long time—his overpowering personality and his frequent disregard for the unwritten book of rules have had much to do with it—but he went out of his way to earn it again on the walrus ivory case.

The investigation should not have been his. It was going to take place on the turf of the Alaska SAC, Jim Houge, so Houge should have been the person who planned it and ran it and selected the undercover agent who was to be the point man—most likely one of his own. The problem was, Houge didn't seem to believe that anything could be done about the epidemic of walrus poaching; given how the laws were written, and considering the remoteness and extreme insularity of the Eskimo communities, the outlaws "couldn't be got." A deep undercover agent would likely get himself killed anyway—some of these Eskimos were fearless of consequences and downright crazy, and a lot of them loathed the white man.

I was not at the SAC meeting where the investigation was first discussed, so all I have to report is hearsay: Dave Hall's version of how he gently persuaded Houge to let him take over the entire case, and the accounts of a couple of other USFWS special agents, who say that Houge's fatalistic (not to say gainsaying) attitude made Dave Hall vent steam from both ears.

Other agents' version:

"There ain't anyone who can't be got!"

"Well, maybe in Louisiana that's true, but it's not true here. Alaska is a totally different place. Subsistence laws aren't waterfowl regulations."

"Like hell . . ."

"What would *you* do, then?"

"Run it."

"Run what?"

"The investigation."

"You want to come up here and run it *yourself*?"

"Yeah, because I know I can pull it off."

"What agent do you plan to use?"

"Myself."

"Your*self*!"

"That's what I said."

"How are you going to run three of the worst states for wildlife violations in the whole country *and* go up to Alaska and run an undercover investigation in a state you don't even know?"

"I didn't say it wouldn't kill me. I just know these outlaws can be got."

Clark Bavin, the head of law enforcement for the Fish and Wildlife Service, was a pure administrator—conflict among his agents was something he could do without—but he had a more than sneaking regard for Dave Hall's fierce will. Letting fellow SACs get into turf wars might be horrible for morale, but the Russians and the State Department had their claws in his back, and Hall was clearly the right man. He looked Indian, and that would help. He knew Alaska fairly well from having worked there when he was young. And even if Hall and Houge ended up loathing each other, he could see in Hall's face, which had turned maroon, and in the lightning flashing from his eyes that he would rather *die* than see this investigation fail.

In March of 1980, having won Bavin's blessing and Houge's not-too-gentle acquiescence, Dave Hall got Doak to agree to let him use his shop as a cover. A few days later, after reviewing whatever intelligence there was on the walrus ivory trade, he told Doak that the suspected dealer he wanted most was a man named Charles McAlpine. McAlpine was reputed to be the biggest ivory dealer in Alaska, if not the entire country, and he had never been caught. He had foiled an undercover sting a few years earlier and had once walked away from two and a half tons of mastodon ivory that was seized coming off an airplane. McAlpine was devilishly smart—he had studied law at Yale or some such Ivy League school—but had spent most of his adult life as a bar owner, big-game guide, and smuggler; he was an educated mercenary, an outlaw-adventurer as the South Africans and Israelis sometimes offer them up. Doak said he had heard the name McAlpine somewhere. Someone he knew had once worked for him as a carver. He said they called him Sealskin Charlie up in Alaska. Doak finally remembered the man's name—Rick Powell—and found him living in Washington state. He called him up and asked if he would arrange an introduction. For a couple of hundred dollars, he would.

On April 12, Doak got through to McAlpine on the telephone. He told him about his shop, mentioned a little of his past, dropped the names of a couple of mutual acquaintances ("Yeah, I know him real well," said Charlie of one, "he owes me money"), then said he was looking to buy about a thousand pounds of raw ivory.

"Well, that's a violation of federal and state law," said McAlpine.

"Yeah, well, if you're in this business you've got to violate a few laws to make some money, right?" said Doak.

"Well, you can't even breathe without violating some law," said McAlpine. "But be very careful because it's no joke. These people are serious."

"Yeah, well, see, that's why I'm in Louisiana. Because in Louisiana, they're not serious about anything."

"If you think it's okay to come up here and buy ivory," said McAlpine, "you're going to get yourself in a whole lot of trouble. And it is not little trouble. It is *big* trouble. It's like kidnapping and bank robbing. They treat it the same way. You think it's some kind of joke or something. When you violate a federal law, the federal agents, the government of this country treats that seriously. It's no joke. It's not, 'They don't enforce the law here in Louisiana.' That's a bunch of *crap.* If they catch you, they will *kick your ass.* They've kicked mine. A guy I do business with back East and I are the biggest ivory dealers in America. And I've historically been the biggest dealer in Alaskan ivory. I know what I'm talking about. And I wouldn't sell unbanded tusks to a guy I didn't know really well. And I ain't gonna give no receipt if I do. Or I take no checks if I do."

"All right, well, how would you suggest we do business, then?"

"Oh, hell, anymore the government will spend half a million dollars setting up a shop and the whole deal. And work for two years setting up every deal in the country and then arrest them all at once."

Doak's heart was beating faster. He wasn't sure whether his capacity to lie was a match for Charlie's needle-sharp defenses. "Well, I'm not the government, for one thing. If you want to check me out—"

"No, I'm just saying the shop and everything—that is the lengths they go to these days. And I'm not telling you stories. I've seen what they can do and what they do—there's very serious heat on walrus ivory by the environmentalists. You and I think it's crazy, but that doesn't mean there aren't hundreds of bureaucrats who are being paid to arrest guys like us. I have got to get it from the Eskimos in a very clandestine manner. And this is all costly. I'm paying thirty dollars a pound for it."

Now Doak was smiling to himself. McAlpine had the same weakness all other outlaws had. Greed. Here he was saying that Doak's shop could be a half-million-dollar front for an undercover sting, here he was saying that ivory smuggling was being treated as a crime like kidnapping, and here he was telling Doak how he would get illegal ivory for him and how Doak would have to pay for it.

"Have your people carved walrus ivory?" McAlpine asked.

"Yeah."

"So you know about the core and the skin and how it is. You need big tusks, is what you need."

"Right," said Doak, "good solid tusks. Your New Orleans market, your South market, these guys over in Texas—they like their big tusks, they like to keep them in a trophy room, they like them on their tables, in their offices and stuff. See, we get a lot of oil money down here. I've sold four pairs of big tusks just since Mardi Gras. That is, in two months. You're talking over ten thousand dollars each pair. What I call big tusks is, you know, tusks that range maybe ten pounds, something like that."

"That's a small tusk," said McAlpine.

"Yeah, right. But see, the thing is, if I have to pay trade port shipping costs and all this type of stuff for those giant-size tusks from Africa, it's not really worth it."

"Well, what I should do, I should send you about a hundred pounds of big walrus tusks. The biggest that come. And I should charge you forty-five dollars a pound. And they should be tagged. And then, afterward, you keep those tags handy and you get it cut up quick as you can and never have more than two or three around, and nobody can prove those tags didn't come off those pieces you've got around."

Doak and Charlie talked a good while longer, with Doak reading off a shopping list—could he get polar bear hides? could he get whales' teeth? did he have access to tiger hides and exotic stuff like that?—and Charlie hedging and saying that it was all illegal, he was crazy to be looking for it, but yes, he could probably get it for him. He was skittish as a foal and gluttonous as a starving bear. The poor miserable sonofabitch, Doak thought to himself, after they'd hung up, tyrannized in equal proportion by greed and fear. But he was also thinking about what got to him. It must have been the Texas money. These Texas good old boys making millions and billions in the oil game, these Sun Belt developers who were building the New South—they were not the pathological skinflints who had made the Old Wealth. They didn't wear their golf shoes until the soles were worn through, even though they owned all the golf courses on which they played . . . This was New Wealth. This was crazy throwaway wealth. These rich southern good old boys took *pride* in throwing millions away. And there were so many of them now, even compared to a few years ago. That discount store magnate, Walton, the Wal-Mart king, hadn't had two nickels twenty-five years ago, and now he was the richest man in America . . . Trammell Crow, who owned half of Dallas . . . the Bass brothers, who owned just about all of Fort Worth . . . the savings and loan Bubbas and Billys . . . all the small fry worth maybe a quarter or half a "unit" . . . a unit being Texasese for a hundred million. "Hey, how many units do you spose old Bobby is worth now?" "Oh, probly two, three maybe, but he done took a bath on that ol' charter airah-line he bought . . ." These Texans were like a bunch of kids who find a huge bag of stolen loot. And they behaved as kids would, throwing parties where you ate caviar with tortilla chips . . . gold-plating their Rolls-Royces . . . building ghastly suburban palaces the size of hotels . . . and stocking them with good old boy stuff. That was what must have flashed through Charlie McAlpine's mind. Good old boy stuff! Custom-built ivory-inlay pool tables with racks of ivory-inlay cue sticks and sets of solid ivory balls—balls he could pick up for six dollars apiece and sell for a hundred . . . polar bear rugs for the parlor . . . walrus and elephant tusks to display on the desk half the size of a tennis court . . . elephant-foot ashtrays . . . eagle-feather head-dresses . . . mounted heads of bighorn sheep and Dall sheep and mountain goats and grizzly bears. These were crackers who would spend a couple of hundred thousand dollars on four sets of trophy horns so they could say they made the grand slam. And if they bought an elephant tusk for four thousand dollars, they would say it cost them ten because bargain shopping was not what these people did. And here was this guy Doak, who knew these people, who had hundreds of them come into his shop every year, who was dealing with a clientele to whom cost *was almost no object.* And he wanted McAlpine to be his supplier—in the one place where Charlie hadn't made many good contacts yet.

Obviously, it was much too much for McAlpine to resist. But before he dealt with Doak, he told him, he was going to check him out firsthand.

Charlie decided to come visit in a hurry, about ten days after they talked. He trusted no one. He wouldn't even tell Doak the number of the flight on which he was coming down; he told him only the day. That was enough for Dave Hall, who flashed his badge for the airlines people and found McAlpine on a Continental flight due in at two-eleven on April 21. He sent a pair of agents to the airport to tail him. When Charlie stepped off the plane, the surveillance men, Owens and Germany, were laughing in their hats. The biggest outlaw ivory dealer in the United States resembled a puffin. He was about five feet ten inches tall, overweight, perhaps fifty years old; he had reddish-blond hair, though there wasn't much of it left, and his mottled red cheeks were blue-penciled with varicose veins. He was dressed in Banana Republic from toe to tuft: a short-sleeved khaki bush jacket with matching trousers, a flyaway shirt, and a pair of white jogging shoes with blue trim. He could have been some degenerate Scottish swell in Kenya in the 1920s.

McAlpine walked down the airport corridor like a hunted man, making eye contact with everyone, stopping now and then to let the flow of passengers get ahead of him. At the baggage counter, he picked up a suitcase, a duffel, and a couple of small boxes. Obviously, the two hundred pounds of ivory he had promised Doak he would bring down had arrived in some other manner.

Doak had not liked it, but Dave Hall had insisted that another of his Fish and Wildlife agents, Kevin Wood, go undercover at Endangered Species, posing as one of his employees. He didn't know how long he could hold McAlpine before he got hincky, so the first conversations between him and Doak could be crucial—they might be the sum total of their case, along with the ivory Charlie had said he would bring down. Doak, on the other hand, was worried. If McAlpine grilled Wood about the stuff the shop sold, the whole case might be blown, because Wood didn't know much about anything he sold. Charlie finally arrived at the shop late in the afternoon, after checking into the Monteleone Hotel. Doak introduced him to Kevin Wood, then decided to get him upstairs to his apartment in a hurry. The first thing McAlpine asked Doak when they were alone was how he could be certain Wood wasn't an undercover plant.

By then Wood had already activated the two tape recorders he had installed behind Doak's bookshelf.

"It's a tough game, with the government into everything," Charlie was saying. "There are an awful lot of government agents up there in Alaska. You go into any little place and, you know, everybody knows who you are and exactly what you're doing, and they tell them. In every village they have guys who work for the Fish and Game Department."

Doak said, "Oh, they come in here, too. They check things over and they ask dumb questions. But what the hell. There's a stuffed gorilla over there, you know—and I've got another gorilla in there. I got lions and all that kind of stuff. That rhino horn in there—that's 'not for sale.' As long as it's 'not for sale'—"

"The government's made it tough," Charlie moaned on. He was absolutely obsessed. "And the laws make it very, very difficult. Jesus Christ, it's—I mean all of the elephants are embargoed right now . . . It just gets to be a hassle. The Alaska ivory is scarce anymore. A lot of people want to invest in it. It was legal for a little while, and then they made it illegal again, which is really a big hassle." Then he brightened. "How do you like to do business? You mentioned cash. That's no problem?"

"Nope. That's fine. I mean, if you got a thousand pounds right now, it's going to be a couple of days before I can get it all together, you know."

"I've got about a hundred pounds of tagged," said Charlie, "and about a hundred pounds of untagged. It didn't come with me. I shipped it earlier, you know. If you want to keep doing business, I could take the tags off and I'd take them back with me, and that way you get—in case there is ever a problem, see?"

Just like the phony certificates for elephant ivory you can have forged in Singapore and Hong Kong, thought Doak. Buyer and seller agree to keep recycling the tags, and no one can prove in court that they were used before. Before long, if the price of ivory kept rising as fast as it was, the tags would be worth more than the ivory, just as a taxi medallion is worth ten times more in New York City than the taxi itself.

Doak got out a bottle of gin and some ice. Charlie drank his with tonic. After knocking back two, he was in a fairly expansive mood. "Hell, me and one of my partners are the two biggest people in America," he told Doak. "Next to us, nobody even counts. And the next people to him and me—he does three mil' and I do three mil' and the next people to us do a hundred and fifty thousand or a couple of hundred thousand, maybe. That's how far ahead of the pack we are."

Over dinner at Pascal's Manale, Charlie didn't let up, much to Doak's delight, since he was now wearing a wire that Kevin Wood had strapped on after Charlie went back to the Monteleone to shower and change. He told Doak who his "partner" was: an Orthodox Jewish gangster from New York named Moses Feingold. Feingold handled mainly elephant ivory, he said, although he bought walrus from Charlie from time to time. If Doak wanted some really big elephant tusks, as long as there were any left, he could get them for him, though they were getting drastically expensive. Feingold was ultra security conscious and dangerous, though; it would be better for Doak to go through him. (So you can skim some profit, you bastard, thought Doak.) He told him about some of the other contraband he sold. "I used to sell tupilaks by the hundreds. The pressure got on that. We were smuggling them in from Greenland and I finally got scared. They got too close for me and I quit doing it." He said he dealt ivory in small lots. "You know, a hundred pounds at a time, every three days." (Earlier, he had tried to convince Doak that only about fifteen hundred pounds of ivory went out of Alaska each year; it was too dangerous to hunt the animals, and that was why it was scarce and the price was high. Now, thanks to an excellent taxpayer-sponsored bottle of wine, he was suggesting that *he alone* sold about ten thousand pounds a year.) He told him about the time he had two and a half tons of fossil mammoth ivory held up by wildlife agents and the state police, and how he had managed to slip away but suffered a quarter-of-a-million-dollar loss. He told him how a governor of Greenland had been a friend and how he smuggled whales' teeth out of there. He told him how "everyone" was buying ivory as an investment because the animals were all going to go extinct someday.

"Several airplanes a day come into almost every Eskimo village," Charlie said. "Several. They're all full of government workers, and they're all buying. They're full of state workers, and *they're* all buying. They're full of teachers, and *they're* all buying. You've got to be there," he said in wonderment. Then, tiring of shoptalk, he began telling Doak about his favorite form of recreation: pubescent Eskimo girls. "From fourteen to seventeen they're good," he said. "The Eskimo's the only girl in the world that goes from nineteen to thirty-nine in one year—in the winter they take all that nice breeding stock off to school. That's just terrible cause all the prime ones are thirteen to fifteen." He asked Doak if he knew of any good cathouses in New Orleans. To Charlie's obvious delight, Doak knew an excellent one, Lucky Pierre's, right down the street.

Dave Hall told me later that he could have taken a seasoned under-cover warden—himself included—force-fed him knowledge about the international wildlife and gem and artifacts trade, given him a three-hour exam to make sure he knew what he was talking about, and Charlie would have eaten him for lunch. "He probably wouldn't have made it as far as New Orleans. He would have smelled bullshit right through the phone. Look how he suspected Kevin Wood the second he laid eyes on him. McAlpine was Wile E. Coyote. But Doak was a rock-solid cover. I mean *rock*-solid. It was like having a big drug dealer working under-cover for you. I don't know what-all kind of stuff Doak did earlier in his life, and the porno stuff, you know, I don't like that *at all.* But the thing is, this time he was workin for *me.*" When Doak told McAlpine about the Ore House and the Gypsy Jokers and making porno films, Charlie was goggle-eyed. He wanted to see the films. At dinner, Doak told him about going to India to buy carvings for ivory inlay, and about smuggling in pornography and being caught and bribing his way out; he told him about buying trips to Thailand and Africa; he told him about having phony export certificates for ivory made up for him in Hong Kong and India; he told him about a radio officer he knew on the *President Eisenhower* and a pilot from Houston who was based in Singapore and how they ran all kinds of stuff for him; he told him about a South African he knew who sold him skins of animals—zebra, mostly—poached in the national parks. Doak had more anecdotes than a field has corn. Nearly all of them, he told me, were either made up or things he'd heard secondhand; in his business, if you keep an ear tuned, you can learn about all manner of illegal activity. The point is that Charlie was lapping them up. By eleven o'clock, when Doak finally paid the bill, he was as sure as he could ever be that, from now on, McAlpine would be eating out of his hand.

Which was not to say that his defenses were down. When Doak packed him off to Lucky Pierre's, Charlie's last words of the evening were "My hotel room is pretty safe, isn't it?"

Out of curiosity, if nothing else, Dave Hall had badly wanted to meet Charlie McAlpine when he came down to New Orleans. Out of prudence, he decided against it. He didn't dare meet someone like McAlpine on his own turf. His office had been in the French Quarter for the better part of a decade, and even if he was rarely there, a lot of people knew him and what he did. Someone might say, as he was walking McAlpine down Toulouse Street, "How's the old game warden business, Dave?" Those seven words would destroy his cover and his case. The humiliation would be unbearable. If he botched this case in any way, he would become a laughingstock—there were more than a few agents in the Fish and Wildlife Service who were dying for him to screw up.

So he wouldn't come near Charlie yet. What was the point of introducing him to an undercover game warden who Charlie, in his wild, paranoid imagination, might think was an undercover game warden? What he wanted to do was make a sweep of Alaska first, stinging all the smaller ivory traders and Eskimo suppliers he could get his hands on. Then he and Doak would come through Seattle on their way back home and buy some more ivory from McAlpine to play him along and buttress their case against him. Then he would move on any other ivory or wildlife dealers whose identities McAlpine revealed. Charlie would be furious when they bought walrus ivory from his own Alaskan suppliers, but by the same token he wouldn't trust them if they didn't. McAlpine's prices were the highest in the business, and no enterprising criminal would buy exclusively from someone like him. Enterprising criminals didn't shop retail, and McAlpine was the outlaw equivalent of Neiman Marcus.

For the next few months, then, for however long it took him to clear away the avalanche of paperwork that had covered his desk, there was nothing for Dave Hall to do but advance Doak more money to keep making small buys from Charlie. The only risk in doing that was the possibility that Charlie would become so comfortable dealing with Doak he wouldn't come near Dave Hall.

Dave Hall had invented an alias. He was going to be Dave Hayes, an uneducated but shrewd Texas good old boy who was making a small fortune in the oil-leasing business and wanted to invest it in palpable assets. Some time before, he had gone to the traveling King Tut exhibit, a Texas cracker seeking culture and enlightenment—this was all part of the story—and had been impressed how, even three thousand years ago, when minerals lay on the surface of the earth and the African wilds were almost untouched, gold and ivory were already the most valued commodities on earth. How could it be any different today on such a plundered planet? Dave Hayes wasn't going to do what all his idiot good old boy buddies had done—invest in shopping malls and condominiums—because the oil bubble was going to burst someday and half the houses in Houston would be on the auction block. (It's strange how prescient you can be when inventing a story; by 1987, one in every four houses in Houston was on the auction block.) He was going to buy all the gold, gems, and ivory he could get his hands on. He was going to sell some of the ivory to his Texas friends and stockpile the rest of it because ivory would attain unimaginable value when the elephant went extinct in the wild.

The alias would work—Dave Hall was pretty confident of that—but on the other hand, he couldn't just appear out of nowhere. Doak had to mention him from time to time when he talked to McAlpine on the phone—which was quite frequently now that McAlpine appeared to trust him. He had to get him used to the fact that he had a partner, a financier really, with whom he would soon be dealing himself. It wasn't easy, because McAlpine usually paid no attention when he brought up the subject of his partner, Hayes. McAlpine was the sort of person who didn't just interrupt—he ran right over you when he had something he wanted to say. On June 6, however, a couple of days before he and Dave Hall were scheduled to depart for Alaska, Doak figured that he had to convince Charlie that Hayes was real. After all, in a couple of weeks they were going to meet.

"Now this partner of mine," he reminded McAlpine, "he's got a couple of shops out of Houston, and he's got a lot of money in oil investments. He leases these oil fields out there in the swamps, you know, and he's been getting pretty rich cause of the oil embargo and all that. And, over there in Texas, they want ivory, you know. For my type of business, I need a couple hundred pounds of walrus every three or four months, or something like that. But he's looking at, you know, like a thousand-pound deal where he can sit on it and supply that area of Texas."

McAlpine finally stopped long enough to listen. In fact, judging from the sudden silence at the other end of the telephone line, Doak figured he must have sat bolt upright.

"Keep quiet about this," he admonished Doak. "I don't even like your partner *knowing* about it. You've got to be real careful—"

"About what?" interjected Doak.

"About this ivory thing. You know, just—"

"What, what ivory thing?"

"I mean the ivory you're going to get from me!"

"Oh, shit! He's all right. Jesus Christ! He's the one that's paying for it! Are you kidding?!"

"I know, I know," said McAlpine, "but you know, the more people that know, the worse it is, if he's the kind of guy that talks and tells his friends and everything—"

"Oh, hell, no, no, no! Jesus Christ! He's, oh, he's a wheeler-dealer, this dude. He acts dumb, but he's smarter than a sonofabitch."

"Good," said Charlie.

"The only thing is," said Doak, "he expects this ivory to be down here, you know. He's a bad guy to cross, now . . . If he gets pissed off, boy, he's the type of guy that likes to shoot up the snowbanks."

Doak ended that conversation by telling him about a drought in the bayous around New Orleans that was bringing alligators right into town. "There are fifty thousand alligators within the city limits of New Orleans. And they've been crawling all over people's yards, and guys have been out there shooting them. And people are saying they've been shooting alligators in their backyards to protect their dogs and their children, right? But everybody is up in arms about shooting alligators again. The environmentalists—"

Mentioning that word seemed to set off a Pavlovian response in Charlie McAlpine.

"All the environmentalists are crazy, man," he half growled and half moaned.

"Yeah, it might be on the news tonight," Doak went on, "because the mayor is over there. I think the governor is in on it, too. So that will be a big stink—"

"Ohhhhhh, the environmentalists are *nuts*," Charlie moaned again.

It was too bad, Doak mused, that he couldn't tell Charlie that the Texas wheeler-dealer he was about to meet was one of the main reasons there were so many alligators around.

"If there's a lousier town anywhere on this planet than Nome," Dave Hall said, "I'd sure as hell like to know where."

As a student at Mississippi State, Dave Hall had spent two summer breaks working for the Fish and Wildlife Service near Dillingham, Alaska. Dillingham is not as bleak as Nome, but bleak enough so that he knew what to expect. Doak did not. Somehow he seemed to have imagined forested fjords and killer whales and cruise ships. Nome sits at the bottom of the Seward Peninsula, a huge, treeless, wind-blasted thumb of land sticking out into the Bering Sea. It is utterly isolated— the three roads that lead out of town end in sightless tundra. Wild and desolate, a brutally magnificent place, the Seward Peninsula is marred only by a large container spill, which is Nome. The figure of speech occurred to Doak as their plane banked and circled the town on its approach. The homes and buildings seemed dumped down there on the earth in random chaos, and the majority of them, in Louisiana, would have qualified as sharecroppers' shacks. Many of the older, seaside houses—Victorian bungalows built with money earned during the gold fever of 1899—had been demolished by a storm surge in 1974. Nome was the world capital of the International Quonset Hut style. Bars and churches were in about equal proportion and were difficult to tell apart; one had no loitering drunks and a cross, the other didn't, but they looked about the same. The landscape was mildly undulating tundra, without trees to the limits of sight. Doak, who liked the dense, semitropical effulgence of southern Louisiana, had never seen a place with no trees. Wearing a trenchcoat and a pair of black gum boots he had bought in Anchorage, he stepped off the plane into a strong, misting, seaward wind, and contemplated Nome as if it were a large, freshly laid pile of steaming dung.

They came in from Anchorage, where they stopped overnight on the way up; Nome had practically no decent lodging, and they didn't want to arrive too late and have to spend the night on the street (many visiting people did, especially Eskimos—especially drunken Eskimos). In Anchorage they already had a stroke of luck. For some reason—instinct, perhaps—Dave Hall had booked them into the Sheraton Hotel, which is owned by the Bristol Bay Native Corporation, one of several subsidized businesses invented by Congress to introduce native Alaskans to the miracles of materialism. After checking in, he went down to the bar—that is what you do in a strange town because bartenders know everything. The bartender at the Sheraton was from Mississippi. He took an instant liking to Dave Hall. When he told him he was on an ivory-buying expedition, the bartender did a double take. He looked around. No one was watching. He quickly opened a drawer below the bar. There were four or five walrus tusks inside. Dave Hall did a double take of his own. There was raw ivory for sale in the fern bar of one of the fanciest hotels in Anchorage. The bartender told him if he wanted more, he could get it for him. One of the officers of the Bristol Bay Native Corporation, who lived in Dillingham, was a good friend of his.

Dave Hall was tempted to head for Dillingham the next morning. It looked as if he had a sure indictment, and a native corporation selling ivory against the law was serious business. He decided to hold to their itinerary instead; Nome was the ivory capital of the northern Hemisphere, and that was where any serious buyer would go first. If he went about this wrong, someone might figure out that he was fishing for indictments instead of ivory. When they got to Nome, they dropped their luggage at the Golden Nugget, the only respectable hotel in town, but did not check in—they weren't sure what would happen on their first day. Then Dave Hall rang up Tom Trainor, the one contact they had there. Trainor was a heavy-equipment operator who had walked into Endangered Species a few months earlier, intimating that he had raw ivory for sale. Dave Hall had taken him to lunch and introduced him to his banker—or, to be more accurate, to one of his many front men, a neighbor who happened to be a vice-president of a large local bank, and who kept a phony account on hand showing that Dave Hayes was worth millions. He didn't have any ivory right now, Trainor said, but he had made arrangements for them to buy some. From whom? asked Dave Hall. It was all right to want to know who your sources were. The King Island Native Corporation, Trainor said.

The Eskimos had their thumbprints all over the ivory trade, but no one suspected the degree to which the native corporations were involved. That much was obvious when Doak and Dave Hall drove over to King Island headquarters and Trainor introduced them around. In contrast to McAlpine, who would have suspected them of being undercover agents had they been a grandmother and a five-year-old, the Eskimos were utterly trusting, as if they hadn't seen a game warden in years. John Pollack, an officer of the corporation, sold Dave Hall his first big load—about a hundred pounds of raw ivory at thirty-five dollars a pound. During the next hour, more and more of them began to appear. It was like being seen in Tijuana with a satchel full of cash. A friend of Pollack's came in with a huge polar bear skin. Dave Hall decided to buy it for twenty-five hundred dollars. So much for subsistence.

While they were bargaining with the Eskimos—Dave Hall was anxious to identify as many individual sellers as he could, but he didn't want to seem *too* eager—Tom Trainor was quietly getting drunk. He had brought a bottle in his jacket pocket, and by early afternoon Doak had counted seven or eight hits. When they were done buying, Trainor told them that they couldn't just leave; in Alaska, when you made deals such as this, you went somewhere to celebrate. The place he had in mind was a roadhouse about fifteen miles north of town—it was, in fact, the end of the line of the Iditarod, the Anchorage-to-Nome dogsled race. Dave Hall didn't like driving with a drunk, but it would have been awkward to say no—and at the rate they were buying ivory, a couple of indictments were probably waiting at the roadhouse, too. They stashed the ivory and polar bear hide at Trainor's and took off, wedged three-abreast in his pickup truck.

The north road out of Nome was surfaced with crushed rock, badly pitted by the spring thaw, and only about a lane and a half wide. It meandered on top of a bluff directly along the Bering Strait; at times, it was cut into the bluff itself. A hundred feet below them was a frozen marsh; beyond, the awakening strait. Great wedges of drift ice were spinning imperceptibly in an uneasy sea. It took some courage, Dave

Hall thought, to go after walrus ivory in an ocean like that—certainly more courage than it took to waste an elephant with a Kalashnikov.

Dave Hall has a stack of pictures he took in Alaska, in which are several of the roadhouse. Whatever alias he happens to be using in undercover work, it usually includes two components: the "gun-totin' fool" and the "Japanese shutterbug." ("I photographed all these mothers," he told me once, "to the point where maybe they got annoyed, but they didn't suspect me. If I'd tried to sneak a couple of pictures, they'd have suspected me.") The roadhouse in the photograph is a ramshackle, windowless dump of peculiar height—it looks about four stories tall, though you can't really tell because there are no windows—surrounded by rusted hulks of various machines. An enormous sweep of wild tundra begins just beyond the junk heaped outside the back door. It is like most of mankind's marks on Alaska: a pullulating lesion, a sore. By the time they reached the roadhouse, it was nearly eight o'clock but still light—as it would be for the four or five hours they were to spend there. "In Nome," Vaughn Doak said, "the economy is basically people making deals. There's hardly any tourists; there's not much fishing or anything—it's just deals. All the deals are made in bars. It's people selling anything and everything and drinking while they do it, and then you drink some more to celebrate the deal, and all the while it stays light in the summer so you don't have darkness to tell you it's time to go home. Alaska was the first time in years I got my old hepatitis back. My liver couldn't take it. I've never seen so much drinking going on."

The roadhouse was no exception. Nor was Trainor. He wasn't just a drunk. He was a dipsomaniac. He backed most of his beers with a schnapps; by the time one o'clock in the morning came around he had had about ten of each. Even for someone of his size—he was six feet seven inches tall—his capacity was prodigious. On the other hand, he had reached it: he was falling-down drunk. So was Doak. Doak had incurred the quiet wrath of Dave Hall—who had held a lot of his liquor in his mouth or his shot glass and spilled it down the toilet during trips to the men's room—by nearly matching Trainor drink for drink. A helicopter pilot friend of Trainor's, who was going to ride back to Nome with them, was in similar shape.

When the four of them—three drunks and an extremely vexed Dave

Hall—finally spilled out into the parking lot and stood by Trainor's truck in midnight twilight, neither he nor Doak nor the pilot was in any condition to drive.

"You ought to let me pilot this rig," Dave Hall said to Trainor.

Trainor stared stupidly. His yellow eyes were watering.

"No one drives my goddamned—vee—hickle—sides—you don—know the—fuckn road."

"I may not know the road, but I sure as hell am gonna get us back safer than you are."

"Crocka—shit."

"My ass, it's a crockashit! I ought to drive."

" 'S—bullshit!"

Dave Hall's mood had gone from bitter to incendiary, but there was no point arguing. Trainor fell behind the wheel, revved the engine to screaming pitch, chortled sullenly, and shifted into the wrong gear. He finally got them going, after a fashion, and Doak promptly fell asleep. Dave Hall was smoldering but held his peace. If he'd argued with Trainor, he might have driven right off the cliff. After ten minutes or so, they could see another truck approaching them, still about half a mile away. Dave Hall said nothing, but he had a bad feeling. The road was narrow here. When the other truck was still a hundred feet away, it seemed as if they would clear it. At the last minute, Trainor swerved to the left and they collided head-on. Actually, his left bumper rammed the right bumper of the other truck, which sent them shimmying sideways in slow slippery lurches. Trainor's truck ground to a halt on the crumbly gravel about ten inches from the edge of the bluff.

Trainor wrestled open his door and sprawled onto the road. It was his fault entirely, but he was furious. He picked himself up and began cursing the driver of the other truck, who was charging him and cursing even louder. When they finally were a few feet apart, Trainor recognized him. He was one of his friends. They kept yelling at each other, but the storm had passed. Or it had until a flashing, crackling Dave Hall managed to scramble over Doak—who, despite the crash, was still nodded-out—got out of the truck, and stalked over to them.

"If you don't give me the keys, *now*," he snarled, "I'm going to take em from you and drive back and leave you here."

Trainor was furious at everything—Dave Hall, the driver of the other truck, Alaska, himself, the universe.

"Fuck you!" he screamed back.

There was no point arguing. Dave Hall shoved him out of his way and marched back to the smashed-in but still idling truck. Trainor tried to grab him, but Dave Hall—a veteran of perhaps a hundred Mississippi bar fights—grabbed his shirt with both hands and slammed him back so hard that he ricocheted off the truck and tumbled onto the ground. He clawed his way back up and was about to grab Dave Hall from behind when he noticed a .38 stuck into his face.

The commotion had finally woken Doak up. All he remembers is that the gun had come out very fast, and that Dave Hall looked fiercer than Geronimo.

"I *am* driving, you *ain't* driving, and that's just the way it's gonna *be!*" he bellowed.

"Put that fuckin gun down!" Trainor bawled.

"If I have to kill you to take over this wheel, I swear by God I'm gonna do it!"

Doesn't this wild-eyed part-Indian lunatic realize he is a *federal law-enforcement officer?* Doak remembers thinking to himself through his alcoholic haze.

"He looks crazy enough to do it," said Trainor's helicopter pilot friend.

"I *am* crazy enough to do it!" This must violate all proper federal procedure in a situation where subject is not bearing firearms or behaving in a calculatedly homicidal manner, Dave Hall was thinking to himself, but dammit, this was a unique situation anyway. A drunken scumbag like Trainor—force was all he understood.

Anyway, it worked. "Drive," Trainor finally mumbled. He could barely stand on his feet. "Fuck . . ."

His revolver loose in his jacket pocket, Dave Hall hunkered behind the wheel and drove them back to Nome. No word was spoken. When they finally got back, it was two in the morning. Dave Hall marched into Trainor's house, got the ivory and baggage he had stored there that afternoon, and marched back out, trying to look more furious than he felt anymore. By now, Trainor had some of his courage back. They were going to pay for this, they had better watch their backs, Alaskans didn't tolerate southern gangsters pulling guns on them.... (Gangster, thought Dave Hall—the fight had aided his cover immeasurably.) Dave Hall dismissed him with a glare, threw Trainor his keys, and yanked Doak out of the truck.

By the time they got back to the Golden Nugget, their room—the last available room—had been rented to someone else. They had wanted to reserve it with a deposit, but Trainor had told them they needn't; there would be plenty of space, and in a pinch they could stay with him. He was a drunk, reckless, cavalier, careless—Dave Hall couldn't find words, numbers, or images to express his loathing. And he was almost madder at Doak. Getting drunk on an undercover assignment was inexcusable. He had deputized him and let him carry a revolver; he ought to have behaved like a *goddamned law-enforcement officer!!!* "I could have killed him," he says when retelling this part of the story, and there is still passion in his voice, years later. The night clerk at the hotel said a woman down the street ran a rooming house that probably had some overflow space. It wasn't much, he said, but it did have a roof, and probably some heat. Dave Hall left Doak at the hotel and took a cab over there. The cabdriver, whose name was Carl Peterson—Dave Hall remembers the names of practically all these people—asked him what he was doing up so late.

"We got into a little humbug at the Iditarod roadhouse," he said.

"Yeah. Figures. I know that place."

"We was just trying to buy a little ivory—"

"Ivory? You're buying ivory?"

"That's why we're here."

"You want more?"

"You got it?"

"I can get it for you."

You could get it everywhere at any time of day or night. People simply had it around, waiting for buyers. Dave Hall wondered who the main buyers were. Japanese? The Eskimos would never forgive them for their depravity in the Aleutians during the Second World War. The Hong Kong and Singapore mafia? They usually preferred elephant ivory. Whatever the answer, Nome was as far off the beaten path as you could get, but when it came to ivory the place was like a bazaar in Multan. He took the driver's phone number and promised to call him later. Then he woke up the old woman who ran the boardinghouse and paid for the room. Then he walked back to the Golden Nugget, picked up Doak and a couple of hundred pounds of luggage, ivory, and rolled-up polar bear fur, and dragged them back for the night.

The rooming house was worse than a sty. When Dave Hall awoke three hours later, he almost gagged. The sheets and blankets were revoltingly stained, and they had shared an attic with a couple of the nastiest, most scrofulous-looking drifters they had run into yet. "It was *bad*," he said, in the voice of someone who has witnessed a massacre. He dragged most of the luggage back to the Golden Nugget, put down a deposit for the next available room, and went back and hauled Doak out of bed. He was semicomatose. His hangover was epic. The two of them walked back to the hotel for breakfast. Dave Hall was getting tired of this walk. After breakfast, they realized that between the two of them, they had many thousands of dollars in cash but no small bills. They decided to go over to the bank and break a few hundreds. The teller said they didn't have that kind of change. Doak, who had suffered too long now, was beside himself.

"How can you call yourselves a bank if you can't even change a hundred-dollar bill?"

"We do have money in the safe, which I'm not at liberty to open."

"What's a tourist who wants to unload some money in this town supposed to do if the *bank* can't make change?"

"I'm sorry, sir."

"I *can't believe* this lousy goddamned town! Who do you suppose can break a hundred-dollar bill? Or do I have to go to Anchorage?"

"You could try the Silver Lode down the street. Or the hotel. We'll give you a letter of introduction."

"The hotel doesn't have it. What's the Silver Lode?"

"A bar. The biggest bar in town. You could ask for the owner—he's a pretty nice man."

"What's his name?"

"He's Wayne Gans."

• • •

With this much serendipity in the beginning, thought Dave Hall, they would end up dead in the end. When he was handed a briefing paper on suspected ivory traffickers before going to Alaska, the person who stood out—he didn't just stand out, he leaped from the page like a grizzly bear—was Wayne Gans. Among all their targets in Nome, Gans was number one. He owned the town. The bigger apartments were all his, as was the Silver Lode and another bar, the taxi service, the heavy equipment service, and a fair portion of Nome's other real estate. "It took me two years to get out of Nome," Charlie McAlpine would say to Dave Hall later on. "It'll take Wayne Gans ten. He owns so much of it it'll take him that long to find people with the money or the willingness to go up." By reputation, Gans was both a charismatic and extremely dangerous man. There were rumors—substantiated by repetition if by nothing else—that he had killed a couple of people by shooting them point-blank on the street, but no one could be found who would testify against him. One murder he had served time for and had been pardoned by the governor. He had been indicted quite recently for possessing a polar bear skin, but in the middle of the trial an Eskimo came out of nowhere, for reasons unknown but easy to guess, and took the rap; he said he had left the skin in Gans's garage. Gans had "friends." There were more rumors, none of them substantiated, that Gans was in thick with the Nome police. His wife was a reputed madam. Their union was less a marriage than a cartel. He was suspected of involvement in all kinds of crime, including ivory trading. After Charlie McAlpine, he was Dave Hall's top suspect, but he had had no idea how to make a run at him. What could be better than a letter of introduction from the local bank?

When they walked into the Silver Lode, Gans wasn't there. The bartender said he was at home, so Doak called him up. They needed to change some money, he said, and told him about the letter. They were in town to buy ivory, he said casually. Gans said to come over.

When I asked Vaughn Doak which actor Wayne Gans looked like, his answer was Brian Dennehy. (Doak, a former actor, compares everyone to actors.) Gans was large, barrel-chested, and blond, in his late forties, with piercing eyes and a bit of residual Oklahoma twang. His wife was "an old Rita Hayworth, or maybe Amanda Blake—you know, Miss Kitty from *Gunsmoke*. Only she looked a lot meaner." Gans was open and cagey and friendly and a little scary; someone who was all of those things at once was someone you reckoned with. He lived in what, for Nome, passed as a mansion—a big bungalow down by the water. He had a huge trove of ivory in his basement—"a lot of beautiful carvings," Doak remembers, "a lot of scrimmed stuff, mastodon ivory, walrus, aboriginal artifacts, the works. It was worth tens of thousands."

Gans said none of it was for sale. In fact, he said, they were crazy even to be looking to buy ivory at all because the government was coming down much harder on ivory deals since the passage of the Marine Mammal Protection Act. When Dave Hall told him he had bought a polar bear skin, Gans just shook his head. "If I saw a polar bear skin," he said, "I'd run in the other direction as fast as I could." He told them that he had been prosecuted for possessing one, though he didn't tell them how he had beaten the rap. He also told them in which outlying Eskimo villages they could probably find ivory, and he gave them some tips on buying it. You began by asking for legal stuff, and the odds were high that someone would offer you raw ivory later on. As they went back upstairs for a cup of coffee, Dave Hall was thinking that Gans obviously was dealing ivory, and he was wondering how to catch him at it when his wife announced that they were government undercover agents.

Doak had tried to prepare himself for such a moment, but he still felt nailed to the ground by a lightning bolt. Dave Hall spoke first.

"Ma'am, I've been called a lot of names, but no one has ever called me that before."

"I'm not saying you are. I'm saying they could be, Wayne."

"What in hell makes you think that?" Gans asked. He seemed genuinely surprised.

"Woman's intuition."

Dave Hall felt he ought to play along. "Well, what kind of government agents would we be?" he asked.

"Forget it," Gans said to him. "She's paranoid."

Doak felt wounded. In his black gum boots and a dumb-looking mackinaw, he felt he would never be suspected of being undercover. For the first time, he also felt a little scared.

Dave Hall asked Gans's wife if she would like to search him for his wire. He was wired, but it seemed worth the risk. She wasn't going to do it; neither was Gans. "You *are* gonna find a gun, I ain't gonna lie to you about that. We've run into so many rough characters up here, I'm glad I brought mine along." He began telling them about the Iditarod roadhouse and the fight with Trainor the night before.

"Tom can be trouble, no question about that," Gans said. Like a lot of people in town, Trainor was on Gans's payroll at least part of the time.

The tension never quite cleared after Gans's wife made her remark. It was best that they leave, although Dave Hall was still plumbing his brain for some way to inveigle Gans into an illegal deal.

Doak was right about Nome. All the town's business was conducted from bars. If you sat in a bar long enough, all things were possible. Dave Hall made a couple of small buys—four tusks here, six there—from people met casually, but these Eskimo sellers bought their ivory from the outlying villages, from where the killing parties embarked, and those were the people he was really after. It didn't take long to get them. In the afternoon of the same day they saw Wayne Gans, they met an Eskimo who originally came from Savoonga, on Saint Lawrence Island, a very large hump of rock right in the middle of the Bering Sea. Of the two hundred thousand walrus still believed to exist in the world, probably half or more passed within killing range of Saint Lawrence Island as the pack ice drove them southward. Dave Hall told the Eskimo that he had always wanted to see how his people hunted, and that he would be willing to pay his airfare if he went along as a guide. The Eskimo was homesick. He said yes.

Nome was sunless and dreary and desolate. Savoonga was utterly so. No vegetation grew taller than ankle height. The flight out there, which took about an hour and a half, was terrifying—a great quilt of fog hung over the strait and the pilot had to pick his way through tiny holes in the cover in order to land. The main ivory traders in Savoonga were the Pellowooks, three brothers and a sister whom Charlie McAlpine had mentioned to Doak; they were "crazy as pirates," he said, and he had given up dealing directly with them, even though Gilbert Pellowook had once served as his bouncer when he owned his bar in Nome. Despite the brothers' vicious reputation, Doak and Dave Hall found them rather friendly; they were impressed that a pair of southern boys had actually set foot on their island, for in no one's memory had that happened before. Dave Hall took Gans's advice and bought only legal stuff, mainly some fossil spearpoints and carvings on display at the local store. Raw ivory was available, however—the Pellowooks made that unmistakably clear—but Dave Hall didn't want to buy any; he told them he was interested in placing an order later. For one thing, he and Doak had already bought so much stuff that they had no idea how they'd get it back. The real advantage of a prearranged but indeterminate sale, however, was the ideal opportunity it provided for a takedown. The conversations his Nagra was recording—he was wired all the time—would capture enough illegal intent to constitute probable cause; all he had to do was update it with a telephone call right before the takedown date, and a judge, seeing that illegal activity was again discussed, would give him a search warrant for a raid. Or so he hoped. A lot of good undercover work has been sacrificed because the legalities weren't handled exactly right.

Dave Hall has some pictures from Savoonga, taken mainly at the dock. In a high-powered skiff is a large pile of walrus tusks. A skinboat—a skiff made of animal hide, with a smaller motor—floats next to it. Blood is the most striking feature in these pictures—the butt ends of the tusks are all covered with it and with long, hanging ribbons of flesh. I asked Dave Hall if the Eskimos were disturbed that he took pictures of their booty, and he said they were not. In fact, they seemed pleased. "They're proud of their hunting tradition," he told me, "and you have to admire them. They go a hundred miles out in these little boats. The ice is treacherous, and that sea—the Bering Sea is maybe the most hostile body of water in the world. They lose people out there all the time."

By the time they returned to Nome, the whole town had heard about them, knew what they were after, and was beating a path to their door. "We didn't have to go to the bars anymore," Dave Hall says. "Everyone came to us. We'd be in our room watching TV and the knock would come on the door. Sometimes it was 'Got any smoke?' Sometimes it was 'Want to buy some raw?' I don't remember how many guys came up to our room or just approached us on the street, it was like beggars in Calcutta, except they wanted to sell or buy. Coke, pot—they were crazy for it. A lot of them wear little pot pipes around their necks. One guy came up to the room and looked around kind of nervous and said, 'Got any . . .' and then he went '*pfff—pfff—pfff.*' He was afraid to say the word. I said, 'No, I don't got any "*pfff—pfff—pfff.*" But I'll give you ten bucks for the pipe.' He said, 'Man, you can't take my grass pipe,' and I said, 'Well, hell, you don't got any grass, so you don't need the damn pipe.' He sold it to me. I've still got that sucker. I've never smoked dope in my life. Man, if you need an example of what alcohol and drugs can do to a people, you don't got to go to these crack neighborhoods. Those Eskimos are so beat down and desolated by liquor and drugs and money, which to them is a drug, too . . . it was sad. It was sad."

Between knocks on the door, they managed to get some sleep. When morning came, Dave Hall took inventory. They had at least three hundred pounds of ivory accumulated through twenty-odd buys, plus their baggage, plus some small carvings and artifacts, plus the polar bear skin, all of which they had to haul back to New Orleans. Except for Wayne Gans—if he was even selling—they had most of the bigger fish around Nome. The ones they were getting now were hatchery trout. There was no point in keeping this up. It was time to get out.

Hunting human prey is like chasing a wounded bear. Theoretically, you are the hunter; in reality, you are being hunted, too. There are stories of hurt bears being chased who lay down in brush and waited for their tormentors to come near and then jumped out and swatted them dead. Whether you are a big-game hunter or an undercover agent or a spy, you never know when your prey has come up behind you; you only know that you must keep your senses in exquisite tune. Dave Hall, who is a little bit of a mystic, believes his years as a game warden, and especially his undercover work, have given him the sensory capacity of an animal. Like a dog or cat that begins to tremble before an earthquake strikes, he knows when things are about to go wrong.

He says he felt it their second day in Nome. Then it was just a vague sense that they were being followed. He mentioned it to Doak, and though it may simply have been the power of suggestion, Doak said he felt it, too. On the way to the airport, however, he began to feel it strongly. And then they were there.

Four men were at the airport. They didn't notice where they had come from or if they had followed them out or were already there, but everything about them stank of trouble. They were the sorts of characters who might work for Wayne Gans—white, big, and bearded. "Yellow-eyed," says Doak. "Tough dudes," Dave Hall says, "tough, tough-looking dudes."

He feared two things, and he didn't know which fear was more rational or if either was. The intelligence reports he had read on the ivory trade in Alaska mentioned buyers having all their ivory stolen on the way out of Nome. The baggage wagons had holes in them, and suspicions were strong that it was the work of Wayne Gans; no one else in town would dare steal stuff right under the commercial airlines' noses. How would it have looked if big-operator Dave Hall had spent tens of thousands of dollars of the government's money buying load after load of ivory and then had it all snatched out from under him?

His other fear was of being arrested.

I never realized how real a fear it was until I told him I found it exaggerated. He was incensed.

"You've never *been* in a town like Nome. You've never been in a place where one guy owns the town. In a place like that, with so much money being made from ivory and polar bear skins and stuff and so much of it being traded for drugs, a game warden is like a civil rights worker in the Old South. Gans had the police in his hip pocket—that's what we'd been told. Say you get arrested. If we'd just been plain old ivory buyers, they would have let us go, and our ivory would have disappeared and we'd have had no recourse. 'Oh, you're ivory buyers. We'll have to confiscate this stuff.' But when they'd've found my badge and wire . . . We were the biggest trouble to hit Nome in years. Obviously, these dealers had no fear. They'd never been burned, except that one time where Wayne Gans beat the rap on the polar bear skin. And he beat it, that's the point. I'm not convinced we would have *died*, but . . . You try and guess how many ways there are to disappear up there. I've heard too many stories of guys who've hung themselves in their jail cell. I was worried about me and Doak never being found."

Dave Hall was mainly convinced that the four toughs were out to steal their ivory. He was a little bit convinced they would flash phony badges, say they were undercover police, and bring them back to town.

There was a pay phone over by the airfreight office. Dave Hall called USFWS regional headquarters in Anchorage. No one was there. He began calling the resident agents' homes. He finally reached the wife of one, Don Coombs. He gave her the flight information and told her that someone had to meet the plane. If they were not on it, they were in major trouble. His own people and the FBI should then fly out by military jet. As he talked to Coombs's wife, he noticed that the four toughs were looking over the piles of extra baggage he and Doak had just checked. When he returned to the main terminal, he saw the rest of their baggage being carted away. He put Doak on the aircraft and ran out to the tarmac. He told the baggage handler that he had a lot of valuable stuff in there, that he had lost baggage before, that he was going to watch each item loaded on the aircraft and see that the door was sealed shut, and, when the handler began to protest vehemently, he told him *That was just the way it was gonna be!!!* He waited until the pilot was revving the engines hard and then bolted for the plane. Two of the toughs had disappeared. The other two were on board.

No one was going to do anything aboard the plane. By now he felt they wanted his ivory or his money—he had about thirty thousand dollars left, all in cash because outlaws didn't use traveler's checks—and, having been foiled in Nome, had decided it was worth flying all the way to Anchorage to try to steal it there. But they didn't. He and Doak got back to the Sheraton without incident.

Dave Hall still wouldn't entertain the possibility that the four toughs had just been standing there. Perhaps, like Charlie McAlpine, he was getting paranoid.

The next day they took a commercial flight down to Dillingham. The

hotel bartender's friend was named Freeman Roberts. He was an officer
of the Bristol Bay Native Corporation. His partner was P. G. Brannan.
Like Wayne Gans, Brannan seemed to own half the town. Roberts had
an office above the Dillingham airport. He seemed to own the rest of
it. Dave Hall and Doak bought walrus tusks from both of them. They
kept it in a small warehouse. "Hundreds of pounds there," Dave Hall
says, "and they had more." In Dillingham raw ivory was not as abundant
as in Nome, but there was plenty of it. A lot more sellers were whites.
The likes of some took them completely by surprise. On someone's tip,
they went to the local hospital and bought ivory from a couple of doctors
working there—young idealistic types who were doing the rounds for
the underprivileged. Their hobby was to overfly the beaches in a Super
Cub—a small aircraft with big soft tires that permit rough landings—
and look for dead or wounded walrus. Dave Hall suspects they shot
some themselves. Round Island, not far from Dillingham, is a favorite
haul-out for enormous numbers of males. From Dillingham they went
to Ekuk, down the peninsula, where Rick Powell, who had set up the
introduction to McAlpine, was working at a cannery. Many of the in-
coming fishermen had ivory. "Everybody had it," says Dave Hall. "Not
a lot of it, but there were so many people who did have it we could've
stayed there and bought for a week. They all kept saying how illegal it
was." He sounded a bit wistful. "Damn . . . if I'd had the money and
we'd been able to carry it all, I could have bought more ivory than Fort
Knox has gold."

Two days later they were in Seattle.

When Charlie McAlpine went up to Nome, he opened a bar right next
door to the Silver Lode, and a general store down the street. That made
him a direct competitor of Wayne Gans, and Dave Hall was sure that
Gans was an important reason why Charlie left Nome after only a couple
of years. A direct competitor of Wayne Gans simply didn't last, particularly if he was some upstart with an Ivy League education. However,
they spoke to each other now and then, and after Doak and Dave Hall
had discussed buying ivory from him, Gans had called McAlpine to try
to figure out who they were. McAlpine was making at least fifteen dollars
on every pound of ivory he bought from the Eskimos and sold to Doak,

and when he learned that Doak had begun buying directly from them he was in a red rage. His cheeks were still giving off heat when they spoke with him at a coffee shop near his office in the Seattle Trade Mart on the twenty-second of June in 1981.

It was the first time Charlie had laid eyes on Dave Hall, and despite Doak's efforts to model him into a journeyman crook, Charlie didn't trust him at all. They had done what any criminal would have done—buy from one supplier, learn who his suppliers were, and go directly to them—but Charlie still wasn't over his fear that they were undercover wildlife cops. McAlpine subjected Dave Hall to a merciless interrogation about his oil-leasing business, his real-estate investments, his knowledge of ivory—it was, Dave Hall says, by far the most worrisome catechizing he ever went through. McAlpine was an opportunistic, predatory businessman who seemed to know almost as much about the oil-leasing business as he did. Dave Hall felt he had passed, but not by much.

"You've got all of Nome talking about you," McAlpine told them and the tape recorder in the coffee shop. "I've been talking—the whole *town* is talking about you. The government knows you bought ivory because everybody knows. I even know who you bought from. I know who went to Savoonga with you. Pierce. Is that right? What they really think is, they think you're dope dealers. I wouldn't take a joint up there myself. The natives are crazy."

Dope dealers, Dave Hall was thinking. If people were really convinced they were dope dealers, that might explain the four toughs at the airport. They might not follow them to the airport and then all the way to Anchorage just to snitch a few thousand dollars' worth of ivory and some cash, but a couple of keys of cocaine or pot was real booty. Dope dealers on foreign turf were easy marks. Was Wayne Gans selling dope? Dave Hall still couldn't figure out why they had been followed. It bothered him. He might have to go back there.

"I'd like to do business with you," McAlpine was saying. "You guys know who I am. You should."

"I don't," Dave Hall mocked.

McAlpine tried to look tough. He still resembled a puffin, especially with his cheeks aglow. He hissed, "You guys have been going through towns I do business in."

"Well, yeah," said Dave Hall matter-of-factly. "We were told you were a rip-off artist."

McAlpine ignored that for a moment. "Did you ask in Savoonga about me? You should have."

"I didn't ask anybody about you."

"Who said I was a rip-off artist?"

"A guy named Sidmoore. He said there were about six thousand dollars' worth of artifacts involved."

"Sidmoore . . . well . . . See, I gave Sidmoore six grand for a buying trip and didn't get anything for it, so I took those artifacts of his. I also beat the hell out of him."

"No!" said Dave Hall sarcastically.

McAlpine tried to take that coolly. "If somebody doesn't like me, he probably has a good reason. Did you talk to Gilbert Pellowook? Gilbert's crazy. He's fearless. There was a plane crash once, he rescued five, six people from that burning plane. He's fearless. He used to work for me. He beat up a guy once, a guy who just put his hand on my shoulder."

Dave Hall turned his coffee cup in slow circles and smiled. Charlie didn't make a very convincing tough. He was very angry, though, and that was good.

"How much white ivory did you buy?" asked McAlpine.

"The stuff we bought up there's already in New Orleans," said Dave Hall. "You don't have to worry about that." It was a lie, but it was better if Charlie thought the ivory wasn't within his grasp. He probably had some hoodlums on call who would steal it right out of their motel room.

"I'll bet you a dollar the way you guys thought you'd get away with it. If they thought you were big dope dealers and they grabbed the ivory, they wouldn't catch you with the dope."

"Well, you're right," Dave Hall averred. "We told everybody there's dope all over New Orleans. And there is, all you want."

The tape is unintelligible here for a couple of minutes due to some background noise, but when it's intelligible again Charlie is back talking about his favorite nemesis: the maniacal, relentless game wardens.

"They got a friend of mine, you know," he said. "It must have cost the government a quarter of a million dollars. There were about seven agencies involved. They were following these guys in a plane. They were working on him with spies, long-range telescopes, shotgun mikes, just unbelievable stuff. They tracked him down on radar, had Air Force planes following him. They used the Coast Guard and Customs, U.S. Wildlife, and Fish and Game in Juneau. They just closed in on him. They knew where he was every minute. They knew more about him than *he* did. See, the government doesn't shit around anymore. A few years ago they did an operation, they bankrolled it and started a guy in the ivory business to build a situation in the ivory business . . . I mean, they make a big deal out of it today. Oh, yeah. They use *money*. It's just like ABSCAM. They literally handed people twenty-five or fifty thousand dollars at a whack of good money. *Good money!*"

Doak found himself dying to tell him who they were. He was talking about *them!* Right to their faces! Describing exactly the sort of net he was swimming in without knowing it. Maybe he was doing this on purpose just to smoke them out. Maybe this paranoia business was all an act and Charlie was just being diabolically smart. You're right, he wanted to say, and it's us. *Us! Us sitting here with you, you miserable, paranoid sonofabitch!*

"Not for *ivory*, they don't do that, do they, really?" said Doak instead.

"Ha! You're kidding yourself! In fact, they *prefer* ivory dealers. Ivory dealers aren't as likely to shoot back as dope dealers. I'm paranoid. I'm paranoid."

"*I* am, too," said Dave Hall soberly. He thought Charlie's paranoia was for real. In fact, he was beginning to think he should take off his Nagra and hide it somewhere.

He didn't do it right away. They went back to McAlpine's office and display room, inspected some of the purportedly legal, carved stuff he had around—legal or illegal, there was no way you could prove it, but no Eskimos carved this well; McAlpine had gotten it raw—and then went back to the coffee shop for lunch. Then Dave Hall saw it coming. "Don't ask me how, don't ask me why," he says. "I just felt it coming. I felt it earlier over coffee, but this time I felt it strong." After lunch, on the way back to McAlpine's office, he went into the men's room, unstrapped the frightfully expensive little Nagra and its stereo microphones, and stashed them inside the towel dispenser. If the custodian came around, they were done for.

McAlpine sprang right away. Even without the recorder, Dave Hall will never forget what he said.

"I hope that's a gun in your boot and not your tape recorder."

"You think I've got a *tape recorder* in my boot?"

"Possibly."

"And you want I should take them off?" For effect, he was going to hesitate for a while.

"Your boots, your shirt . . . the jacket. We're both going to feel better if we know who we're dealing with. If you're a federal agent, I'm going to feel better if I know who I'm dealing with."

"How do I know *you're* not a federal agent?"

"Because they're *after me* all the time. What the hell do you think?"

"How do we know that? You could be making it up."

"I am *not* making it up."

"If I'm one of them agents, what're you gonna do?"

"Jesus . . ."

Dave Hall yanked off his boots. He unbuttoned his shirt and started to drop his pants.

"Boy, you can get those off in a hurry," said Charlie. "You must have a lot of practice."

"You satisfied, or should I get buck naked?"

"Oh, hell, it was just a precaution—"

"Now you get your goddamned ass up against the wall!"

Doak was finally feeling amused. Actually, he was feeling enormously, overwhelmingly relieved. Why hadn't Hall had the recorder strapped on? He hadn't seen him get rid of it. This was the *only* time in over a week he hadn't worn it. It was uncanny.

"What are you, nuts?"

"Get them shoes off!"

"They're tennis shoes, you goat!"

"I don't care what kind of shoes they are."

"How could I have a recorder hiding in tennis shoes?"

"You could be setting us up."

"Man, I don't know what you think!" This Dave Hayes looked serious, though, Charlie must have thought. And he was really a vicious-looking southern hoodlum, with the acne scars on his cheeks and that arrogant Indian nose. And that *sneer*.

McAlpine untied his shoelaces and took the shoes off. Then he lifted his shirt and slightly dropped his pants. Doak wanted to laugh. The moment was inspirational.

"Charlie," he said to him, "when you're dead and gone, what do you want inscribed on your tombstone?"

Oddly, Charlie seemed thoroughly prepared for this one. It just came out of him, as if his epitaph had long been written:

> *Here lies Sealskin Charlie*
> *Who's had three hundred young Eskimo girls,*
> *Five young Eskimo boys,*
> *Two sled dogs,*
> *and an ourik.*

Dave Hall and Doak stayed in Seattle for another couple of days, waiting for the arrival of a shipment of ivory Doak had ordered from McAlpine several weeks earlier; somehow it had been held up. It was worth the wait. Now that he was done being mad and done being paranoid—at least for now—Charlie seemed to want to make amends, especially since he was doing business with them again and about to make a couple of thousand dollars' profit on the shipment they were waiting for. He let something out that Dave Hall had always wondered about: how he had managed to send tens of thousands of pounds of ivory through the mails and airfreight without being caught. His main man in Alaska, he told them, was Harvey Johnson, a half-breed Eskimo who lived out in Girdwood, a small town along Knik Arm, about forty minutes from Anchorage. Most of his ivory was shipped via priority mail from the Girdwood post office—first, because the government needs a search warrant to open first-class mail, and second, because one of Harvey's relatives worked there. "She keeps everything cool for us," Charlie said. If someone wanted something sent by airfreight, that was no problem either, because another relative worked for Wien Airlines as a freight handler. Charlie gave Harvey a decent cut from his profit, and Harvey gave some of it to his relatives. "A few cents a pound," said Charlie, "but when you deal as much ivory as I do, it's worth it to them. Worth it to me, too. They've been helping me for years." Sometimes, if Charlie felt some heat was on, he had Harvey ship ivory to himself from Anchorage to Seattle. Harvey Johnson would address it to Harvey Johnson, and Harvey Johnson would fly down himself to pick it up. It was expensive to do it that way, but technically it was legal. The law said Eskimos could sell to Eskimos; it did not say it was illegal for an Eskimo to ship ivory to himself.

"I went to law school, but Harvey thought that up himself," said Charlie. "Harvey's one in a million. He went into the Army as a private and came out as a captain and a pilot. Most Eskimos, they're so dumb they go in as a private and come out lower than a private. Harvey's really half-Eskimo and half-human."

For a week's work it was an exceptional haul. They had evidence that could send Charlie McAlpine to jail, as well as Harvey Johnson. The Pellowooks, Tom Trainor, Freeman Roberts, P. G. Brannan, the doctors in Dillingham, leaders of the King Island Native Corporation, leaders of the Bristol Bay Native Corporation, a dozen sundry dealers in Nome who had sold them ivory—all were now indictable. There was physical evidence; in most cases, there were tapes; and there was corroborating testimony from Doak. It would have been tempting to take down the case right away. For one thing, you wouldn't have to update probable cause; all the buys were recent enough so that the Fish and Wildlife Service could immediately send a legion of agents to Alaska, obtain some search warrants, and throw everyone in the soup. Also, the longer you held up a false front, the higher the odds were that it would crumble. Dave Hall was not, after all, a "deep undercover" agent—he was a USFWS special agent running all over the South sans disguise; he was a nonstop proselytizer for the conservation cause whose picture had been in the local newspapers dozens of times. It had been in hunting magazines and newsletters. All it would take would be for Trainor or McAlpine to sell some ivory in the South and talk about the crazy part-Indian good old boy buying ivory and whipping out his guns for a spark of recognition to ignite in someone's memory. If McAlpine saved his old hunting magazines, the odds were reasonable that he had Dave Hall's picture sitting somewhere in his *house*. He had been in *Field & Stream*, in *Sports Afield*. There wasn't another undercover agent in the country who let himself be photographed as often as Dave Hall did.

But he still didn't have Moses Feingold, reputedly the biggest importer of illegal elephant ivory in the United States. He didn't have Douglas O'Neill, a former biologist for the Alaska Department of Fish and Game who was suspected of being a major dealer now. He didn't have the retail dealers in Lahaina and the carvers in Bellingham and on Cape Cod who were knowingly buying contraband ivory and feeding demand. He didn't have Wayne Gans.

And Endangered Species was a beautiful cover. Bomb-proof front operations are such a rarity in undercover work—in any kind of undercover work—that they are valued almost lovingly. Dave Hall couldn't bear the thought of dismantling such a cover, a cover so good it might yield him members of the international ivory cartel, the most destructive organized wildlife criminals of our time. For all he knew, he could tie evidence to the tails of the ivory princes of Hong Kong or the African heads of state who were praised by the United Nations wildlife-conservation do-nothings while their families earned millions from murdered elephants. When you had such a cover, you hung on for dear life. He was going to rev this investigation beyond the red line. Or he was going to crash.

Charlie McAlpine became a different person after the strip search in Seattle. He lost his edge. Reading his voluminous case file, you can find a few transcripts of telephone calls in the ensuing weeks where, when Doak picked up the phone, Charlie's first words were "Tape recorder running?" but now he seemed to be saying it as a joke. If he was worried about anything, it was that Dave Hall and Doak would buy directly from his Eskimo suppliers again. His threats were never overt, but he implied that if they went on another buying spree in the villages, bad things might happen.

Dave Hall was kind of curious what he might try to do, but he had enough evidence already to indict the people he assumed were the main suppliers on the ivory coast. He wouldn't need to go back there. He would give McAlpine his business back. Now he wanted to start moving upward through the higher echelons of the ivory trade. He wanted *respectable* people. In July he flew to Hawaii to meet Charlie and his wife, Geena, because he wanted to get a feel for the amount of contraband ivory offered as legal stuff in the hyperexpensive Lahaina shops. (Outside Hong Kong, Singapore, Taiwan, Ōsaka, and Tokyo, the old whaling town of Lahaina, on the island of Maui, may then have sold more ivory than any place in the world.) He figured that a razzle-dazzle cracker-barrel entrepreneur like Dave Hayes would either go to Hawaii to meet women or bring one in tow, so he recruited Marie Palladini, the USFWS agent who had played A. J. Caro's girlfriend on the Kelly-Klapisch case, to go with him. (When I asked Marie what it was like to spend four or five days in that role—as Dave Hall's secretary or paramour or whatever she was—she rolled her eyes. "It was exhausting," she said. "All he did was try to marry me off. When it comes to women, he's an extremely traditional guy." When I asked her what she thought of McAlpine, she said, "Slime.") They stayed at a small, rather elegant condo resort called Lahaina Roads, where Charlie McAlpine was a fixture. Obviously, he was selling a lot of ivory in Hawaii. In some of the shops, carvers were working raw walrus tusks behind closed doors, and Dave Hall had no doubt that some of the elephant ivory they were using was of illegal origin, too. "They just lied," he says. "They were selling to a lot of people who were asking if animals were killed for this ivory, and they said, 'Oh, no. These carvings are made from *found* ivory. These walrus and elephants all died of old age.' Bullshit! We'd just seen white tusks in the back rooms that had to come from animals that had just been killed."

It was in Maui that Dave Hall had everything he'd heard about Nome—and particularly about Wayne Gans—confirmed.

"Nome—right now that's the end of the world," Charlie said to him and Marie and the Nagra one evening over cocktails. "If they figure you're carrying heavy bread or something, hell, your life's in danger, you know. When you start talking about ten thousand dollars to people up there, why, Christ, they'd kill you for five hundred. And if they think you're carrying ten thousand, which is small money to be doing any business with, why, your life's in danger. That Wayne Gans has been in prison for murder, did you know that?"

"I didn't," Dave Hall lied. "I thought he—".

"He was convicted."

"He told me that he'd killed several guys when he got out, but I didn't know—"

"He's killed several and got put in jail for it once, and he got like a fifteen-year sentence and then he got a governmental pardon after serving a couple of years."

"He did?"

"Yep, got the governor."

"Well, I tell you what," said Dave Hall. "I liked that guy."

"I like Wayne, too, and Wayne'll talk turkey, but what you have to understand about Wayne Gans is, he has no morals. I mean there's nothing he won't do. He'll kill, he'll rob, and he'll talk turkey, too, but there's a point—a lot of times you'd never know Wayne was going to hurt you until you was already so hurt you couldn't do nothing. He's a heavy-duty dude."

"Oh, I believe that."

"There's convicted murderers, felons, AWOL GIs up there—and they all work for Wayne Gans. Every one of them. He'll walk into your place with a couple, three of those guys, and he'll walk around with his hands in his pockets and you're intimidated. You're thinking, Oh my God, what am I doing to get Wayne Gans mad at me? I—whatever it is, I better stop."

"Why did he let us come up there in his territory and buy some merchandise and not—"

"I don't know. You never know. I mean, one guy he might hurt, the next guy he might not. If it's convenient and you've got something he wants, he'll just off you."

"That's what I was afraid of," said Dave Hall. "That he was gonna— that he had connections with the airlines and when our baggage went out of there, we'd never see it again."

"Well, even he—if he wants to hurt somebody, he just tells some guy at the airlines, 'Heh, ah, these boxes coming through with his name, you're gonna be rich if you get me those boxes.' And those guys who work on those airlines, they don't care about the FBI and all that shit, you know. They couldn't care less. They just—those boxes just disappear!"

"Well, I can see why you left Nome," said Dave Hall.

"Well, I was up there for the adventure, the flying, but who needs that? God, guys carry pistols in their goddamn hats and stuff, and it's cold, and it's windy, and it's black all the time, and the young girls are off to school, all there is, is some old . . . you know . . . Christ. . . . And everybody *hates* each other." (Dave Hall couldn't believe Charlie was talking about his addiction to pubescent girls in front of Marie, but at least his wife was not there.)

"Well, those villages up there—do you think there's going to be a continuous supply of ivory coming out of those villages?" asked Dave Hall.

"Let's put it this way. Since I've been in business, a lot of things have changed. We have things today like government interference and all that. But we still have a lot of inventory. And one good thing—two good things about the government. Number one is they're stupid. Number two, they're lazy. If government guys were like you and me, this country would be in real trouble today."

Dave Hall spent the next few weeks in Louisiana, running after the usual brotherhood of alligator snaggers, waterfowl baiters, deer spotlighters, bird smugglers, fish netters, turtle poachers, and Cajun gourmets. It was, after all, July. Right around the Fourth of July, the population of yellow-crowned night herons—Cajuns call them *grosbecs;* they are a protected species because they were clobbered in the past—goes into free fall in southern Louisiana because they are the traditional delicacy on that particular holiday. "If you're a Cajun and you don't got a *grosbec* in your pot on the Fourth of July, you're some kind of Communist or something," says Dave Hall. "We're always on *grosbec* patrol around then." The resident game warden at the Rockefeller Refuge, James Nunez, ran down a pilot who had abandoned his downed plane in the swamp in the middle of the night, and netted about twenty-eight million dollars' worth of cocaine, then the largest haul in the state's history. A couple of Dave

Hall's agents came upon a crystal-methedrine laboratory in the woods. These things aside, it was a rather uneventful summer, except for two developments. An ivory dealer from La Honda, California, named Larry Cohen flew in with some sperm whale teeth and offered Dave Hall and Doak fresh walrus ivory and several narwhal tusks, which they later purchased (a narwhal tusk looks like a unicorn horn). Once again, business was coming to them. The more promising development was a visit late in the summer by Junior Feingold, the son of the man McAlpine said was the biggest ivory smuggler in North America next to him. (Dave Hall figured he was probably a much bigger dealer than McAlpine, given Charlie's grandiloquent tendencies.)

Dave Hall was taken aback, to put it very, very mildly, by Feingold's son. He had never encountered an Orthodox Jew before, and Junior was a bona fide one. When Dave Hall and Doak took him out to dinner at Pascal's Manale, he interrogated the waiter at length about the chef's choice of cooking oil, then decided he didn't trust him and ran into the kitchen to make sure they weren't frying his green noodles in animal fat. Feingold was overweight and hyperactive, a spoiled punk of a kid who seemed strung-out as a trip wire and went on incessantly about his collection of guns. Dave Hall apparently believed that violin cases carried by Jews really hold violins, but Feingold was a reputed member of the East Coast mob, so the kid's obsession with guns made some sense. He had brought a small quantity of ivory with him, which Dave Hall bought, promising to make a much larger purchase later in the year. He wanted to go to New York himself to see what quantities the Feingolds were bringing in.

A few months earlier, in January, one of the USFWS agents in Alaska, John Collins, had made a run at a suspected ivory dealer in Fairbanks named Douglas O'Neill. Collins's people had been after O'Neill for a long time. He had worked for some years as a biologist with Alaska's Department of Fish and Game, specializing in marine mammals. He knew many of the Eskimos on Saint Lawrence Island and around Nome, and he still went out there regularly to buy merchandise for his shop, in which he sold, among other things, Eskimo-carved ivory and artifacts and gems. O'Neill was as cautious as McAlpine and just as clever; he had never been caught with raw tusks, even though the Fish and Wildlife Service was convinced he was buying hundreds, if not thousands, of pounds every year. Collins's attempted undercover buy was foiled in an almost ludicrous way. He simply walked into the shop one day after several months of fruitless discussions and tried to talk O'Neill into selling him something illegal. O'Neill was just about to make the deal, and Collins was feeling enormously pleased with himself, when a hunter whom Collins had hooked on a big-game violation came in the door and recognized him instantly. Since O'Neill now knew he was being watched, he was considered untouchable, and that was why, in September, Dave Hall moved him to the top of his suspect list.

By then Dave Hall had decided he needed a surrogate in Alaska. Going up there all the time was too exhausting. The person he chose was Wally Soroka, a young agent for the Fish and Wildlife Service in Massachusetts. Soroka was relatively new to undercover work, but he was tough. "He's got ice water in his veins," Dave Hall says. He also looked right. Soroka was wiry, bearded, and seemed just a little sinister—*shifty* might be a better word. With a little chain grease on his jeans and a cigarette dangling from his mouth, he looked as if he could get inside a motorcycle gang, and he would.

Dave Hall requested Soroka's transfer to Soldotna, Alaska, in August; then he began trying to pry loose another big wad of purchasing cash from Washington. Soroka was ready to pay O'Neill a visit less than a week after he'd arrived. Dave Hall told Soroka to try to pass himself off as his and Doak's buyer; it would at least steer the conversation toward white ivory. To Soroka's surprise—he felt he wouldn't have any more luck than Collins had—it worked.

O'Neill had heard all about the gun-toting good old boys with the shop in New Orleans, and knew what they were after. "The white ivory is extremely hard to get ahold of," he told Soroka, who had wired himself up before going into the shop. "If you could get ahold of any quantity, it would be mammoth."

"What do you think would be a fair price for white ivory in Nome?"

"Well, *if* you could buy it—because it's totally illegal."

"I've heard that," Soroka said. Then he lied, "I bought some yesterday in Nome." He was going to have to be fast on his feet if O'Neill asked for details.

O'Neill kept a big .45-caliber pistol quite visible in an open briefcase that sat on the floor. Soroka had to consider him dangerous. He said, "Right now, through the store, I'd sell it for forty dollars a pound."

"How long do you think it will stay at forty dollars a pound?" Soroka asked.

"I can see it going up the next trip out."

"The next trip up to the villages?"

"Yeah. It's held at forty well over a year now, and even through all these price rises and everything it hasn't risen, but I've seen a lot of pressure from the Eskimos in the last three months. What I'm getting at is walrus has been depressed for a long time, and it's probably the most versatile ivory you can get. If your friend is really interested in buying the white walrus, I'd have to talk with him for a while cause we're all very careful. All they've got to do is catch us once, and there's a year in prison or a ten-thousand-dollar fine."

"They're strict up here?"

"Yeah, they're very strict. It's much easier to catch someone up here than it is back in Boston."

"These are ivory agents?" Soroka asked.

"They're Fish and Wildlife."

"Oh, game wardens," said the game warden.

"They're all tied in with the FBI and everything," said O'Neill. "See, coming back—you either have to come back through Nome or Barrow. And very few white men will go out there. Once you've been through a village, it's not hard for an agent to find out. You could stay out there for as long as you want, but you've got to get that ivory back, and there's only one way to get it back, and that's through Nome . . . so all they have to do is sit and wait for it. See, last year we brought over six thousand pounds of ivory in, oh, four fairly large deals. If they want to cut off a large supply of ivory, all they have to do is catch one person: me. And the Eskimos—the Eskimo, he'll sell to you, you'll head for Nome, and he'll call Nome and say this guy just stole my ivory. He'll get your money, and he'll get his ivory back, too. It's so goddamn risky— I'm one of the few white guys who'll even go out there and buy."

O'Neill would go no further than this—he wasn't going to sell him anything yet. Soroka felt it would be counterproductive to push him too hard. He wrote Dave Hall and gave him the gist of the conversation; if they wanted to get O'Neill, he said, he would probably have to come up himself. Exhausted as he was, Dave Hall was itching to pack his bags. Six thousand pounds was a very substantial quantity of ivory to sell in a year. O'Neill alone might be responsible for a thousand dead walrus annually; that was half a hundredth of the estimated surviving world population. It was more if you figured that for every two or three walrus that were shot, only one was recovered; the others died and sank. When you added that quantity to the ten thousand pounds McAlpine said he sold in a year, and then accounted for the King Island and Bristol Bay native corporations, the sundry small Eskimo dealers, and the thousands of fishing boats—many of which were probably selling ivory in the coastal ports or to Japanese and Taiwanese ships on the high seas—when you added everything up, it was easy to imagine the walrus becoming at least commercially extinct. The Russians were right, even if you ignored the large number of walrus they were undoubtedly killing themselves.

Dave Hall had several telephone contacts with O'Neill before going up to meet him personally. He found he could play him like an instrument. He traded him some sperm whale teeth that the Department of the Interior had confiscated from someone for a small shipment of walrus ivory and enclosed a few photographs taken inside Endangered Species—of the huge pair of elephant tusks Doak kept in the window to lure people in, a tiger's head, some elaborate native carvings. O'Neill was very impressed. He was even more impressed that Dave Hall and Doak had gone to places like Saint Lawrence Island to buy ivory from the Eskimos. "The Pellowooks, now—they scare the hell out of me. You never see these type of Eskimos in Anchorage. They're *mean* motherfuckers. And they're *animals* when they get mean, all the Pellowooks are." The way you really got to Douglas O'Neill, however, was by taking a collector's interest in ivory. He wasn't at all like Charlie McAlpine, who, when talking about a beautifully carved walrus or elephant tusk, was really talking about the amount of money he could sell it for. Charlie was the ultimate capitalist; if he caused the walrus and elephant to go extinct, he would make his living selling more durable goods—Eskimo girls, perhaps. O'Neill valued ivory as he would a gorgeous mistress. One day, in New Orleans, Doak told Dave Hall, quite casually, that Michelangelo had worked in ivory from time to time, so the next time he spoke with O'Neill, he told him that Doak had just returned from a buying trip with a small statue he had found in Hong Kong, which, according to a London museum—where he had taken it to have it appraised—was certainly the work of Michelangelo or one of his better students. Dave Hall told O'Neill how the veins in the arms and hands were absolutely perfect and how the eyes could have cried, and when O'Neill said it was wonderful how someone could bring all this out of a piece of stone, he told him the statue was made of ivory—and then almost had to restrain him from hopping the next plane down. O'Neill would have sawed off his arm without anesthetic to own a piece such as this. "It's ivory?" he almost cried. "Ivory?!"

And then, on the other hand, there was O'Neill talking bloodlessly about the numbers of walrus being killed.

"I don't know how long they're gonna last," Dave Hall prompted him, "cause up in Savoonga they were sure killing a lot of em."

"Yeah," said O'Neill. "They take a lot of them. Well, best estimate, and I'm using my background with the Department of Fish and Game— Fish and Game has records that they are taking approximately three thousand animals a year. And we know that an Eskimo, being the poor hunter that he is, he loses approximately fifty percent, so that jacks the figure up to six thousand. And knowing what I do from the Department of Fish and Game, I would jack that figure up to twelve thousand."

When Dave Hall wondered again if what they were doing might some-day cause the walrus to cease to exist, O'Neill said, "Well, this is my living and I don't look at it in terms of breaking the law."

Dave Hall answered with a "Yeah." He waited. He knew from his encounters with southern poachers what was coming next.

"And what we're doing, Dave, is—Jesus Christ, I'll have to sit down and talk to you sometime, but it's minimal compared to what's go-ing on."

Sure, thought Dave Hall. It's all the Eskimos' fault—just as the wors-ening shortage of ducks in southern Louisiana was the fault of the thousands of people in Chicago and Memphis who shot them from rooftops as they flew south. And of the Canadians.

Sometime before Dave Hall went up to Alaska to meet Douglas O'Neill in person, a private investigator from Saint Louis flew to New Orleans on an odd assignment. She was to find a shop called Endangered Species, in the French Quarter, and try to determine whether it was "suspicious" in any way. From the tone of the letter she sent back to O'Neill, the investigator couldn't quite fathom what O'Neill was looking for. Was he worried that the place was a front for the law? A drug laundry? An ivory operation that might try to undermine his? It didn't really matter because the investigator never called to ascertain that the shop would be open when she went down, and, as it happened, it was closed. But it was a real shop, she wrote O'Neill, certainly not an obvious front—there was a gigantic pair of elephant tusks in the window, behind heavy bars, that alone was probably worth tens of thousands of dollars. Inside there seemed to be carved ivory all over the place, and some tiger skins and a lot of expensive-looking primitive arts and antiquities. She couldn't imagine that he had anything to worry about. If this Endangered Species place was some kind of front, it was the quirkiest one she had ever seen, and she doubted anyone in government had the imagination to set up something like this.

When Dave Hall finally got back to Alaska in October, he flew to Fairbanks with Wally Soroka to make his first direct buy from Douglas O'Neill. O'Neill kept his white ivory in a camouflaged bin at the back of his shop; all of his receipts and documentation he kept at home, in case the shop was raided. The buy from O'Neill was really superfluous, since he had already indicted himself by sending white ivory through the mail. Dave Hall had gone up mainly to establish personal contact with him, and also to get as much information as he could on a rumored ivory and wildlife smuggler named Jerry Kingery.

Kingery's name had come up two or three times before, in conversations with other dealers. He was a familiar if phantomlike figure to the Alaska state troopers and the FBI. In California, where he lived before moving to Alaska a few years earlier, Kingery had been the first lieutenant of Sonny Barger, the vicar of the Hell's Angels motorcycle gang. In those halcyon days before the Crips and the Bloods, the Angels were about as tough as street gangs got. Most of them were not full-time criminals, as members of the crack-dealing black gangs tend to be, and an Angel was more likely to be equipped with a yard of chain than with a Kalashnikov. But the average biker was a swilling, belching, farting cartoon ape who crawled from under some rock and had no future in mind, and the simple *idea* of respectability gave him fits. Visits by hordes of Hell's Angels had turned whole cities into garrison states. When Hunter Thompson wrote what you have to call a sympathetic book about the gang, he was stomped half to death.

In Alaska, Kingery had organized a gang that called itself the Brothers. The gang claimed no affiliation with the Angels, but the police were fairly sure Kingery had been sent there by Barger to capitalize on the pipeline money and the demand for drugs and women it was sure to create. The Brothers were believed to own a couple of Anchorage's topless-bottomless bars and had girls working in its brothels; what else they did for a living no one knew. Kingery himself was a partner, with his real brother, in the Kingery Brothers Trading Company, whose business was a mystery. Dave Hall felt sure from what he had heard that the Brothers were dealing ivory. Bikers were into just about anything that was against the law.

That Kingery was apparently involved with a gang that had knocked out many, many sets of teeth and had broken a museum-size collection of ribs didn't particularly bother Dave Hall and Wally Soroka. Douglas O'Neill had been almost too easy anyway. They simply looked up Kingery in the telephone book and got him on the line, saying they were ivory buyers. Kingery told them to come over to his house. Dave Hall took his extra revolver out of his duffel and stuffed it in his boot. Then he slipped the Nagra inside his secret liner and ironed out the bulge.

Kingery lived in a semirural, down-at-the-heels working-class area on the outskirts of Anchorage, in a trailer set down on a substantial yard that was littered with one of the more interesting collections of machinery and castoff junk Dave Hall had yet seen. There was a huge semitrailer rig parked outside, a couple of truck differentials lying around that were the size of igloos, some battered snowmobiles and motorcycles, and a couple of sheds. Kingery himself was no cookie-cutter three-hundred-pound gang member; he was small and wiry and intense and actually trimmed his beard. Dave Hall thought he was a dead ringer for the young Charles Manson, cleaned up for trial.

Kingery did not seem the least bit afraid that he might be set up. Dave Hall wasn't sure if that was bad or good. Kingery was cautious enough, however, to keep his ivory at the home of another Brother, whose name was Randy Smith. They drove over to Smith's and picked up the ivory. Kingery would deal only in cash, but aside from that and the human skull, the sale went without a hitch.

The skull was in Kingery's trailer, sitting on the tabletop. It was on a plate. Dave Hall couldn't get it out of his mind.

"That's a hell of a conversation piece," he said to Kingery. "What'd you do—go out grave robbing or something?"

"Nah."

"Well, I better not ask you who it was."

"It was my ex-girlfriend."

Kingery's voice was mirthless. Either he possessed a deadpan delivery or it was true.

"You lookin for anything besides walrus?" Kingery asked as Dave Hall and Soroka were about to make a grateful departure from Smith's house.

"Well, like what?"

"I'm asking *you* if you're interested in anything other than walrus mounts."

"Well, sure I am. My partner, he's got a shop in New Orleans that sells a lot of wildlife pieces. He's got, you know, tiger skins and trophy heads and stuff like that."

"We have a lot of that shit."

"You do?"

"It depends what you want. We can get you some good bearskins if you're interested. Brown bear and polar bear both. We got us a few sea otter pelts. Ever seen one of them?"

"Never. That's a critter we ain't got where I live."

"It's the best pelt there is. Soft as a pussy hair. It got real, real expensive before they listed it on the Endangered, but we can give you a pretty fair price."

"Well, we ain't furriers, but I'd like to take a look at it. If it's really rare, maybe I'll buy one for myself."

"It's a real nice skin. Soft as pussy."

"You got it here?"

"Nah. We keep it somewhere secret."

"Close to here?"

"It's a little ways out of town. We got a place in the mountains there. It's like a hideout. Usually no one but a Brother is supposed to go up. You might be the first, if we let you."

Dave Hall nearly took the bait. He spat it out. It was too impulsive. "If it's a bit of a drive, I got to go some other time. I got business appointments most of the afternoon."

"Like I say, we got the stuff. You got to tell me if you want to see it."

"I sure do want to see it, but maybe it ain't gonna happen this trip."

"You're gonna be back here, then?"

"Yeah, we've found so much merchandise for our shop, we might be coming to Alaska fairly regular."

"Deal with Kingery Brothers. It makes a hell of a lot more sense than going all the way to fucking Nome."

Dave Hall was wondering whether they should have gone to the hideout right away. It seemed insane to go up there, even with Soroka, without having some backup nearby. The place sounded extremely isolated, and these were the last people on earth you wanted to be isolated with. The more he thought about it, the more he was convinced that they shouldn't go up there at all. In Alaska, because of the extreme cold and poor soil at higher elevations, there are almost no trees above two or three thousand feet, except down in the warmer Panhandle. The Chugach Mountains were like a great uptilted prairie—there was no cover, no place to hide. If some Fish and Wildlife Service or FBI agents tried to set up a scouting post near enough to the Brothers' chalet so that they could get there in time to rescue Dave Hall and Soroka, they would likely be seen. Backup DEA agents hide in nearby buildings or vans; backup wildlife agents actually hide behind trees, or in trees, or anyplace that offers cover. Around the chalet, there would likely be none.

On the other hand, the sea otter pelts added a whole different dimension to this case. One of Dave Hall's concerns was that after all the effort and risk he was putting into it, the net result might be a few suspended sentences and some affordable fines. "I wanted jailtime," he says. "It's all criminals understand."

Whether or not they went to jail would depend, to some degree, on the public reaction to the crimes. Every judge has his finger held up to the political winds, and if he sensed outrage flowing from the body politic, he might sentence someone to years in prison—five years was the maximum for a Lacey Act offense—where he might otherwise have meted out a fine. Dave Hall had wetted his finger to appraise the political winds, too. The walrus was an avuncular sort of creature, but a surly one, and was rarely seen except in zoos. The walrus did not occupy a high throne in the anthropocentric animal kingdom. It was an interesting curiosity of an animal, not one that a lot of people care much about. But the sea otter—the sea otter, though taxonomically a weasel, was enshrined and anointed and ordained by humans as saintly, a creature as loved as the giant panda and the koala bear. It had been practically wiped out because of its fabulous pelt; in 1914, when it was finally protected by international treaty, there were thought to be no more than two hundred remaining in the wild. All through the 1700s and 1800s, after some of Vitus Bering's men, who had been hunting seals, discovered the otter by accident while marooned on the Alaska coast and dazzled Europe's furriers when they brought a few pelts home, the Russians and British and Americans had hunted them in a frenzy, perishing by the hundreds in Alaskan storms, raiding one another's ships—it was a musteline gold rush in which the last legal pelts sold for many thousands of dollars each. Even though the animals had, by the 1970s, made a fairly good recovery—there were probably tens of thousands in Alaska alone—the slaughter had been so appalling and the otter was so appealing that Americans were in no mood to let them be hunted ever again. In the 1800s, hunting sea otters was commerce; now it was child killing. Killing sea otters almost surely meant jail.

A jail sentence, in Dave Hall's view, made certain risks worthwhile. He was going to the Brothers' chalet.

• • •

The most difficult thing in undercover police work is knowing when to let yourself be afraid. You are at least a little apprehensive all the time because your identity is an elaborate lie held together by flimsy thread, and loosing one stitch can make the whole thing unravel. You are apprehensive because you know the wrath of someone artfully deceived is more explosive, more thoughtless, than the wrath of one who is just surprised. Street cops are merely shot; undercover drug agents are sometimes sadistically murdered. If your cover is halfway good, however, and the people for whom you work are not corrupt (you are utterly at the mercy of those to whom your real identity is known), then the odds that you are safe are usually good—unless you imagine that you are suspected. Then they can turn bad. People with overactive imaginations who try undercover work usually give it up fairly soon. You must *believe* that your cover is intact, because a hardened criminal, like a good undercover operative—like an animal—has finely tuned senses, and he knows the smell of fear. On the other hand, if your cover is seriously threatened or lost, you must know that, too, before it's too late. If you are convinced your cover has been blown, you can try to save yourself by admitting who you are, on the theory that most criminals know and fear the consequences of killing an undercover cop. Undercover cops are protected by other cops as by a mother bear who avenges harm to her young. On the other hand, if someone feels he can get away with killing you, he might. You must also know *why* you are threatened, when you are. If you have been targeted as a convenient source of free cash—working undercover often means having a lot of money on your person—you have to decide whether your odds of surviving a robbery are better as a cop or as a make-believe crook. Do you tell the man holding a gun to your throat that you are an undercover agent, or do you not? Undercover police work is a tightrope act, a constant series of minor adjustments and calculations to get you from one side to the other as smoothly as possible. If you are on a tightrope and compensate too much for a wrong motion, you fall off.

When, in December, on his third buying trip to Alaska, Dave Hall got into the back seat of Jerry Kingery's car on the way to the Brothers' mountain chalet, he felt himself about to slip.

In Soroka's undercover truck, they had gone once again to the house of Randy Smith, the Brother who kept Kingery's ivory stash. Everything had seemed routine. They had no backup, but both agents had acclimated themselves to that fact. At least they had a vehicle if they had to leave fast. As they climbed back inside the truck to follow Kingery and Smith to the chalet, however, Kingery told them to get out.

"Why get out?"

"We're gonna go up in our vehicle."

"Well, we'll just follow you up."

"We don't let no one up there except with us. No other vehicles."

Dave Hall didn't know what was going on, but he didn't like it. The cardinal rule of undercover police work when you have no backup is never, *never* sacrifice your means of escape.

"I don't see what difference it makes. Your car or both cars, what's the big deal?"

"It's Brothers' rules, man."

"Look," said Dave Hall, "I don't got a lot of time, and I came a long way to make some deals. If you all are gonna spend the whole damn day up there, that's just a waste of time for me, and it sounds to me like it's too far to walk back down."

"We'll drive you back whenever you want to go."

"Well, I hope that's damn well true."

Dave Hall was more nervous than he'd been in a long, long time. He looked at Soroka, who was already in the back seat of the Brothers' car. He looked plenty scared, too. "You could see it in his eyes," said Dave Hall. They had no idea how many of the Brothers there would be. If there was any trouble and they didn't have their own car, they were not going to escape.

Dave Hall decided to get in. He wasn't entirely convinced he would let himself go all the way up. But he had to try to get a feel for what was going on. Was it conceivable they had been found out? Not likely. Did the Brothers really let no other cars up there? Were they after his cash? He had another fat roll in his pocket—ten thousand, twenty thousand, he didn't even know how much—and Kingery probably knew he did.

Had Kingery gotten hold of his photograph somehow?

"Look," he said as they drove, trying to mingle calm and menace in his voice. "I'm a businessman. I came up here to make me some money. I've never been in a deal like this, where I can't even drive my own fuckin vehicle. You all know that I'm carrying a lot of cash. But you also got to know that I'm carrying this here"—he had the bigger revolver in his hand—"and I got another one in my boot, and if there's some kind of funny play goin on, I may die, but somebody's gonna die with me."

Jerry Kingery laughed. The gun didn't faze him. He had seen plenty.

"You gotta be crazy, man. There ain't gonna be no funny play. I know where you're comin from." He looked at Soroka. "You got a couple of them things, too?"

Soroka forced a grin.

The road wound and wound along the rounded contours of the Chugach foothills, climbing fifteen hundred, two thousand, perhaps twenty-two hundred feet over Anchorage before it leveled off for a while. It was a perfect day, and the view went to infinity. There were worse places to die—but you couldn't think such thoughts. They could see everywhere: Knik Arm stabbing into the Kenai range, and the Redoubt Volcano and Mount Iliamna, blue in the distance across Cook Inlet. These bikers had taste. At least they appreciated scenery.

They entered a rutted dirt drive. It sloped down into a swale, climbed out, and rounded a stand of small shrubs—blueberries or elderberries or some such thing. That was where their backup agents might have had to camouflage themselves. They would have had to dress up as bears. The chalet came up ahead of them over a brushy hump. From the road, because of the rise and swale, it had been completely obscured from view. It was well situated. The place was big, an A-frame three stories high, which you might buy for a couple of million dollars in Steamboat Springs or Vail. Dave Hall remembers its being eerily quiet. No other houses were in view. Even though it was very cold up there, a small child was playing in the yard. A young woman—a very good-looking woman for a biker's old lady—ran out as they drove up and scooped up the child and ran back inside, as if to get him out of harm's way.

Soroka tensed. Dave Hall tensed.

Kingery and Smith led them into the house. The chalet seemed even larger inside. There were a number of doors on three levels, around a center atrium, most of them closed. A couple of them were padlocked.

"One more rule we have is, don't go in any of the rooms without our permission," Kingery said.

"We won't."

Kingery took them out on the deck to look at the view. Dave Hall decided to play Japanese shutterbug. He took several pictures of Kingery, grinning as he did it. Kingery did not grin back. Having his picture taken seemed to upset him considerably.

When Dave Hall and Soroka went back inside, they were taken inside one of the locked rooms. There were three or four brown bear hides, a couple of polar bear skins—big ones—and a lot of walrus tusks. There were also large elephant tusks.

"Are these mastodon, or are they elephant?" Soroka asked.

"Elephant."

"Elephant!?"

"Elephant."

"I never thought I'd see elephant tusks in Alaska."

"You just saw em."

Dave Hall wondered how the Brothers possibly got elephant tusks. If nothing else, this showed that wildlife smuggling was quite a big deal to them, not just a minor sideline. They went into another room, which had a small pile of sea otter skins, a couple of trophy Dall sheep heads, and more furs that Dave Hall couldn't immediately identify. Through the walls they heard voices, male and female, coming from other rooms. It was still possible they were going to be jumped. If you were robbed while committing an illegal act—as they would have been doing had they been who they said they were—you didn't run to the authorities, and the Brothers knew that. They were still vulnerable. Had it just been Kingery and Randy Smith they were facing, they would have been prepared to shoot them, if guns began to come out, and bolt. But they weren't going to outshoot half a dozen of the Brothers.

Dave Hall said he would have to call Doak to see if he could really use hides. He wasn't sure you could sell an Alaska brown bear skin in

New Orleans, let alone a sea otter. If he said yes, they would be back.

Kingery said that was fine. They sat around for a while and talked. Dave Hall was confident enough now to fish around, very gingerly, for some clues about the gang's other sources of income. He didn't want to push very hard, and all he got from Kingery was that they were involved in some of the downtown strip bars.

Dave Hall finally insisted that they go. If the Brothers were going to make their move, now was the time. His nerves were so hypertrophied that he was surprised when they didn't. When they were finally back in the car and heading down the mountain, he and Soroka realized that for the past two hours their hearts had been quietly pounding the whole time. "I don't like to think that this or that could have happened," he said later on. "You just try to picture what it's like to be with a gang like that on top of a mountain in the middle of nowhere, with no way out, and you can guess what it felt like. It would surprise me if these guys haven't killed people before. They weren't the wild-ass types people associate with motorcycle gangs. They were just hard guys. They were businessmen bikers. That's the most dangerous kind."

Before leaving Alaska, Dave Hall paid a visit to Charlie McAlpine's Anchorage shop. It was in the middle of downtown, and it was quite fancy, though not as nice as some of the Lahaina stores. Charlie's brother-in-law, Gib Alpert, ran the place when McAlpine wasn't around, even though he seemed to dislike Charlie intensely. Gib, thought Dave Hall, was no more likable than Charlie—they were the perfect pair. Gib introduced Dave Hall to an old Eskimo named Romeo, who was sitting in the back of the shop so motionless and quiet that at first you might have thought he was stuffed. It was obvious that Charlie used Romeo to launder a lot of the illegal ivory he sold. He shipped his raw tusks to his stable of carvers and scrimmers in Bellingham and Lahaina, who shipped them back so Charlie could claim they were carved by Romeo. If you saw Romeo work a piece, you realized that his talents as a carver were minimal, and he worked so slowly that he might produce half a dozen pieces a year, but from Charlie's point of view it was worth keeping him on the payroll, doing essentially nothing. He could sell a lot of ostensibly legal pieces, finely carved pieces, over the counter for hundreds or thousands of dollars more than they would have brought had Romeo carved them himself.

Dave Hall stayed around for another couple of days, looking for more ivory dealers in Anchorage's bars and the girlie joints and coming up mostly empty-handed. He also called some of the contacts he'd made on his earlier trips. The most promising were the Apgars, Ruth and Steve, who owned the Golden North Hotel in Skagway—the gold-domed Victorian structure whose picture appears in nearly all the cruise ship brochures. Ruth had sold Doak a load of walrus ivory a few months earlier at Endangered Species. The Apgars were up to their elbows in walrus ivory smuggled out of Savoonga, where they once lived. He set up a buy from them and went back home. Being Dave Hall, he would have been frustrated if there was a single ivory dealer he hadn't stung, and there were probably plenty. Mainly, though, he was exhausted.

There were about two hundred telephone messages on his desk. He worked sixteen- or eighteen-hour days for the next week, making thirty calls a day and shoveling paperwork like a front-loader. It had become a pattern with him: he would be gone for weeks, then come home and spend practically all his waking hours at his office. David, his son, was seventeen, and his daughter, Pam, was thirteen—they would soon be out of the house—but he rarely saw them anymore. Sarah Hall was not just sleeping alone but living alone. Dave Hall becomes belligerently defensive when you bring up his absenteeism from family life—"Why the hell can't our women appreciate the importance of what we're doing?"—which a psychiatrist might jot down as prima facie evidence that it troubles him deeply. Yet at the same time, according to his peers, his work obsessiveness has become more and more extreme over the years. It was during the ivory case that his behavior became worthy of clinical interest.

"He realized as soon as he got on that damned ivory case that he was in over his head," a fellow USFWS agent who, like some others, admires him greatly and resents him deeply, told me once. "He about wrecked his health and his family life and his marriage over that case. Sarah finally had it up to here with being the sweet dutiful southern-belle wife, and Dave began to see that she has a will as strong as his, and the sparks really began to fly. He's been gone from home so much of his life anyway, you couldn't blame Sarah for suspecting that he was screwing women in motels all over the country, or going on gambling binges, or drinking, or what-not. But Dave is as old-fashioned about screwing women as a priest. He doesn't gamble and he hates drunks. Usually, he won't even shoot a game of pool. He's got no time for games cause he can't stand to lose. He works—that's it. Work is the only area where he's weak, and only because he doesn't know how to limit himself. He takes on more and more and he doesn't get any sleep, and he gets irritable as all get-out and so intense you think he's gonna crack. And then he takes on *more* work. It may have been a blessing for his family to have him gone as much as he was. He loves them, but he doesn't know how to show it. He thinks he's saving the world, that's what he thinks, and that no one can do it better than Dave Hall. On that ivory case, after our Alaska SAC, Jim Houge, said to him, 'Okay, Mister Big Operator, you think you can put Charlie McAlpine in jail, why don't you try?' it became like the final proof of who he was. He'll rise to almost any challenge, one that a normal person would laugh at, it's such overreach. All through 1980 and 1981, he lived, breathed, ate, slept, and fucked ivory for month after month. But he toughed it out. He'd have rather died."

Dave Hall would never admit that exhaustion or family stress were motivating factors in deciding finally to take down the ivory investigation. His no-sleep-macho complex is the most full-blown I have seen—he complains bitterly about lack of sleep, but it's a crucial part of his identity—and the stress of his family life was nothing new. Nonetheless, after a lifetime of excellent health and no vices except work, his health was deteriorating fast. He, Houge, and Clark Bavin, the chief of law enforcement for the USFWS, decided on February 3 or 4 as the takedown date. The last piece of unfinished business, which Dave Hall would try to complete immediately before the takedown, was to try to make a case on the person reputed to be the biggest importer of poached ivory in North America.

Moses Feingold was the only suspect who had half fallen into their net who was importing large quantities of elephant ivory into the country. Elephant ivory presented another legalistic nightmare: some African nations still allowed exports, whereas others did not, so exporters in countries with a legal trade often laundered ivory from other countries where it was banned. It was difficult, if not impossible, in most cases, to prove wrongdoing. The best hope would be to establish probable cause to raid Feingold's business files—there might be a paper trail leading to some duly recorded illegalities. Feingold was an attractive target anyway, because there were too many stories floating around about his involvement with criminal elements. And the Fish and Wildlife Service wanted to assess the size of his operation, if only to let Congress know how much poached ivory was coming into the United States from Africa.

Actually, Wally Soroka had visited Feingold earlier in New York and sold him some illegal walrus ivory, so probable cause already existed. What Dave Hall now had to do—not just in Feingold's case but with the dozens of others from whom he had bought wildlife contraband—was update it. Most Americans think the police can go to a judge and say they think so-and-so is defacing the flag inside his home, or stockpiling explosives, or practicing cannibalism, and the judge will issue search warrants like scrip. A search warrant is actually very hard to obtain. Even though, in June, Dave Hall had bought ivory and a polar bear hide inside the King Island Native Corporation headquarters, and had a tape transcript in which the corporation's leaders mentioned illegal activities about two dozen times, that did not constitute probable cause for search and seizure. It had happened too long before. The standard used by the courts is largely temporal: if you can show probable cause within the preceding few hours or days, then your odds of obtaining a warrant are good. If your probable cause is weeks or months old, then they are almost nil. Everything Dave Hall had done during the previous eight months was groundwork; now, over the course of four or five days, he would have to repeat everything again. The actual buys would all be made by surrogates. Nearly half the USFWS force of two hundred special agents was going to Alaska to help take down the case; they would pose as brothers or uncles or business partners of Dave Hall or Doak, make some buys, and the nets would fall. But he and Doak would have to make all the arrangements, which meant hours and hours on the telephone followed by frantic transcriptions of the recorded conversations to take to the judge. He began about the thirtieth of January and was on the phone pretty much nonstop for the next couple of days. On the thirtieth, he got four hours of sleep. On the thirty-first, about three. On the first, four or five. On February 2, he flew out to New York to visit Feingold.

Dave Hall thought Feingold was potentially dangerous, so he took Dave Cartwright, one of his Louisiana agents, with him. They rented a car at the airport and called Feingold's son, who gave them directions to his latest business location. They had corresponded several times over the past few months, and in that time the address printed on the letterhead and business receipts had changed twice. Feingold, it seemed, picked up his operation and moved it a couple of times a year. Even McAlpine didn't go to such lengths. Feingold's ivory business was tucked inside a warehouse in an industrial section not far from Yonkers. According to Dave Hall, the amount of ivory crated and stacked inside was "staggering," though he wouldn't guess how much there was. He did count more than thirty workers in the place. Most of them were cutters because Feingold rendered most of his raw ivory into jewelry. There were some walrus tusks lying around, but Feingold's stock was mostly elephant. It was New York, but it could have been Hong Kong.

Moses Feingold was about fifty. He had steel-wool hair and an athletic build, unlike his fat son, and again unlike his son, who was histrionic and excitable, he projected a guarded, slightly menacing taciturnity. He didn't seem as paranoid as Charlie McAlpine, but the quality of menace was an ingredient McAlpine lacked.

The father was busy, but Junior Feingold insisted on taking them to lunch; then he wanted to run them by the Feingold home. He was absolutely determined to show Dave Hall his collection of guns. The kid was twenty-three, going on two; he had a kinetic, infantlike energy. If you flashed your badge while Junior was cooing over one of his rifles, you could imagine him impulsively blowing off your head.

Feingold's ivory factory, Dave Hall thought, had represented the last opportunity for things to go really awry. Sitting back in Feingold's Cadillac Seville, dead tired, he was so relieved—so finally and overwhelmingly relieved after more than eight months on this case, with its horrible weather and dreary villages and wretched drunks and biker gangs and

corrupted Eskimos—that he told Junior perfectly sincerely that it would
be a pleasure to see his house and his guns. That was when young
Feingold told them, quite offhand, that his father had recently installed
bug-detection equipment about as sophisticated as they use in the White
House—an LEA Combo Detector and a Gunderson TTRD-800—and that
the premises were patrolled by two armed guards. If anyone walked
into the house wired, Junior chortled, he'd be blown away.

They were no more than five minutes from the house, and Dave Hall
was sitting in the front seat of the car. There was no way he could take
off the Nagra discreetly. He turned around to say something to Cartwright and gave him a now-what? look. Cartwright looked as if his mind
was racing, too. Now that they had promised to look at Junior's guns,
they couldn't *not* go inside the house. He had built everything perfectly
all these months, and now this infantile Jewish Little League punk was
going to make the whole edifice tumble down. He raced wildly from
excuse to excuse—nausea, a critical telephone call, a daughter's illness,
anything that could keep them out of that house—and nothing would
work. He insists he wasn't worried about the guards—if the bug detec-
tors sprang the alarm, he and Cartwright were going to have their guns
drawn before they could move. The time advantage was all theirs. He
was worried about the case. If the alarm went off at home, it would
probably set off a keyed-in alarm at Feingold's factory. He would know
immediately what it was about. Even if they busted Feingold and his
son, their lawyers would have them out on bail in a few hours. They
would get on the telephone to their network of ivory suppliers, and
every record and receipt, every stash and stockpile in North America
would disappear instantly. There would be nothing but old evidence
and hearsay, and that didn't make a case.

Everything depended on technology. Could the most sophisticated
tape recorder in production sneak past what was purported to be an
espionage-level bug-detection trap?

The Feingolds lived in a three-story house in one of the fancier suburbs along the Hudson River. It was a big Victorian house, built of wood,
a somewhat rococo and expensive house that belonged in San Francisco. There was a long, sweeping circular front drive. The two guards
who came out to meet the car were Mexicans; they were squat like

Mayans and rough-looking, but they wore coats and ties. Young Feingold had a very fine collection of guns. And the Nagra, with its soft motor drive and lightly magnetized high-resolution tape, did not set off the bug-detection system.

On that day and the following one, about seventy agents of the Fish and Wildlife Service flew into Anchorage. They came from Atlanta, Miami, San Francisco, New York, Chicago, New Orleans, Phoenix, Texas—from all over the country—and sometimes ended up by accident on the same flights. When that happened, they did not acknowledge one another's existence. There were to be no clues that something major was going on. When a group of them flew out to Nome the next day, they booked themselves into the Golden Nugget as a conclave of meteorologists. To add a dose of credibility to the lie, several women agents were in that group. More agents went to Seattle, to New Jersey, to San Francisco, and to Hawaii. At practically the same moment, they all struck.

The amount of ivory confiscated was spectacular—something like five tons of it in Alaska alone. Together with the guns, drugs, and everything else that was seized, it was a multimillion-dollar haul. An underground bunker at Elmendorf Air Force Base was requisitioned for it, and it was guarded around the clock. The seventeen agents and state troopers who went into the Brothers' chalet came back outside carrying a lot of automatic weapons and several human skulls.

The trials went on for years. Jerry Kingery and the Brothers had some of Anchorage's better-quality legal talent at their side in about half an hour. McAlpine assembled a small battery of lawyers, too. Naturally, the whole loosely knit mafia of ivory hunters, buyers, dealers, and exporters unraveled completely; everyone began offering evidence on everyone else to save his skin. McAlpine offered mounds of new evidence on Feingold; the Eskimos offered more damning information on McAlpine and Douglas O'Neill. "It was a free-for-all," says Dave Hall. "A mudfight."

McAlpine couldn't get over how he had been duped. He thought of all the times he had asked Doak, on the telephone, if his tape recorder was on and of the body search and other precautions he had taken with

Dave Hall; he thought of the times he had eaten with him, had cocktails with him, and opened his heart about as wide as it would go. "Man," he had said to him once, sitting by the pool back in Hawaii, "I'm fat, I'm losing my hair, I'm getting tired. You think I want to die traveling around with a suitcase full of scrimshaw? Bullshit! I want to die in the saddle or on a sailboat or lying on a beach somewhere. I don't want to die walking in a store, sweating, and saying, 'Look, I'm Sealskin Charlie from Anchorage, Alaska, and I want to show you some fine scrimshaw.' I don't want to die that way." Charlie couldn't believe Dave Hall hadn't broken down and confided who he really was, when he had said that. But he didn't seem angry so much as shell-shocked. He was too mortally wounded to be mad.

I once asked Dave Hall if he felt sorry for any of the people he had duped. He said he felt sorry for the Eskimos because they had been "conned into the white man's culture." Since that culture is represented, at an extreme, by Charlie McAlpine, he felt no pity for him. "He was a goddamned yuppie, that's what he was. An over-the-hill Alaska yuppie. These crooked brokers on Wall Street, these big government-contractor scandals—he's one of them. Charlie is the kind of guy likes to get up in the morning, read *The New York Times*, have his maid bring him breakfast, go for a swim in his pool, talk about the girls he's screwed— *having* is all that means anything to him. He doesn't give a shit about the state of the world, the environment, nothing—he just wants to get his fat piece of the pie while there's still any left. The environmentalists were the ones that put him in the biggest rage of anything. He'd cuss and moan and go on as if trying to preserve anything, or protect anything, is just plain *crazy*. The one unusual thing about him is he's a lowlife with a pedigree. He's well educated, he's got a legal education, he's extremely intelligent—he can have just about anything he wants legally. But he's got to break the law. He's like the Wall Street crook who's making three million dollars a year, but he's got to make twenty million, so he breaks the law. If he was making twenty million, he'd have to make a hundred million. Charlie McAlpine is everything that's wrong with America today. He is *us*."

Moses Feingold was never convicted; Dave Hall believes the government blew the case, and it makes him so livid—still today—that you feel like hopping the next plane just to get away from him. Jerry Kingery and the Brothers were never even indicted; one theory is that the government attorneys in Alaska feared that they or their families would be harmed if any of the Brothers were sent up. Sealskin Charlie, however, ended up convicted. He served time in a minimum-security prison and was hit with a large fine, which he is still paying off. On top of his legal fees, which cost him over a hundred thousand dollars, it pretty much wiped him out. He is listed in the Anchorage directory now as selling real estate.

I called Charlie McAlpine one day a few years later to see what he had to say about Dave Hall, the ivory case, the walrus, the Eskimos, and wildlife law enforcement in general.

I lied to Charlie. I wanted to give him an opportunity to retell the story from his own perspective and to exonerate himself as best he could, but if I had told him I was writing a book about Dave Hall, he would have been off the telephone in five seconds. (As it was, he hung up on me after three or four minutes, suspicious that I was recording the conversation and that I wasn't who I said I was, but he called me back the next day and held forth for almost an hour.) I told him I was working on a story for *Field & Stream* about harassment of hunters by the Fish and Wildlife Service. I am mindful that I was violating a canon of journalistic ethics, but since it was done to get Charlie to tell his side of the story, I decided to hell with it.

Charlie said that he felt he was entrapped. "They're the moral equivalent of the Gestapo," he said. "And Hall is the moral equivalent of the SS. He came on like such a gangster, whipping out his guns and talking about his drug-dealing friends. He pushed me and pushed me to sell him ivory, to buy ivory. It's a goddamned disgrace that the government spends taxpayer money on vicious harassment like this, but when they get you, there's nothing you can do. They have the tapes, they seize your documents, and they have *complete control* over what's used in court. If there's a tape where you say, 'Hey, I wouldn't be selling you this if I thought it was illegal, but I think it's honestly a gray area and it's probably legal,' they don't use that one. If it's a tape where you're talking about making money or seducing girls, they *do* use that one. Hell, they'll do absolutely anything to get you. Not just ivory but on any goddamned petty infraction or compromising situation they can trap you in. That Doak took me to a whorehouse in New Orleans. He *took* me there! They figured they might not get me on any real charge, so they'd better make a lecher out of me."

Had he done anything illegal, then?

"No. The ivory I bought, I had carved by my Eskimos. That's perfectly legal. I have been a *great benefactor* of the Eskimo community. I give them jobs, I make them money—or I did until these bastards forced me out of my business. Only they chased me into real estate where I can make *more* money; the sonofabitches must regret that. But they don't *care* if you've done nothing illegal, cause once they decide they want you, they get you—even if they have to fabricate their whole goddamned case."

Weren't there some hardened criminals involved in the ivory trade?

"You're talking about Wayne Gans. I don't know if Wayne's a hardened criminal. He killed a guy on the street and got sent up. Maybe it was justified, I don't know. They sure consider him an upstanding asset to the community in northwest Alaska. He's the richest person up there by far, and he employs a lot of people. Jerry Kingery, well, he was just a guy who had run with the Hell's Angels and came up here and started his own motorcycle club and had a native girlfriend. If he bought ivory and she worked it, I don't know if that was illegal. All cops hate motorcycle riders, that's why they went after him. And he had a lot of guns. Jesus Christ, you should have seen the pictures of when they raided his house. There were eighteen of them! Eighteen! And they had machine guns, Uzis, I don't know what. They held him in confinement for hours without letting him talk to his lawyer. I'm telling you, this government runs some things just like the Gestapo. It's a fucking disgrace, and you're going to quote me even if you say you won't, and they'll come after me again. I consider Dave Hall to be a dangerous man. Even some of his own people do. They told me privately he is way out of line. They think he's psycho. And you know what? They're right!"

So the whole case was pure harassment and had nothing to do with any serious threat to the walrus's survival?

"The walrus was never endangered! That's just the kind of bullshit they put out. Their own biologists never said it was endangered. It's never been listed. There are more of them now than ever. They're probably overpopulated. It's just that some environmentalists put a lot of pressure on the government to stop this or stop that, and they feel they have to do it. That's the kind of power the environmentalists have these days."

What about other animals that are officially listed as endangered? Are undercover operations necessary to stop people from poaching them?

"Well, I don't know. These people don't really care that much about endangered animals. It's all a political power trip to them. They just want their cases plastered all over the front pages of the newspapers, and they got that with me. They even made a video that used a picture of my shop that was aired on national television. They'll ruin you any way they can."

So if I, a white man, had asked Charlie, a white man, to sell me some ivory—which would have been illegal, whether he thought it ought to have been or not—he wouldn't have done it?

"No. If I had some in my collection, I might have said, 'Look, you want a piece of ivory, take this one.' I might have *given* you one."

During the summer of 1989, Sam LaBudde, a marine biologist, conservationist, and intrepid undercover journalist—one of his pluckier exploits was to ship out with a tuna boat and surreptitiously film the crew netting dolphins illegally—flew up to Alaska and spent several weeks both in a small chartered airplane and on foot, surveying the beaches of walrus habitat for evidence of recent kills. As death censuses go, it was not a particularly scientific one; plenty of walrus wounded by hunters at sea are eaten by other marine animals before they wash ashore, and those walrus taken back whole to the villages (rather than left to rot) were not counted either. LaBudde's tally, whatever it was, was certain to be much lower than the actual kill. Nonetheless, he managed to count two hundred walrus, which, judging from the relatively fresh condition of the corpses, had been killed within the previous few months. Hundreds more lay around in varying states of decay, sometimes half-buried in sand; there may have been others completely buried that he did not see. In a couple of places, dead walrus were piled on beaches like giant driftwood. Not a single one had tusks.

LaBudde, whose account appears in the fall 1989 issue of *Earth Island Journal*, also visited a number of Eskimo villages to see how easily one could find raw ivory for sale. It was everywhere. The main difference between 1989 and 1980, when Dave Hall and Vaughn Doak went buying in some of the same villages, was the price. In 1989, if you offered cash, walrus ivory was up slightly, to about fifty dollars a pound. (That, in any event, was the price from which you negotiated.) If you offered drugs, on the other hand, you could have it for much less. The U.S. attorney's office in Anchorage had prosecuted a case a short while earlier in which ten walrus head mounts, nominally worth five hundred to seven hundred dollars each, were traded for an even ounce of marijuana, an exchange rate that works out to about four dollars a pound for the ivory. A bottle of vodka, LaBudde reports, was payment enough for a pair of small tusks. Had he brought cocaine or methamphetamines, he could pretty much have set his own terms of sale, within reason.

Walking through an Eskimo village in 1989, LaBudde wrote, is "like touring a graveyard for wildlife. The outer walls of many homes are layered with collections of hides, skulls, tusks, antlers, and whalebone. These bleaching remains are hung in such profusion that it is difficult to fathom their utility. Hundreds of reindeer hides are rotting all over the village. A pile of about thirty decaying pelts have been dumped on the beach for the tide to take away. Several fresh polar bear hides are hanging out to dry, and I spot three more scattered about going to rot. Outside one house I count the skulls of six polar bears—the great ursine teeth bright against the dark flesh clinging to the bone."

Everything LaBudde had to report is corroborated by the Fish and Wildlife Service. During the fall of 1986 and spring of 1987, USFWS special agents prosecuted fourteen cases involving the illegal sale of wildlife products by Alaska's native population. In ten of those cases, illegal drugs constituted all or part of the payment. More recently, in 1989, USFWS agents confiscated a big crate of tusks from an Anchorage resident—who was white—along with $28,100 in cash and five pounds of cocaine. The ivory-for-drugs trade, according to officials, is on the up-and-up; if you go on a buying expedition to Nome these days, you needn't bother to bring cash.

•   •   •

The last time I spoke with Dave Hall about his ivory case, I finally asked him the question I had always been afraid to ask: How, by any reckoning, could he consider the whole effort worthwhile if there is more ivory poaching going on in Alaska today than ever before?

The case nearly ruined his health. As soon as the undercover work was over, he ended up in the hospital with a severe bout of colitis, a chronic inflammation of the lower bowel that can kill you and rarely disappears for good. He spent two weeks in the sick ward, losing a lot of blood and receiving massive infusions of corticosteroids. His near-total recovery, nine years later, seems almost miraculous, but considering what the investigation did to him, I thought he would explode when I suggested that it had been pretty much worthless.

He just shrugged.

"I guess if you think in terms of long-term impact, a lot of what we do is worthless."

"How can you take serious risks to your life and almost ruin your health on a case you think is worthless?"

"What are we supposed to do? Give up and say screw the walrus and the elephant? Let McAlpine do his thing?" Now he was mad.

"How you justify it personally is what I'm trying to figure out."

"The police work and the indictments are the most meaningless part of the job. I've always said that. What justifies the case is when you manage to convince a few of the people you've indicted that they're ruining everything for themselves and their children's children's children. If I got two Eskimos to see that, then the case was a success."

"Did you?"

"I don't know. I think I did."

"How would you change things, if you could?"

"The subsistence exemption hasn't helped the Eskimos any more than it's helped the walrus. Traditional Eskimo culture is dying out a lot faster than the walrus. The difference between what I saw up in the villages as a college student and today is enough to make me think traditional Eskimo culture has got maybe one generation left. Then it'll be gone. The old ways will be gone, the crafts and the carving, dog sleds, the boat making—it's all gonna disappear. The only thing that will stop it from happening is if we repeal the exemption. 'Subsistence' is a joke. Buying drugs and buying into the white man's culture through walrus hunting is not subsistence. It would be less of a joke if the Fish and Wildlife Service was more serious about enforcing the law. The hierarchy is what I'm talking about. The bureaucrats and politicians who run us. There's so much game playing going on. You arrest a bunch of Eskimos, and that's heat, man, that's *serious* heat. Discrimination! Racism! You get the senator and the congressman down on you. You get the native-rights people all alarmed. Who needs that? So let's just leave things the way they are, arrest a couple people now and then, and, you know, say, *We've solved the problem.*

"I'd actually be sadder to see the Eskimo culture disappear than the walrus. To me, it's like losing the tribes in the Amazon. We just won't admit that we're letting it happen, just like we won't admit that we're destroying our own rain forests. We lecture the Brazilians about the Amazon, and we log off the whole Tongass for Japan. Man, we are in the same league as Jim Bakker when it comes to hypocrisy."

Dave Hall says he would junk the subsistence exclusion and replace it with a quota system for walrus similar to the one that's been created for whales. Each village would be allowed a predetermined kill every year, with no strings attached. The quota would be minimal and aggressively enforced. Then he would permit something most environmentalists abhor: a sport-hunting season on walrus. "It's got to be a primitive hunt. Maybe you can use some power on the boat, but it's got to be a skinboat, or use a dog sled. No snowmobiles! That's the only way we're gonna keep the art of making skinboats and dog sleds alive. You got to have an Eskimo guide. We could do the same thing with polar bears. A sport-hunting season. But no airplanes. No snowmobiles. Killing males only. You'd have to allow guns but no automatic rifles. It means you let the rich white guys come up to hunt an animal that only Eskimos are allowed to hunt today, sure, but everything else about the hunt—almost everything—is traditional. The anti-hunters want to ban all hunting. I don't know who's gonna enforce the law, but they'd better be ready to spend billions if they really want it to work. And if it's really enforced—if we get the walrus kill down to zero—we get an overpopulation of walrus and they start starving to death. If we leave things the way they are, we'll lose the animals and traditional Eskimo culture both.

If we outlaw all killing, we'll lose the Eskimo culture for sure, and we'll overcrowd the walrus habitat. One way or the other, we're gonna create the worst of all worlds cause that's what happens when you let politics dictate nature, which we do all the time."

"So if you could change your looks and come up with another front like Endangered Species, you'd never run another undercover operation in Alaska because it would be pointless and because politics ruins everything in the end?"

"No, I'm not saying that."

"What are you saying?"

"Sure I would."

For now, keeping the elephant from going extinct will be a far greater challenge to wildlife conservation than saving the walrus. Despite heavy poaching—and thanks, in part, no doubt, to the undercover operation Dave Hall ran, though one could never prove that conclusively—the world walrus population, now confined mainly to the Bering Sea, has been quite stable, at around two hundred thousand over the past ten years, a decade that saw the elephant's numbers reduced by one-half. It is much easier to kill elephants than walrus. Their huge tusks are worth much more money, and, if you include Asia, there are about two billion humans living in elephant habitat. There aren't two hundred thousand people living near walrus habitat. Africa, its land and resources overwhelmed and ravaged by its exploding population, sinks every day into deeper, unplumbed, and perhaps irreclaimable ruin. The continent becomes bare; ivory is its remaining gold. Even in countries such as Kenya and Zimbabwe, where game patrols are now under orders to shoot all poachers on sight, the ivory hunters skulk daily toward the wildlife preserves. Many invade from neighboring countries. Most poachers in Kenya today are Somalis; there is every indication that the Somali regime approves of their activities and skims off either profits or poached tusks. In Tanzania, where at least a quarter of a million elephants have been slaughtered over the past decade, representing 70 percent of Africa's greatest remaining herd, the species is merely endangered. In those countries that are not serious about saving their elephants or where they are being written off—a government spokesman from the Congo recently stated that "the extinction of the African elephant is inevitable"—the apocalypse is at hand.

Until the human race matures or destroys itself, the elephant is at the mercy of four terrible forces: extreme poverty, overpopulation, corruption, and unappeasable demand. If it is to remain on this earth, outside of zoos—and the African elephant rarely breeds in captivity— at least two of these four forces will somehow have to be brought under control.

The first and second, Africa's poverty and overpopulation, are so intractable that it's pointless to think about working for the elephant's salvation from that end. Out of a population of six hundred million, nearly all of whom are poor (if you exclude South Africa, the entire continent's economy is smaller than Belgium's, and a few dictators own half the wealth), there will always be millions of potential ivory poachers. The potency of the lure is irresistible; until recently, before the price of ivory began to fall, a couple of large tusks were worth ten years' average income for most people. With its exploding and illiterate population, its ravaged resources, and the horrifying spread of AIDS, Africa faces fathomless misery. Things will get much worse, hard as that is to imagine. But even if Africa were someday to join the "developed" world, as much of South Asia has begun to do, that is no guarantee that elephants would be better off. In South Africa, the most developed country on the continent, only about eight thousand elephants survive, nearly all of which are inside Kruger National Park; an elephant that tries to eke out a living outside the park ends up in a farm field or a development or on a highway, and its odds of survival are near zero. Elephants are huge, unruly creatures, unwelcome in an overcrowded human world. The best thing—the only thing—elephants have going for them elsewhere in Africa is the fact that they are important to village society, whence most of the poachers come. In drought periods, they stamp open water holes that villages without wells and other wildlife may use; they play a crucial role in maintaining the savannah by clearing brush and knocking down trees; in their great, warm guts, they germinate acacia seeds. Elephants have for so long played such a dominant role in maintaining the stability of wild African ecosystems that ecologists shudder to think how these ecosystems might come undone without them. Elephants also bring in tourists, who are, to some nations, the most important source of hard currency.

Ten years ago, not a single African nation was calling for a world ban on ivory trade. During the past two years, with the African elephant population dropping at a rate of around two thousand animals a week, nearly all of them have. (Among those African countries that still have elephants, the only holdouts are South Africa, Botswana, Namibia, and Zimbabwe.) But even such a drastic change in official policy is no guarantee that the elephant will survive, since in Africa corruption and brutality are almost as endemic as poverty, and nowhere more so than in the case of elephant killing and ivory smuggling.

In 1988 Craig van Note, representing the Washington-based consortium of environmental groups called Monitor, provided detailed testimony to a congressional committee about elephant and rhinoceros poaching by UNITA, the right-wing revolutionary group that for years has been trying to overthrow the leftist government in Angola. By Van Note's estimate, UNITA rebels operating under Jonas Savimbi—who has received massive military assistance from South Africa and considerable moral and logistical support from the American CIA—may have poached as many as a hundred thousand elephants over the past several years to finance its war. Most of the ivory was shipped through South Africa en route to Hong Kong—almost certainly, Van Note said, with the cooperation of the South African Defense Force, the country's elite military unit. The charges upset so many South Africans that SADF was compelled to set up an internal inquisition, which, not surprisingly, cleared itself of all culpability. But a South African military officer, Colonel Jan Breytenbach, who commanded an elite parachute unit that assisted UNITA, recently wrote in the *Johannesburg Sunday Times* that "elephants were mown down indiscriminately by the tearing rattle of automatic fire from AK-47 rifles and machine guns" in the hands of Savimbi's troops. "They shot everything," Breytenbach reported, "bulls, cows, and calves, showing no mercy in a campaign of extermination never before seen in Africa. The hundreds of thousands of elephants became thousands; the thousands became hundreds; and the hundreds, tens."

Savimbi himself has since confirmed that UNITA has used ivory profits to repay South Africa for armaments, and several shipments of ivory coming into South Africa from Angola have since been seized. These allegations are by no means the only ones implicating members of the South African military in wildlife smuggling. In 1988, for example, criminal indictments were handed down in Connecticut against three Americans and several South Africans—including a major in the SADF—alleging that they smuggled AK-47 assault rifles and rhinoceros horn into the United States. According to England's Environmental Investigation Agency, "it has been [the South African] government's policy to allow the illicit ivory and rhino horn trade to flourish . . . as long as it serves the government's perceived interests."

As it has sought to overthrow the government of Angola, South Africa has for years been a supporter of Renamo, UNITA's counterpart in Mozambique. Renamo's brutality is unsurpassed by any guerrilla organization in the world except perhaps the Khmer Rouge; it has reportedly killed a hundred thousand civilians and has been accused of mind-numbing atrocities, such as tossing babies onto bayonets and disemboweling pregnant women. (Renamo has some prominent supporters in the United States, too, notably Senate Minority Leader Robert Dole.) Lately, Renamo and its principal military advisers, former members of white Rhodesia's Selous Scouts, have been implicated in rhino and elephant poaching perhaps as destructive as UNITA's. Mozambique's socialist government, however, has been implicated, too. According to the Environmental Investigation Agency (EIA), "Mozambique is said to be willing to issue . . . permits to allow [poached] ivory to be legally exported—for a price." In this as in many similar cases, direct hard evidence supporting such allegations has not emerged; however, in the past, many of the rumors and accusations publicized by groups such as the EIA have turned out to be true.

Zimbabwe, which still has tens of thousands of elephants, is one of the few African nations that also permit an annual legal "cull," even though its director of wildlife, Rowan Martin, admitted in 1989 that "in the past two years the escalation of illegal hunting for ivory within Zimbabwe is very noticeable [and] as elephant populations decline in countries to the north, the pressure on elephants is expected to intensify." The worst poaching incident was the recent slaughter, in Gonarezhou National Park, of about one thousand elephants, almost a quarter of the park's estimated numbers. The EIA, which interviewed people in the area, claims the poachers were mainly members of Zimbabwe's Red Berets, a paratroop unit trained in North Korea, and maintains that the park's superintendent was personally involved. North Korea's imposing presence in Zimbabwe may help explain why so many elephants are being poached there; among the Communist nations, it is, next to China, the principal entrepôt for elephant ivory and rhino horn. In the past seven years, North Korean diplomats have been apprehended several times with illegal ivory; according to the EIA, practically the whole Korean embassy staff in Zimbabwe and Zambia are involved in ivory and rhino-horn smuggling.

Somalia is one of the most brazen of all African countries when it comes to illegal ivory exports. Somali soldiers have been caught poaching elephants by Kenyan game wardens and have returned fire when pursued; the government issues pro forma apologies, and it happens again and again. A Kenyan newspaper recently printed a copy of a letter signed by Somalia's president, Mohammad Siyad Barre, "authorizing" two traders to enter Kenya and bring back ivory—an authority that was news to the Kenyan government. According to the *New African*, Barre has personally dispatched poachers and smugglers into Ethiopia, too. With only forty-five hundred elephants of its own, Somalia has managed to export tusks from an estimated thirteen thousand eight hundred elephants in the past three years. And those were merely the tusks for which documentation was provided; undoubtedly, countless others were smuggled out, most of them poached in Kenya and Ethiopia.

In Africa, diplomats of all kinds are involved in the outlaw ivory trade; they are usually well connected and can always claim diplomatic immunity if they are caught. In January of 1989, a giant metal container box—the kind that goes on a cargo ship—which was registered in the name of the Indonesian ambassador to Tanzania, Husein Joesoef, and which happened to contain three tons of poached ivory, was seized by police in Dar es Salaam. (The ambassador was forced to resign.) Nine months later the son of Portugal's president, Mario Suarez, was one of three Portuguese members of Parliament who barely survived a plane crash in Angola; the aircraft, a small Cessna, was flying unscheduled and below radar screens and may have crashed because it was drastically overloaded with elephant tusks. A Tanzanian member of Parliament was recently apprehended with a hundred and five poached elephant tusks. A Roman Catholic priest was found in possession of two hundred twenty-four. A Chinese trader based in Pretoria was seized on the border between Botswana and Zambia with, among other poached wildlife parts, two tons of contraband ivory and ninety-four black rhino horns, a haul worth at least two million dollars.

But worst of all, according to conservationists, is the corruption that has permeated the CITES secretariat itself.

CITES—the Convention on International Trade in Endangered Species—is the principal government-level wildlife-conservation authority in the world today, a conservation equivalent of the United Nations (the secretariat is, in fact, housed in the UN offices in Switzerland). One hundred and two countries are members of CITES, which means, in theory, that they must abide by majority rule; if the member nations agree to list a species under Appendix One of CITES rules, which declares it officially endangered, then none may permit imports or exports of that particular species. But where a ban is less than total—or in any gray area—the secretariat has great discretionary authority.

The secretary of CITES, a Canadian named Eugene LaPointe, for years strenuously opposed listing the African elephant under Appendix One, despite pleas from one member nation after another—Kenya, Tanzania, the United States—for full protection. LaPointe's alternative was a system of ivory "trade controls" and quotas, which was adopted—largely through his intervention—in 1986 and which proved so hopelessly flawed that the member nations ultimately voted to scrap it, but not before the world elephant population declined by another 20 percent.

The quota system allowed any member nation to export as much ivory as it wanted, so long as it informed the secretariat in advance how much it planned to export so it could be held accountable. The quotas had absolutely nothing to do with sustainable "harvesting" of elephants. A country whose ruling regime is directly involved in the ivory trade—Somalia, for example—could legally export the ivory of its entire surviving herds in a single year. Nor was "accountability" anything but a chimera; by CITES's own admission, the quotas were exceeded by at least 150 percent. The system also exempted "worked" ivory, on the grounds that it was too difficult to monitor; the result was the almost instantaneous creation of carving factories in Dubai, Singapore, Taiwan, Macau, and Zaire, where workmen performed some rudimentary work on tusks that were then shipped—legally under the CITES rules—to Hong Kong, whose four or five thousand master carvers finished them. Confiscated ivory was allowed to be legalized by governments instead of destroyed, as some African leaders—Daniel arap Moi of Kenya, for example, who torched twelve tons himself for the benefit of an international television audience—insist it must be if the ivory trade is ever to stop. The trade controls also gave the secretary authority to legalize stockpiled ivory himself.

It was this last authority in particular, and LaPointe's willingness to exercise it, that infuriated organizations such as the EIA and even the governments of some African nations, not to mention Europe, Canada, and the United States. In 1986, for example, acting on the paid advice of Ian Parker, a former professional elephant hunter who has killed thousands of the animals in his lifetime, LaPointe issued CITES permits to eighty-nine *tons* of ivory stockpiled in Burundi. Because Burundi's elephant population is completely extinct, every one of the eight thousand elephants sacrificed to the charnel pile is likely to have been poached. LaPointe did the same thing again in Singapore—where he unilaterally "legalized" *three hundred and fifty tons*, most of which was again poached—and again in Somalia, Djibouti, and several other countries. The secretariat's argument, then as now, was that a legal ivory market must be allowed to exist; if the trade were to go completely underground, as in the case of cocaine, prices would skyrocket and things would get even worse. But Ian Parker later admitted that he had taken a seven-hundred-fifty-thousand-dollar bribe in Burundi in exchange for including, in his "amnesty" recommendations, several huge shipments of poached ivory then about to be added to the stockpile (it came in from Zaire, Tanzania, and other African countries). And LaPointe himself later accepted tens of thousands of dollars in contributions to the CITES secretariat from several notorious Hong Kong ivory dealers, who, by EIA's estimate, realized about twenty million dollars in profits from the ivory he arbitrarily "legalized."

Officials with the Fish and Wildlife Service have politely described such actions as "incomprehensible" or "counterproductive." David Currey of the EIA calls them "flagrantly criminal" and "diabolical," or worse. "LaPointe consorts with ivory poachers and he takes money from them. The scale of abuse is so obvious that there's no longer any doubt about the ivory trade's grip on all major decisions made by the secretariat. He's delivered CITES on a silver platter to the poachers and smugglers."

In October of 1989 the member nations of CITES finally voted in a turbulent biennial meeting, by a margin of seventy-six to eleven, to list the African elephant under Appendix One, giving it world status as an endangered species and prohibiting all ivory trade. All stockpiled ivory was to be destroyed within months, although Hong Kong appealed for permission to work and sell its remaining raw ivory stocks—estimated at nearly seven hundred tons. (In the spring of 1990 British Prime Minister Margaret Thatcher decided to give Hong Kong six months to sell off its stockpile; Kenyan Wildlife Service Director Richard Leakey said her ruling "has almost nullified the gains made in trying to save the African elephant over the last months.") Even so, in response to CITES's historic action, the world price of ivory has plummeted lately, to as little as two dollars a kilogram in East Africa, which is exactly the opposite of what people like Eugene LaPointe predicted it would do. How long it will remain depressed is anyone's guess. The reigning ivory "families"—the George and Tat Hong Poons of Hong Kong and Dubai, the Lais of Hong Kong, the Pongs of South Africa—have bought and sold enormous quantities of poached ivory for years; they are as comfortably established in the ivory business as the Colombians are or were in the cocaine trade. (The EIA, which has ferreted out some remarkable information—assuming it is accurate—recently disclosed that George Poon's income is about one million dollars a week.) Unlike the cocaine cartel, the ivory mafia has displayed little inclination toward violence—although the poachers in Africa are capable of extreme brutality—because they don't need it; even though the Tanzanian government estimates that 94 percent of the ivory entering Hong Kong is illegal, the Poons and Lais of Hong Kong have never been indicted for anything. In both Hong Kong and Singapore (which, together with Japan, China, and Taiwan, are the world centers of ivory trade), the ivory mafia employs thousands of people and contributes significantly to the local economies. Given all this, there is a strong likelihood the ivory trade will continue underground. At what level depends entirely on international demand.

The number-one ivory market in the world is Japan. Sixty-five percent of all the elephant tusks imported by Japan are rendered into *hanko*— small, inscribed cylindrical seals sold by the millions as commemorative pieces. In the past, the seals were wood with a tiny ivory tip; since Japan began sucking in all the world's wealth, most are now made entirely of ivory. There is no obvious reason why they cannot be made of wood again. Most U.S. ivory imports become jewelry—the United States has traditionally represented about 10 percent of the world ivory market—but many stores and jewelry chains now refuse to carry it in any form; nowhere, except perhaps in England and Germany, is revulsion over the elephant slaughter more profound than in North America.

What all this means, in the end, is that the fate of the world's elephants (and walrus, too) is largely in the hands of Asian countries where ivory carving has been a venerated tradition for hundreds or thousands of years: Japan, China, Taiwan, Korea, India, Hong Kong, Singapore, Thailand, and Malaysia. Once these countries were mainly exporters; now that most are so much wealthier, they are ivory consumers. None of these societies has developed much of a conservation ethic; several have long-standing traditions of raiding other nations' resources. One can only hope that they are serious about saving the elephant and manage to curtail demand. The curtailment must be drastic and unprecedented—the price of contraband ivory will probably have to remain at a few dollars a pound for years before the elephant population can ever begin to stabilize or, inconceivable as it may seem now, rebound. In 1989, however, ivory was still being sold, by one estimate, in three thousand shops in Hong Kong alone, and people from all over the world were buying it. Also, in that year, for the first time, the skyrocketing human population outnumbered the plummeting elephant population by a million to one.

For the elephant and the walrus to survive, people all over the world will have to conclude that ivory is far more valuable on a live animal than taken from a slaughtered one—even if few of us will ever see an elephant or a walrus in the wild and even if the species' value cannot be measured by any conventional standard. As Flora Lewis wrote in *The New York Times*, the ivory wars are only the beginning of a vast new human dilemma.

Part III

SACALAIT

Part III

SAGALAIT

THE Redwood Inn is in Jackson, Mississippi, on Terry Road, in a draggle-tailed, down-at-the-heels neighborhood. Whoever built the place was a minor-league impresario—it is constructed of genuine redwood lumber shipped from northern California through the Panama Canal—and the inn was once a quite respectable establishment, the sort of piney traveler's rest you used to find along all the workhorse U.S. highways before the interstates were laid down parallel and cannibalized them. U.S. Highway 57 used to handle most of the northern traffic going to or from New Orleans, and U.S. Route 80 sped motorists east or west; in those days the cash register sang. Now the traffic rumbles by on the interstate, the franchises pick the travelers' pockets, and the Redwood Inn has gone to seed. Tattooed roughnecks wander in and out of the bar, the food in the restaurant isn't fit for man or beast, and the motel rooms rent by the week. There's a porno emporium across the road—the only one in Jackson—in a deceased Winn-Dixie supermarket. You could be after coke dealers, a Korean call-girl racket, a chop-shop ring, or, as Dave Hall was in this particular case, a gang of rough and tough Louisiana good old boys selling millions of pounds of poached game fish in half a dozen states. You just couldn't find a better front for an undercover sting.

Willie Disch was already working the Larto Lake gang before the Second World War, when he was the resident state game warden—one of a handful who weren't on the take—in the parishes of Catahoula and Concordia. The gang was seining fish out of central Louisiana's big oxbow lakes, mainly Concordia and Larto, lakes that produce fish as Kentucky bluegrass raises horses and Illinois soil sprouts corn. The Larto gang specialized in white perch, or crappie, a delectable fish with an insulting name, which Cajuns call sacalait—"bag of milk"—because of the sweet white flesh inside the fishes' stretchable skin. (Sacalait rarely go over twelve inches, but, like largemouth bass, they are voracious, porcine eaters and can grow ludicrously fat.) Before airfreight and fast highways and refrigerated trucks brought fresh ocean fish to landlocked America, sacalait was ubiquitous in fish markets throughout the South and Middle West. The fish were especially savored by blacks— they still are—and when rural southern blacks began migrating north to urban jobs in the 1940s and 1950s and pined for their Friday-night Baptist fish fries, the Larto Lake gang started running the piscine delicacy all the way to Saint Louis and Chicago and Cincinnati, five thousand pounds at a time. When a six-and-a-half-ounce Coca-Cola cost a nickel, fresh-caught crappie was selling for a dollar a pound. That is why sacalait, like redfish today, was beginning to get scarce; that is why commercial fishing was banned; and, as Prohibition begat Al Capone, that was how a bunch of crackers with fourth-grade educations and gummy mouths were making what amounted to lucre back then.

Willie Disch's problems had to do with politics—more specifically, with the raw, red, pullulating rash of corruption spread by the regime of the Kingfish, Huey Pierce Long. That Huey had been assassinated just six years before Willie Disch began his game warden's job meant nothing as far as Willie Disch was concerned, because the legacy of the Kingfish was a lot of little Kingfishes, who cropped up in his wake as a mother wart spawns little baby warts.

In Concordia Parish, from the 1940s to the 1970s, the resident Kingfish was the sheriff, whose name was Noah Cross (the name, perhaps not by coincidence, of John Huston's prince of darkness in *Chinatown*). Cross's main source of extra income was not bribes, as was the case with most parish sheriffs, but a string of brothels and gambling bars in which he owned a part interest. His deputies' chief function was to collect the gambling receipts and beat up girls who held back too much.

But Cross had an interest in illegal fish and game, too, as Vincent Darby and Russell Landry, the first undercover game wardens for the Louisiana Department of Wildlife and Fisheries, were to find out. In the late 1960s they had gone up there to investigate reports that tremendous numbers of game fish were being poached. The evening they arrived, posing as fishermen, they had their camp shot to pieces when they were out; a few hours later Cross's deputies, who were likely the ones who shot up their camp, came by and arrested them—to be held without charge. (Obviously, someone at Wildlife and Fisheries had given them up.) *Habeas corpus* meant nothing to Noah Cross, so the only way Landry and Darby could get out of jail was to confess to him who they were. The deputies took them to the sheriff's estate early the next morning, where they found him nursing a highball. He offered them one and then, after learning their identities, told them to help themselves to another drink and then get the hell out of his parish and never come back. Neither did. (In 1973 Cross was finally convicted of jury tampering in federal court and sentenced to four years in prison; he developed cancer there and was released to die at home.)

Avoyelles Parish, just south of Concordia, was the home of a much rougher crowd, which everyone called the Dixie mafia. Based more or less in Simmesport, the Dixie mafia was—and still is—a loose confederation of criminals involved in everything from contract killings to hard drugs to poached deer. After World War II, before a lot of remnant wilderness was converted to soybeans and cow fodder, the Dixie mafia made a fair piece of change selling illegal venison. Russell Landry tried to shut down that gang, too, but all he got for his efforts was a death threat and a warning never to set foot in *that* parish again.

Connected in a vague way to both the Dixie mafia and Noah Cross was the Larto Lake gang, whose principals, since the 1940s or even earlier, were members of a family named Book. The Book clan went back several generations in Louisiana history—not as far back as the Battle of New Orleans, but far enough so that the hamlet nearest Larto Lake is named Book. The leader of the Larto gang in Willie Disch's time was Charlie Book. Perhaps by coincidence and perhaps not, the chief of enforcement for the Department of Wildlife and Fisheries over in Baton Rouge was Charlie's brother, Julius. The local game warden who was later to replace Willie Disch was Julius's nephew Nelson, also known as Beetle. Beetle Book was an indefatigable country-boy entrepreneur who made his first money at the age of six, picking insects off a local judge's crop; that was how he earned his nickname. The idea of Beetle Book working as the game warden in Concordia Parish might have struck the locals as Kafkaesque, had anyone known who Kafka was. He was himself arrested thirty-four times for game-law violations, but he never spent one night in jail. Beetle produced four sons he knew about, at least two of whom, Randy and Darwin, were to become members of the gang. There were Books and Book types everywhere you looked, grazing their little cowpatch of graft. For month after month, they managed to keep a step or two ahead of Willie Disch. If he went out at night to patrol Larto Lake, they went seining somewhere else. If he went somewhere else, they hit Larto. "Nobody is that smart or that careful. They was getting tipped off, is what was goin on. I didn't know if there was anyone in my department I could trust even to mail a letter for me."

Willie Disch is sitting in his kitchen as he says this, drinking coffee that could dissolve an engine block. He lives on the north side of Baton Rouge, across the road from the stolid phalanx of refineries and chemical plants that has bestowed on the Mississippi River, industrial America's cloaca, the moniker "Cancer Alley." Willie Disch, in 1987, is a strong, hearty, and nonmetastatic eighty-five. His forearms are hams; from the neck down, he could be a salaried lumberjack. Reaching into a file folder, he extracts a canceled check and offers it with a grim smile. The check is forty-three years old and is made out to him by the state of Louisiana in the amount of twenty-five cents.

"I finally found me an informant. They was awful hard to come by, on account of everybody bein a-scared of these outlaws. If you gave your name, you didn't know what would happen to you. If you didn't give your name, well, Wildlife and Fisheries could deny it ever received a tip. Do you see how it was? But I finally found one because some of them local folks, they was exercised over this Larto Lake gang. I was informed they was supposed to come out with a big load of white perch back there in about December of 1941. That's what was said to me. Now, I wanted to see who I could trust in my department, so I shared this tip with some of the other wardens. I made mental notes of who they were. Then I went out there on the Memphis highway so I could snag those boys coming through. I was told these fish were going to Memphis, and that was all I knew. Well, now, of course, they never come out. They was supposed to be driving a big green Chevrolet coupe, and don't you know I stayed up all night and no such vehicle come on through. The next morning I called my supervisor, who I still thought was a good straight man, and he told me, 'Willie Disch, you go back to headquarters, make tell some story about going someplace else tonight, and you go right back there and wait by that highway until they do come. And Willie, don't you tell a *soul.*'

"So, now, that's what I did. I waited out there all of Monday night in the cold, and again they never come. I waited all of Tuesday night, and they never come. It was *dang* cold that night. I waited all Wednesday night, and still they never come. I knew a game warden can't expect much sleep, and I was gettin in a few nods during the day, but I was beginning to think that I was taking my job just a wee little too serious, when don't you know on Thursday night—it was about one o'clock, two o'clock in the mornin—they come on through. They had themselves a big green Chevrolet coupe just like I was told they would. And they had that vehicle *loaded,* I mean, that rear bumper was hanging down two inches above the pavement. They was layin a trail of fish slime all the way to Memphis cause in those days freezers was expensive and they shipped fresh."

Willie Disch had his car cached behind some trees. He planted the flasher on the dash and tore off in pursuit. There was no way the gang could outrun him in a Chevy with a flat-head six and eight hundred thirteen pounds of fish on board. They had removed the rear seat so they could cram in a couple hundred extra pounds. "Now that car *stunk!*" said Willie Disch. "It was so loaded that in a panic stop they was gonna be buried alive."

At, say, thirty cents a pound wholesale, eight hundred thirteen pounds of fish, divided equally among those who netted and trucked that particular load, probably meant something like fifty dollars a man for a day's work, back when fifty dollars a week was a fine wage. It was simply too much money to let an honest game warden stay on the job.

"First thing happens is, we got a budgetary crisis. They got to lay me off, so they say. And they done it, too, for several months. But we had a lot of sportsmen who were awful peeved about the Larto gang sucking up all them game fish, and they had their own political connections in Baton Rouge, so they found me my job back. They called up one day and said, 'Willie Disch, we found us some money in the budget. We're gonna reinstate you! Ain't you some kind of lucky cuss!' What they did was, though, they made a roving ranger out of me. They run me up and down this state, to hither and yon and back again. 'Willie Disch! We got us some deer spotlighters workin up by Shreveport. Go see what you can do!' Or it was *grosbec* or alligators or some other thing, so long as I was kept away from Larto Lake. You know how they handle those dissidenters in Russia, don't you? Well, here they drove you crazy other ways. They promoted you to a desk job somewhere, or they just run you into the ground like they did me. They took our travel expenses out of our own paychecks in those days, and here I was travelin like a circuit preacher. Made us buy our own guns, too. They just wore me down to the bone. Maybe I got more pride than some others, but I couldn't take this treatment forever, so I decided I might as well quit sooner than later."

Willie Disch retrieved the canceled check for twenty-five cents and held it up like a souvenir. "This here was my last paycheck. This is what I was worth for trying to enforce the game laws of the state of Louisiana."

World War II came and went. Korea. Joe McCarthy. *Sputnik.* The Kennedys. Vietnam. Nixon and Watergate. OPEC. Jimmy Carter. Iran. Reagan. Gorbachev. Vanna White. The Larto gang remained in business the whole time. It remained in business because Louisiana's oxbow lakes, like the Georges Bank and the Yellowstone River and the Columbia before all the dams, are not so much lakes as protein factories; their biological output is so heroic that you can put fishermen elbow to elbow around the shores or seine the daylights out of those lakes and they keep yielding more fish. But the gang was also hell-bent on ensuring that if its own greed didn't put it out of business, the state of Louisiana wouldn't either.

"The sheriff, now, don't worry about that part of it, man, he'll sit down and eat a goddamned load of white perch with us," said Beetle Book one day in 1986, conversing with the undercover game warden who would ultimately bring the roof down on all their heads. "The district attorney, he's one hundred percent with us, son, you're goddamned right. You ain't foolin with no goddamn rookies, Dave, you ain't foolin with no goddamned ignorant motherfucks neither. Now I may sound like a goddamned country boy, but let me tell you somethin, son, I know some shit. If you get caught, you're not gonna have to spend a night in some muthafuckin stinkin jail. We got the right bunch in office now. This is *outlaw* country! The outlaws done removed the good boys from office, and we ain't gonna have none of them problems again for a long, long time."

In the early fall of 1985 I asked Dave Hall to let me get into a covert operation with him. I did not envision such a request bearing fruit. I had heard of reporters allowed to cruise around in police cars for a night, but I knew of none who had actually gone undercover, even for a day. I decided the best way to make something happen was to suggest to Dave Hall that he was overstating the risks of undercover wildlife-law enforcement—that they didn't stack up to much against those routinely faced by covert agents of the DEA or FBI, or even Customs. It was good strategy. At first, I was rewarded only with a scalding version of the boiler-plate Dave Hall Lecture on How the FBI Is a Half-assed Outfit That Couldn't Even Manage the DeLorean Case and Uses a Mob of Backup Agents for Each Undercover Agent and How the Fish and Wildlife Service Has the Most Incorruptible, Highest-Scoring Agents in All of Law Enforcement and How the Special Agents Have No Money and Rarely Use Backup and How the Federal Marshals Bringing Criminals to Justice Say They Fear Hard-core Poachers More Than Anyone and How People Who Talk Half-cocked Like This Don't Know What the Hell They Are Talking About. About a month later, however, I received a call and a sort of apology, in which he said it was against all regulations and he would certainly lose his job if anything happened to me, and he was probably making a stupid mistake, but there was a new operation involving a fish-poaching ring he was just starting to work into, and if I wanted some experience with covert law enforcement, I should fly on down.

It was the usual story: Dave Hall was in Tupelo or Pine Bluff or some such place when I arrived, and the directions he gave me over the phone were cryptic. "It's near where Highway 80 goes under the interstate, kind of on the southwest side of town. It's in a bad neighborhood. Look for a restaurant made of redwood that's sort of a dump. Let's meet there for dinner." How did I tell a restaurant made of redwood from one made of, let us say, Georgia longleaf pine, or perhaps even Canadian red cedar? "You're from California," he said in all seriousness, "I figured you'd know." What do we call dinnertime? "Whenever you get there."

After looking up the Redwood Inn in the telephone directory and learning that it is on Terry Road, I found the place after half an hour of searching. It was four o'clock in the afternoon. I wandered into the bar. I'm sort of a masculine-looking fellow, and I had my cowboy boots on, but I was appraised as if I were wearing a pink tutu. I racked a table of billiards and began to shoot by myself. A chain-smoking skinny guy with an armful of tattoos, wearing a sleeveless T-shirt and a cat hat, came over and asked if I wanted to play some eight ball. I have played a fair amount of pool in my life, and I ran off a couple of my best games ever, making radical cuts and table-length rail balls and even a massé shot. In a strange place, you tend to play pool very badly or very well. The skinny guy congratulated me in a sarcastic manner that suggested I might get my butt kicked after dark in the parking lot. When Dave Hall walked in the door a few minutes after five o'clock, the skinny guy went over and shook his hand. He was with the Mississippi Department of Fish and Game.

Toward evening more game wardens began arriving, dressed mostly in roughneck clothes. A couple of them puttered about in a surveillance van outside—something about a florist or a catering company, I can't remember what, was printed on its side—while Dave Hall set up a video camera and a microphone in the kitchen. He asked me to find the camera after it was concealed. I couldn't. It was inside a giant napkin box. I did notice that the splatter of thirty years of fry-cooking was sticking around the ceiling vent, covered with woolly black grime. Two black women cooks, one enormously tall and the other enormously fat, watched the proceedings with the barest of interest. They had seen it all before. Eventually a thickset white man, about fifty years old, wearing a clean white shirt and a cheap narrow-brimmed fedora of the type that Lee Marvin rarely took off during his years on *M Squad*, and smoking a stogie, wandered in. He actually looked a bit like Marvin. Dave Hall introduced him to me as Lonnie "Buck" Pridgen, the proprietor and his oldest friend. When Dave Hall mentioned that I was a reporter from California, Lonnie "Buck" Pridgen looked me over as if I were vermin. "Buck's a character," Dave Hall told me later on in the bar. "He acts real tough, but he's sort of a pussycat. His wife just left him a few weeks ago. She gave him a couple pieces of furniture. Ol Buck's livin with his mama now, around the corner. She's real old. Livin there with all that old lady chintz and all them doilies, smokin his stogies and pinin away for his no-good wife. He lived for her and for huntn ducks, and that was about it. Now it's just ducks. He and I used to go down to the Mississippi when we were kids—we still had a lot of ducks on the river back then—and hunt every day after school during waterfowl season. We'd lower a boat down those steep banks with a rope and jump in. We went out in any weather. We were out there once when a tornado came through and we about died. I think those were the best times of his life, and maybe mine, too. We liked it a lot more than dating girls. Buck is an extremely old-fashioned kind of guy. He's always had a strong sense of hunter ethics. He's real correct around women. He's a thousand percent for law and order. It all seems strange, this place of his being the dump that it is now, but it's true. There's a *bad* problem on this row with drug dealers and hookers and pimps. Go outside in a couple of hours, you'll see them up and down the street. I think ol Buck would as like to clean em out with a machine gun. He had a pimp hanging around one of his motel rooms just a few days ago. He went after that sucker with a baseball bat and about beat his brains out. This was a tough young black dude, but Buck ain't afraid of anybody when he gets mad. He loves to let us use this place for covert operations. It gives his life some meaning or somethin. I'm kinda worried about old Lonnie 'Buck' Pridgen right now, he's not in the best shape I've seen him in."

Dave Hall leaned in to me a bit. "You have to get used to old Buck," he admonished. "He acts a little rough, but ordinarily he wouldn't harm a fly. Like a lot of us southerners, he's still fightin the Civil War. To him, a *California* Yankee just might be the worst of all worlds. But all you got to do to get him to like you is ask to see his guns."

I asked right after dinner, a meal I will never forget. I can remember hoisting an onion ring on my fork and watching droplets of grease form on the bottom of it and rain on my plate in a small, steady stream. The steak could have resoled shoes. The salad dressing, poured over year-old lettuce, tasted like melted candy. I skipped dessert.

"That was a fine meal, Buck," I said.

"We do our best," said Buck.

"Could I see your guns?"

"Why? You want to start a revolution or somethin?"

"Dave says it's one of the finest collections in the South."

"It is." Lonnie "Buck" Pridgen led me out the door with an abrupt jerk of his head, which is his basic means of communication. If you told him that someone had bet you a hundred dollars you couldn't get him to say three words, his response would be the same as Calvin Coolidge's: "You lose." We walked in absolute silence a couple of blocks to his mother's house. It was a simple cottage in a humble neighborhood, crammed to the rafters with her old-lady bric-a-brac and Buck's stuffed ducks.

"You know this duck?" he asked, pointing to a redhead, which at the time I could not identify as a redhead. (I have since made a point of being able to identify damn near any duck.)

"No."

"Redhead. What about this one?"

"Merganser?"

"Pintail. This one?"

"Mallard?"

"Mallard. Right. At least you got one. What about him?"

"No idea."

"Teal. You ain't much of a duck hunter, are you?"

"No. I love ducks."

"Hunting is our heritage."

"I guess so."

"It's our birthright."

"Right."

"It's part of what's the matter with us today."

"What is?"

"Duck hunters goin extinct. That's why ducks are going extinct."

"You may be right."

"Damned right I'm right."

Buck led me upstairs to the attic. There were enough guns there to outfit a garrison. There were Civil War guns, buffalo guns, rimfires, World War I carbines, ancestral repeating rifles, giant-bore shotguns, fowling pieces, Colts, Lugers, Smith & Wessons, Harrington-Richardsons—about sixty of them lovingly identified by Buck over the course of half an hour as I stood by, feigning profound interest. He said he didn't know anymore how many he owned, but he guessed about eight hundred. "This country will never fall," he told me solemnly, "long as we keep our right to bear arms. Send a planeload of us boys over to Russia with our guns and we'll kick their Communist butts." We went downstairs again, and Buck introduced me to his mother, who was rocking in a chair, watching television. She was about the sweetest old lady I think I have ever met. Then we went back to the Redwood Inn. That was when I first learned what I was doing there.

"We've basically been after this gang for forty years," said Major James Gueho, aka Uncle Junior, the head of covert operations for the Louisiana Department of Wildlife and Fisheries. He was middle-sized and portly and bearded, a country-boy Falstaff, but he was all business and his eyes were cold. "They're really entrenched over there. But we've had one of our guys in the gang for the past few weeks. First time we ever successfully used covert operations on them. He's moving in deeper a little bit at a time. They're gonna make a delivery of about five hundred pounds of sacalait tonight. This here's our second big buy."

"Is your guy going to be one of the guys making the delivery?"

"Yeah. Try and guess which one."

"What do you want me to do?" I asked Dave Hall.

"That's right," he mused, having forgotten that he promised me some kind of role in this thing. He thought for a minute. "We'll give you a white apron and put you in the kitchen with me and Buck."

"What's a California Yankee doing in the kitchen of a place like this?"

"You can say you came down here to teach us how to do that California cuisine."

The Larto gang was supposed to arrive at midnight. We sat around for three hours, shooting pool, drinking (Dave Hall nursed one beer the entire time), and telling stories. A lot of undercover work is just sitting around, like a private detective whiling away hours in his car outside some errant husband's girlfriend's house. The stories were mostly about hunting, and often about blacks—who were often called niggers—hunting. Southerners can behave quite charitably toward blacks and be incorrigibly racist at the same time. I guess northerners can, too. One of the Mississippi wardens, the sweetest of the whole bunch, talked about his neighbor, an old black dwarf who was always hunting rabbits with his hounds. He could never keep up, and when the hounds got too far away, he flagged down the next car, hopped in with his shotgun almost half a height taller than he, and asked the driver, whoever he was—a salesman, a tourist—to stop every few hundred yards so he could listen for the dogs. When they bayed "rabbit," he thanked the driver courteously and hopped out. Everyone nearly died laughing. Dave Hall taped all of it; it would go into his voluminous library of southern folk history and outdoor memorabilia. Listening to stories like this is about the only time he seems genuinely happy and relaxed. Finally, at a few minutes to midnight, the telephone rang. The Larto gang was five minutes away.

I don't know what I was expecting. The same old Chevrolet coupe in which the gang had tried to outrun Willie Disch? A 1953 Hudson Hornet? A Barracuda? Somehow you don't expect a pair of Louisiana poachers to deliver a quarter ton of fish in a Pinto. The little car was so impossibly loaded that the rear bumper hung a couple of inches above the pavement, just like the Chevrolet coupe's. I saw why when I peered inside: a big deer—a buck—lay sprawled across the plastic ice bags filled with frozen sacalait. The driver, who said he was Darwin Book, was about six feet three, gaunt as Lincoln, missing a couple of teeth, filthy with grime and blood, and extremely nervous. The passenger introduced himself as Dave Trahan. He was about five feet ten, a bit more filled out than Darwin, wearing steel-rimmed glasses and a dirty pair of overalls and what can only be called a shit-eating grin. He was by far the more voluble of the two.

"God dawg!" Trahan literally burst into the kitchen. "We about ate it with the law back there on the Interstate." Trahan's accent was that of a warbling coon-ass, Darwin's a sullen hillbilly's. "De car ahead of us, man, dey smack this deer full broadside about a mile north of the Brookhaven exit. Darwin say, 'We got to get us dat deer.' I say, 'Hell, man, dey kilt it, it's dere deer.' Ol Darwin say, 'No, no, man, we gonna say we hit it too and finished it off, dat sucka is *our* deer.' We run on up, it's some lady in de other car, she doan know what to do with de deer, to leave it lay or what not. We say, 'Hey, now, we done smacked dat deer, we done give it de *coup de grâce*, we gonna drive off with it, if you doan mind, ma'am.' And dis lady, she doan know what to think, meanwhile old police cruiser come on by, slows down a bit, and we thinking, Oh, man, now we are *fucked!* but he done drove on off. Meanwhile, nother guy in a truck, he's stopped for de deer, too, he's about to load it up, so Darwin, he run on up and say, 'Hey, man, whatchoo doin wid dat sucker?' So we had us a little argument, but it's us two and him one, and we got us de deer. Darwin gutted it right off the highway. God dawg, man, I was impressed! Then before that we had us a flat tire, on account of all the weight, and oh, man, we got paranoid again. Dis car here, it's Darwin's girlfriend's, see, he just got him a spare before we came up or else we'd be sittin back dere with all this messa fish waitin for the highway patrol to help us out. Oh, man, what a trip! A few more like this one and I'm gonna have a coronary."

All of this came out of Trahan's mouth like gibberish. Uncle Junior and Jim Pridgen listened with amusement, but also, I thought, with a certain distaste for this guy.

"How many pounds are there?" asked Dave Hall. I had to begin thinking of him as Big Jim.

"Four hundred five pounds," said Darwin.

"This ought to be the time of year to be gettin em."

"They ain't doin too much now. I had to hustle to come up with this much. You ain't got a permit, Jim?"

"I ain't got no permit."

"Well, I had to ask. See, you get some of them Arkansas fish-farm permits, you just get some blank ones and write in the weight whenever we deliver, and if they check you, you can say these are farm fish. Works real good."

Big Jim Pridgen was supposed to be a lowlife hustler extraordinaire, so he didn't want to talk about bogus legalities, not quite yet.

"How much notice would you need to get a thousand pounds?"

"These here are a couple bags of bream," Trahan interjected. He and Uncle Junior were unloading the sacalait like firemen running a bucket brigade. The tiny hatchback seemed to hold a limitless number.

"Them white perch are good-size, too," said Darwin. "A week ahead we could get you a thousand pounds. Y'all don't got any of them permits, do you, Jim, hunh? Daddy told me to ask. If you got them, you'd be safe. See, we crossed a state line, and when you do that it's a federal offense, for you and me both."

"Dis is a *sure-nuff* felony federal offense." Trahan grinned.

"We got some good contacts up in Memphis," mused Big Jim almost to himself. "I know I can sell a thousand pounds up there. We can figure out some deal where you make some money and I make some, too. Trouble is, they catch you up there in Memphis, that's your *ass*."

"If they catch us *here*, you're gonna do time," admonished Darwin. "You're gonna do time *here*."

"Them lakes over in Louisiana, they just keep crankin out these fish, hunh? I hear you boys sell a damn lot of em."

"We get a lot, and we got a lot of people workin for us," said Darwin. "We take em all over the place. Chicago. Saint Louis."

"You never got into much trouble, though, hunh?"

"We got things pretty well taken care of over there, least we do now. You get lucky sometimes, too. I flipped a truck once, had three thousand pounds of fish in it. There was perch all over the road, man. They just gave me a two-hundred-dollar fine and gave my fish back to me." Darwin pulled hungrily on a cigarette. He was shivering.

"They didn't say it was illegal?"

"Didn't know or didn't care."

"Tell Big Jim how many deer you kilt last year, Darwin," Trahan said.

Darwin seemed extremely anxious to get out of there. He looked animal-like at all of us.

"Twenty-seven. Only two does."

"He blind-lights em is what he does," Trahan said gleefully. He launched into an extended description of how you spotlight deer, cruising around with a powerful portable headlamp until you see one; often you can freeze the creature without even getting out of the car—deer become absolutely paralyzed when a bright light is in their eyes—and shoot it from behind the wheel, using the side mirror to steady the rifle. Spotlighting deer is probably the most common serious game-law violation, claiming many hundreds of thousands of deer every year, nationwide, and Dave Hall's office has prosecuted hundreds of poachers for doing it, but he listened with what seemed like genuine interest, as if he had never heard of the technique before.

All the while I could see the black eye of the video camera watching us from inside the napkin box. The thing looked nakedly exposed to me, now that I knew where it was, but neither Darwin nor Trahan seemed to feel the slightest suspicion that they were being filmed or taped. Finally, at about one-thirty in the morning, Dave Hall reached for his wad and dealt Darwin $506.25 for the fish and the deer, and he and Trahan climbed into the battered little car and drove away. Dave Hall almost ran to the tape recorder to see if it had picked everything up. Then he shoehorned out the video camera and began replaying the scene. I believe these videos are a far greater entertainment to him than movies.

Gueho had been eyeing me since Darwin and Trahan left, as if to judge my reaction to the whole affair.

"Not quite as exciting as you thought undercover work was gonna be?"

"Interesting, but not really *exciting*, no."

"It can get exciting. More than you want. What did you think of that pair?"

"Darwin I could tolerate. The other guy was a rip-snorting asshole."

"Thought he was an asshole, huh?"

"Didn't you?"

"Sure enough did."

"Maybe if he'd've wiped off that shit-eating grin now and then."

"I happen to know he's been workin pretty hard on that grin."

"Well, such a dude is gonna make us Yankees feel some prejudice against southerners. I hope you lock him up good so—"

"Been workin at being an asshole, too."

It dawned on me. What an idiot. *What an idiot!*

"You did say that one of these guys was going to be your man . . ."

Gueho, who had been almost utterly mirthless up until then, began to shudder like a big bowl of Jell-O in a moderate earthquake. I had never seen someone convulsed in laughter not actually laugh.

"Yup."

"And it wasn't Darwin, was it?"

"Nope."

The next morning, on four hours of fitful sleep, I drove down to Natchez to meet Dave Hall and Lieutenant David Tullos of the covert operations unit of the Louisiana Department of Wildlife and Fisheries, aka Dave Trahan. After Tullos and Darwin had left, Dave Hall told me that Tullos and Gueho had started working a case on a river rat named Sam Ferry, who lived across the Mississippi from Natchez on the wrong side of the levee with a verminous brood of sons and daughters and cousins and brothers, and that no deer, duck, goose, alligator, heron, egret, squirrel, rabbit, crow, raccoon, or turtle had much chance of survival if it wandered within Ferry habitat. "They're like the mountain men," Tullos had told Dave Hall. "Eat just about anything except night crawlers. Old Sam, for all I know, he could be a cannibal. I'm a country boy myself, but these people are way below country on the ladder of evolution."

Dave Hall said Tullos had managed to persuade Sam Ferry to take him duck hunting the next day, and he was going to go, too. "If this here wasn't exciting enough for you, then you ought to come with us. See some of the people we got to fraternize with on this job. Tullos says Sam Ferry is as bad-lookin a dude as you'll find in these parts. He says he looks like he stepped off the screen in that movie, the one about the city boys who go rafting and run into the mountain men, what was it called . . . ?"

"Deliverance."

"That one. Them two mountain men, remember?"

"Jesus."

"I don't know what it's gonna be like or what kind of humbug we might get ourselves into, but these people are blastin a big hole in the migratory waterfowl around those parts, so we ought to check em out. You can come or not, but you got to assume all risk cause they sound like bad dudes."

"Can I carry a piece?"

"We're all gonna be heftin shotguns."

"I mean a pistol."

"I can't let you. You'd have to be deputized. Anyway, it's gonna be all right. I'll probably have two pistols on me, and Tullos will have his. If there's any humbug, we're gonna have the advantage."

"Even if we're outnumbered?"

"We've been trained for this type of thing."

"Will you arrest them all?"

"I doubt it. This here is just reconnaissance. Besides, they might not do anything illegal."

After a typical country breakfast at a truck stop—a serving of scrapple and eggs that could have caused an elephant coronary, washed down by coffee too weak to revive a fibrillating mouse—I drove west out of Jackson on Interstate 20. Interstate highways look worse in the South than anywhere else because the vegetation is so verdant. In blond western deserts, and on the sere Plains, you hardly notice interstates, and the Eastern Seaboard is so cemented over you hardly care, but in the South such a highway is like a slash across a face. I pulled off the Interstate twenty miles out of Jackson and got on the Natchez Trace, a federal parkway that cuts diagonally across western Mississippi. Aside from the Blue Ridge Parkway, the Natchez Trace is probably the most picturesque road in the South. In De Soto's time it was already a well-traveled Indian trail, and De Soto followed it for a ways, murdering Indians on sight, until he died of a fever amid a sprawling Mississippi flood. Meriwether Lewis died here, too, either by his own hand or as a victim of highwaymen. In the nineteenth century there were so many bandits lurking in the surrounding forest that the Natchez Trace was supposed to be the most dangerous road east of the Mississippi. On a cold and brilliant December day in 1985, it was peopled by only a few leisurely drivers and a clutch of puffing locals running a charity marathon. There were no bandits. Hamadryads seemed to hover in the spacious woods, which, on closer examination, proved not so spacious; the National Park Service has a narrow right-of-way, and at its edge, beyond the leafless trees, I could see brick ranchettes and a Wal-Mart the size of the Pentagon going up. The southern hardwood forest was our most efflorescent wilderness, a wonderfully diverse community of animals and plants—some oaks were ten to twelve feet in diameter, like redwood trees—but today there are only a few virgin square miles left; most of the rural South is corn and soybean fields and the tree farms timber companies brag about in magazines ("We plant twenty trees for each one we cut!"), without showing you what they really look like—coniferous corn.

Natchez, one of the prettier towns in the middle South, sits on the bluff side of the Mississippi. Louisiana, across the river, is level as a pond—the colossal Mississippi River levee is the highest point of land—but the Mississippi did not dump millennia's worth of alluvial overflow across the state that borrowed its name, so the two banks represent topographically different worlds: on the Mississippi side you have relief, bluffs and creek hollows and almost-hills, while Louisiana is baking-pan flat. In a social sense, the contrast is even more extreme. Natchez, once the richest town anywhere in the South, the center of the cotton empire, is still quite flush, its economy now based on residual wealth and tourism rather than slaves, while Vidalia, which sits on the Louisiana bank beneath its haughty sister, looks Third World. Somewhere over there, almost within view, in a stilted shack facing the river's full flood rise, lived the gap-toothed hillbillies with whom I was to go out murdering ducks that afternoon. Behind me, in the parking lot of the red-brick Ramada Hilltop Inn, a couple of buses were disgorging tourists from distant locales, resplendent in polyester finery.

Dave Hall's blue Ford LTD was nosed into a slot at the end of one motel wing. I knocked, the door opened, and the threshold was filled by a grin. David Tullos looked exactly as he had the night before, and the motormouth was still turning at maximum RPMs.

"Hey!"

"Good to meet you."

"Hey, man, it's good to meet a Yankee. Sorry I couldn't introduce myself last night."

"You were great."

"Now they say I fooled you."

"You did."

"They didn't tell you who I was?"

"They did, but I forgot."

"You *forgot!* Dawg, I must've gave you the red ass."

"You fooled Darwin, I guess that's what counts."

"I guess so, too, but I had my doubts for a while."

"It looked to me like you had him completely short-sheeted."

"No, not there at the inn but back in the car. Damned drug-snortin, fish-smellin, hillbilly hippie Darwin—"

"Darwin was snorting cocaine?"

"Not that stuff. Pot. Marijuana. He smokes that reefer like Buck Pridgen draws on those nasty cigars. All the way up in the car, he was suckin away and blowin like a smokestack. He kept offerin that shit to me, but I've never smoked it, wouldn't even know how, and besides, all Darwin got to say in court is this game warden was smokin reefer with him, and the judge and jury think, Oh, yeah, that's bad moral character, unprofessional, probable entrapment, whoo! But Darwin's buddies, they all smoke that stuff, so I had to make up a little story on the spot, and I came up with this thing about my poor mama and how she died. 'Darwin,' I say, 'I used to smoke that shit all the time, man, until they caught me and threw me in the reformatory for three weeks. It was while I was in there that my mama done passed away. Just all of a sudden like that, and I can't ever, ever see her again. One of her last words was "I can't see my boy!" Man, I just can't smoke it no more. The stuff makes me think of my mama and I get crazy and weepy.' And ol Darwin said, 'Oh, man! I understand! I understand!' and like that. I passed that grade. That Darwin Book, he is one fine piece of work. Like on the way back to Larto Lake from the Redwood Inn, we were ten miles out of Natchez when his pecker about popped out of his pants, he was thinkin about Nellie Jackson's, that's the local whorehouse, he figured he come into some fast bucks and he wanted to unload his wad right away like all these bush rednecks do, he says to me, 'Come on! Come on, man, let's spend at least that hundred we made on dat deer, that's lagniappe, man, we wasn't expectin that!' So I got to poop the party one more time—you can't have an undercover game warden going to a whorehouse, that don't do wonders for your moral credibility—but man, I had to be fast on my feet this time, I say to him, '*Look* at you, man! You all covered up with *blood* and *guts* and you smell like goddamn *dead animals*, you want to go to Nellie Jackson's like this with deer blood all over our clothes, they're gonna guess we just *killed* someone. They gonna think we're a couple of sure-nuff crazy killers on a spree and call the cops on us.' See, now I had to tell Darwin I was single. If I said I had a wife, they coulda pinned me down, found out where I lived or tried to, snooped around, and maybe they would've found someone who knows I'm an undercover agent, you know. So I'm always single and I always have a shifty address. But now, someone like old Darwin Book, he thinks any single boy who won't go to a whorehouse is either queer or *crazy*. So I had to keep it up about all the blood and guts and how we was gonna get pinched in there with our peckers up and our pants down and maybe they'd try to pin some unsolved murder case on us, the Mississippi law is worse than the police they got in Louisiana and all that. That got him kind of scared, so he gave in. It was close, though."

In New York City, you get a cabdriver like David Tullos now and then, someone who has you where he wants you and tells you stories until you are pulverized. That Tullos didn't know me from Adam and had met me seconds earlier didn't faze him in the slightest. He knew I was writing a book, and his ego was large enough to fill every cubic inch of its half-formed architecture. Dave Hall, meanwhile, was in the back of the room paying no attention the whole time Tullos held forth; he was futzing with a piece of video equipment that had been causing him some kind of chronic trouble.

As usual, he was all business. "We ought to get movin."

"Let's go," said Tullos. He was wearing a greenish set of Farmer John overalls, a white shirt, and a pair of gum boots under a checkered shirt-jacket. The effect was almost clownish, as if he were a four-year-old out for a romp in the playlot instead of a game warden on a deep-undercover job.

"These boys ever say anything to you about them clothes you wear?" asked Dave Hall.

"They think I'm some kinda fashion dandy."

"Hey, we got to get our cover straight," said Dave Hall. "I'm gonna be Dave Hayes again on this thing."

"You can be whoever you want," said Tullos. "I'm stuck with bein Dave Trahan, though I wouldn't mind trying some other alibi. Hey, wait a minute, you can't be Dave Hayes!"

"Why not?"

"Cause these Ferrys know all the Larto gang, and they're gonna know you as Big Jim cause of the deal last night with the fish."

"You're right," said Dave Hall. I would have felt better if they had figured all this out earlier.

"Besides, what am I talking about, Darwin and Beetle talked about you last night when we got back to Larto Lake. And before that. You were already Big Jim." Tullos turned to me. "See, Beetle didn't like us making the delivery in Mississippi cause we were crossing state lines. That's a federal offense. That's why I arranged the whole thing—cause these clowns never get put in jail by the so-called local justice. Ol Beetle, he said, just as we were fixin to drive off to Jackson with all those fish, he say, 'Darwin, I'm kinda leery about this. They could be settin us up for a federal offense.' And I'm just lookin straight ahead and, whoo, boy, I'm glad my pants stayed dry. But when we got back late last night, ol Darwin, he said, 'Daddy, I wished you'd've met this Jim Pridgen. He is *sneaky*, man. Always pacin and duckin like a raccoon. He don't even have a telephone. He's on the lam from his woman and the law for I don't know what. And his brother Buck—if he ain't a killer, I don't know *what* he is, cause he looks *mean*, man. You don't got to worry about these Pridgens, Daddy, them boys are a couple of genuine *hoodlums*.'"

It was the first of Tullos's stories at which Dave Hall smiled, because it was about himself. "That Jim Pridgen, he is some heavy-duty outlaw, hunh?" he said.

Tullos asked me if I was ready for a real undercover job. I said I thought I was but was a little worried about doing something wrong. I didn't say *panicking*.

"Don't sweat that. You've got the habilité. This ain't going to be quite like last night, though."

Why not? I knew the answer.

"First, you ain't never seen someone as ugly as Sam Ferry. He make rat-faced ol Darwin Book look like Liberace. Sam's got a bunch of brothers; they're all part-time oil-rig workers and tough as shit. They could come along, I don't know. We're gonna be with them in the bayou with a lot of guns, and it's gonna be *boom, bang, pow*."

I didn't know we were going with the brothers. I thought it was going to be the three of us and Sam Ferry.

"You'll do fine, though. Just treat it like any other chasse au canard."

It had been years since I'd hunted anything, and I really can't kill ducks. I can't eat them, either. I would have to shoot to miss, though that might come naturally.

"If Dave and I make like to shoot anything that moves, don't let that bother you, man. We got to play the killin fools."

"Who am I supposed to be?"

Dave Hall said, "You can be my buddy from California. We're in the oil-leasing business together. You don't got to know anything about oil leasing. These dirtbags are too ignorant to know anything about it themselves. Just act like this is all new to you."

Tullos said, "I don't know, man, those brothers have been around oil all their lives. They may know a bit."

"Yeah, but not about oil *leasing*. That stuff is so Greek to them they ain't got the concentration to learn anything about it."

"Hell, he's from California; we can say he's a movie star. 'Hey, doncha know Marc Reisner, he's on *Hill Street Blues* every week, man!' These suckers will believe anything about California."

• • •

Park Avenue debouching into East Harlem, Piedmont cheek by jowl with North Oakland, the North Shore upwind from the South Side housing projects—none of these urban contrasts quite prepares you for the worlds within worlds in the rural South. On one riverbank stands Natchez, with its resplendent gardens and mansions, its plantation-inspired Ramada and Hilton inns—its colonnaded Days Inn, for God's sake—its organized tour groups of Germans and Japanese, its hoop-skirted matrons leading formal house tours. On the other side, Vidalia, where the better-looking homes qualify as Natchez shacks, where the poor live in dressed-up pigsties, and where the river rats like Sam Ferry live in elevated hovels on the wrong side of the levee, shacks built of a few poached slats nailed to some plywood planks, with a cheap corrugated roof covered by a plastic sheet held down by bricks, the whole precarious scrap edifice standing on stilts that would probably splinter during severe lovemaking or wash away during a moderate Mississippi flood.

We drove by several of these shanties as we went out of Vidalia on the crest of the giant earthen bulwark, which is wide enough for two cars to pass. "The wrong side of the levee," fretted Dave Hall. "Hell of a way to live! The problem with these people is they got no sense of *management.* They aren't necessarily *bad* people, though some of them are. They just don't want anything to do with what you'd call civilization. They don't want a real job. They may plant a pea garden, but they don't want to run a farm. Look over there. That's cow pasture protected by the levee, when *they're* not! *Cows* have a higher goddamned social status than they do, and they don't care. All they want is to get by easy. Pay no taxes, obey no laws. Some of them make pretty good money trappin and fishin and sellin illegal waterfowl, and hell, their expenses are low. But they ain't gonna take that money and save it or invest in some property. A lot of em never saw the inside of a bank. They never wrote a check. It's all here today and gone tomorrow with these hillbilly-types."

Tullos said, "This here is sure-nuff Faulkner country, still today, it is."

The levee curved away from the main Mississippi and followed a long oxbow. "His little shack is right here somewhere," said Tullos. "That one!"

It was no different from the other wrong-side-of-the-levee shanties we had passed, though perhaps a bit larger. The big new LTD seemed utterly incongruous parked out on the weedy drive. About three minutes passed before Sam came out of his elevated shack, fixing his threadbare shirt inside his baggy black trousers. He came down the rickety steps with a slightly arthritic bounce. Sam Ferry was in his early fifties, I would have guessed, about six feet tall and strongly built. He had a neatly trimmed mustache riding a couple days of beard stubble. He was actually fairly presentable with his mouth closed. He smiled wolfishly as he shook hands with Tullos and then Dave Hall and me, displaying large spaces and black gums where there ought to have been teeth. A wad of chewing tobacco lodged in his cheek like a tumor. He stank.

The yard in which we were standing looked as if a tornado had brought over every appliance within five miles, about twenty years before. There were two penned mules in the yard and a homemade houseboat, which some river people keep for emergency quarters during floods. A respectable-looking truck sat in the drive, and through the woods behind the shack—woods that are often underwater but were now dry—I saw a couple of aluminum boats with powerful outboards on their transoms. The trees were painted with silt lines about ten or eleven feet high. Out back was a small fenced garden and some chicken and pig sheds.

"Pleased to meetcha," Sam was saying.

"Jim Pridgen," said Dave Hall. "And this here's Mark Rice. Brought us down a Yankee from California today. He can't believe that some of us people down here in the South still live off the land."

Sam squinted and gave me his best Pepsodent grin.

"I'm a partner of Jim's in the oil-leasing business," I said, which was totally stupid and unnecessary, and I almost lost it on the "Jim."

Sam grunted. His family, or whoever they were, had come up to us. Besides his squat, squawlike wife, there were a teenage girl with a voluptuous body and a brutally misshapen face, an older girl who wasn't bad-looking and had an engaging, taunting smile, an obviously retarded fat boy of about fourteen, and three of the meanest, roughest, most blackhearted-looking rednecks who could possibly exist.

Sam introduced us. The two girls and the retarded boy were his children. He had more. The evil caricatures were his younger brothers. He had more of them, too. Not one of them had a firm handshake.

"Here for a little duck hunting?" Sam offered.

"Trahan here says you know this bayou inside and out and got a boat, so we figured it would be good to have you as a guide. Mark here, he ain't ever been duck huntin' before."

"Naw!" said Sam. "I thought everybody'd been duck huntin."

"Quail, grouse, you name it," I said. "Never ducks."

"Well, they ain't gonna be flyin till around four, but we can get over to the island and get set up."

Dave Hall and Tullos went to the car and got their heavy shotguns out of the back seat—the trunk was full of incriminating equipment and couldn't be opened under any circumstances—and two of Sam's brothers went back to the house and got their guns and Sam's, a gigantic old long-barreled single-shot that took a special shell. Then we began walking over to the boats—four of them, three of us, and me unarmed. The closer we got to the boats the more certain I was that they were play-acting just like we were, that our cover had already been blown, and they were leading us to an underwater grave. Who was zooming whom?

Sam's aluminum boat was flat-bottomed and beamy. It was surprisingly spacious. The motor had the cowling removed and was very loud. It looked big enough to put out a hundred horsepower. The oxbow at whose edge we stood was nearly as wide as the main Mississippi channel, and several miles long, going north and west. We shot across it in tandem with the brothers' boat toward the opposite bank, where a solid wall of trees stood. Sam was going full-throttle right to where we should have smacked the shore, but I realized, after momentary heart failure, that there was no shore. The trees all stood in several feet of water. Sam throttled down quickly and we made a giddy, twisty course between the trees and around deadfall. Old bleach bottles were hung and posted everywhere as markers; you could easily get lost in here. The trees were big stately hardwoods, mostly oak and pecan, but a few large cypress still stood, cypress that must have been at least a couple of hundred years old. I looked back and couldn't see open water anymore. We were completely enveloped by the forest, as if a set of bars had clanked down behind us.

Sam's brothers had split from our course before we entered the drowned forest. I caught a last glimpse of their boat, trailing bubbles and hydrocarbon vapors in its wake; then it was obscured. This, I thought, must be part of the plan, something to put us off guard. The brothers might be going back for long-range rifles to pick us off later on, so even our heavy-bore shotguns wouldn't do us any good. I forced myself to think about something else, or my nerves wouldn't have survived even this routine little caper. That was what Dave Hall had called it in the car. Surely, if he had said that, he wasn't expecting any trouble. Not really. Surely he and Tullos would sense it if they suspected us.

"Them game wardens give you much trouble around here?" Dave Hall asked Sam.

I paled.

"Nah," said Sam, spitting a goober into the water. "Not much trouble. We been rough on them motherfuckers."

"You give them bastards a hard time, hunh?"

"Yes, sir. Not like we used to, though. It used to be them fuckers would *never* come in here after dark."

"Age kind of mellowed you out a bit, huh?"

Sam wasn't sure whether he ought to take this as an insult. "Maybe. But I'd still shoot a fuckin duck off the bow of a game warden's boat."

"Man, I tell you, that is something I just do not *understand*," said Dave Hall with utter conviction. "Who the *hell* would want to be a goddamn *game* warden?"

"We get more trouble from the fuckin state warden now than from them federal ones," Sam averred. "We had it real quiet there for a while. Had it so they left us alone, pretty much. But they got some new guy now out of Ferriday, big tall motherfucker, and he's been givin us trouble again. Sumbitch knows better than to come in here at night, though." Sam grinned toothlessly.

Dave Hall pulled up his jacket. He was wearing a belt with a big brass buckle that read GARDE-CHASSE. It was an official province of Quebec game warden's belt buckle.

"Look at this here," he chortled.

"Well, goddamn it!" said Sam. "Where'd you get it?" Sam knew some French.

"Buddy of mine gave it to me," he said. "He told me it came from some game warden who got himself revenge-killed."

Sam guffawed.

It is uncanny how easily one becomes disoriented in a drowned bottomland forest. The trees all look the same, and there are no ground features—stumps, rocks, ravines—that help you get your bearings. And in a moving boat you are constantly watching for obstacles, weaving and doubling back, and you lose all sense of where you have been. Even Sam Ferry, who had lived there all his life, always checked the suspended bleach bottles to orient himself and stayed along the plastic trail. At the prevailing water level, he told us, the strip of forest that had gone underwater was only a mile or so wide, but left to myself I probably would have circled around in there for a week and a half before finding a way out.

Sam found a spot he liked—there was a break in the treetop canopy that would let us shoot at overflying ducks when they began coming in to roost—and shut the motor off. There had been a wind blowing back in Natchez (which seemed two thousand miles away, even though it was almost within rifle range), but where we were it was indescribably still. It was not the quiet of an Everglades sedge or mangrove border; there is an Impressionist light throughout the Everglades, a mottled openness, a quiet, expansive sense of freedom; here the stillness was dark and heavy and dank. Sitting there in the boat I felt suspended: the forest canopy sealed us off from the sky; the scum-frosted water denied us the reassurance of the earth.

We heard the odd, shrill, unducklike whistles of a pair of wood ducks. "Them fuckin woodies ain't got no sense," Sam said. "They're easy to kill but hard to see."

Dave Hall said, "I bet you can kill a lot of them wood ducks in here. This here is wood duck Shangri-la, man, with all them wild nuts."

Sam said, "I blasted forty-four of them motherfuckas in one day once."

The mark of a good undercover game warden is to react to such a remark without the slightest split-second hint of disgust; that is why they are few. Dave Hall grinned leeringly and said, "Man, that's the kind of shootin I would love to do. I ain't never had a bag like that."

"And that was shootin' em," Sam said haughtily. "When we trap em over bait, we can do a hell of a lot better than that."

"Man, I ain't heard of anything like that since the market hunters," said Tullos. "I thought those days was gone."

"Not around here, they ain't. We could kill ducks twenty-four hours a day and not dent em. And we *got* ducks year round, too, especially woodies."

"I bet you're good at trappin them ducks," said Dave Hall.

"We're river rats," said Sam. "We can trap, shoot, fish, run a boat, outwit them game wardens"—he grinned savagely—"and just about do it all, man, so long as it's about livin off the land."

"You really make a living off the land?" I ventured.

Sam shot me too long a stare. "Well, now, I don't know what you'd call a living. In California, seems to me everyone out there is a fuckin millionaire. I make a living, yeah. We ain't starving. You saw my house. It ain't no great house. You might not even call it a house. To build a real house you got to have somethin. I ain't got nothin. And I don't *want* nothin. It's just somethin to worry about. You got a nice car, you got to worry about it being smashed. I want to get by, and I don't want no motherfucker tellin me what to do." He launched another slug of brown spit into the swamp. "Them are my goals."

"I can appreciate that."

"Now that island over there, through them trees. That belongs to a bunch of rich folks. They bought it a few years ago and say we can't hunt there. Well, shit, my daddy settled us in these parts fifty years ago, and we always hunted there. That island has put a lot of food on the table. So what am I gonna do when they tell me I can't hunt there anymore? *I'm gonna go on huntin there*—that's what I'm gonna do!"

"A man's got to eat," said Dave Hall. "You ain't gonna be excluded from nature's table just because you ain't rich."

"Fuckin right."

"Whereabouts did your daddy come from?" I asked.

Sam ignored the question. "We got to lay low, though, durin huntin season, cause they post their own damn game warden over there. Some of them private game dicks can be a bigger pain in the ass than these wild and fisheries boys."

Sam paused a moment, then said, "My daddy came here from Italy. He was a dago sonofabitch. Ferry's a bastard name. In Italy it was somethin else. Raised up nine of us. And a lot of that time he warn't even there."

"He was a travelin man?" asked Dave Hall.

"No. He got sent up. Got sent up to the penitentiary."

"For what?"

"Killin a man. He did a paid killin once and got fingered, and they put him away for some long years."

"He must have been some tough coon-ass," said Tullos.

"He was. And a good provider. He figured there ain't nothin wrong with killin a guy if the money is gonna feed his family." Sam threw all of us a taunting look. "And I tell you what, I ain't no different. I'd go kill somebody if the price was right. Most of us would. Tell me that ain't so!"

"You got to be right, there," said Dave Hall solemnly. "Most of us probably would."

The thought of looking into this murderous hillbilly's black hole of a mouth just before the blur of shrapnel screamed out of the barrel and sang my head away was more than I could handle. I tried to think of something else. All I could think about, though, was how I would have liked to take Sam Ferry and heave him off the edge of a cliff. Or hold his head in duck dung until he had been asphyxiated. Hatfields and McCoys are romantic until you hear the twistedness in their hearts and smell the stink of their sweat.

Dave Hall was more interested in Sam's exploits as a poacher. Sam was soon telling us about jacklighting deer ("I shot eight of them fuckers in one night; made a good pile of money off them"); about stringing monofilament nets between trees at levels where wood ducks tend to fly, then herding clusters of them into the nets; about setting traps full of bait for swimming mallards; about seine-netting fish in the river right below Natchez; about standing at the locks downriver with a big-beam flashlight at three in the morning and spearing trapped channel catfish and paddlefish and garfish (which can weigh over two hundred pounds) with a gaff; about the old days when they used to wing alligators with a .22 (he seemed to have given that up). He ended, somehow, by talking about Nellie Jackson's whorehouse. "Nellie brought a lot of us up," he said. I didn't want to think about what it would be like to be in bed with a woman who had been in bed with Sam.

Tullos went to work then. "Man, I kin hardly believe that shit! I ain't never heard of that monofilament trick!"

Sam swallowed the bait. "Well, you don't believe me, I'll show you sometime."

"I got to come up for that. That is one trick I never saw." I had forgotten that both Dave Hall and Tullos were wired. They were always building their case.

The temperature was about thirty-four. I had on hip-length waders over tight dungarees, and I could have been standing in ice water. I was uncomfortable and showed it.

Tullos looked at me and said, "They got a swamp like this on Beverly Hills Drive?"

Sam guffawed. He had never heard anything so funny.

"You remind me of my brother-in-law from Missouri," he said to me.

"How come?"

"I don't know. You just do. He come down here, and he can't believe the way we live either."

"I'll tell you one thing, Mister Sam. I didn't believe it when D"—the *D* came out before I stammered in a *JIM*—"when Jim told me about it, how you folks still live off the land."

I was stricken. Dave Hall paid no mind, however, and Sam didn't seem to catch it. I decided to shut up for the rest of the day.

"I ain't Mister. Just call me Sam."

"OK. Sam."

"Bet you never dreamed a place like this even existed anymore."

"I didn't."

"You sure do remind me of my brother-in-law," he said again, grinning his black and raw-red gap.

In the next three seconds a small flock of ducks came racing over the trees, three shotgun barrels whirled and pointed skyward, five deafening booms murdered the stillness of the air—followed by two more—and the ducks banked wildly and flew on unharmed. I was still recovering from the shock when a rain of shot trinkled into the water a few yards from the boat.

"God*damn!*" said Dave Hall. Unlike many of his fellow wildlife agents, he still loves to hunt on the job and hates to miss.

"They're gonna start flyin' now," said Ferry.

The hunters opened the breeches of their guns, and blue smoke came out with the spent shells. It's hard to believe that a three-inch shell can make a sound like an atomic bomb.

It dawned on me that the other two blasts came from Sam's brothers' guns. They were close by again.

"Well, we bit it," said Dave Hall.

"We can't leave here without gettin a duck," said Sam.

"I guess it ain't legal, but it's still a little light."

"Fuck that! Fuck that!" said Sam.

A squirrel chirruped in a nearby tree. Tullos looked its way avidly. The squirrel was high in the branches, but it seemed intent on making its way down.

"Hey, Sam, can I shoot a squirrel?" Tullos asked.

"Fuck, yeah!"

We sat stock-still. The squirrel danced down a few feet, stopped and peered at us, sprang to the next lower limb, and stopped again. It was almost within shotgun range. Poor little idiot, I thought. It jumped to a higher branch, but then I saw that it was trying to get to another tree closer to our boat. It made a line-drive leap and clutched some whippet branches, then clambered up to a groin near the trunk, then plastered itself against the trunk, its back pointed at us.

Tullos's gun boomed.

The squirrel went flat as a road kill, then rebounded as if launched from a trampoline and dropped like a rock in the water. When we poled over to it and retrieved it, it was spread-eagled and slightly pancaked by the blast, as if someone had prepared it for mounting. Its body was pocked by two dozen pellets.

"Iced that muthafucka good." Sam grinned.

"Love me a squirrel," said Tullos. He eats a lot of them.

We waited. It was just light enough to see. I heard the whistling of their wings even before I saw the ducks, then heard the great deep-throated blasts. There were five or six ducks, small ducks—wood ducks, probably—and one was hit. His wing beats stopped momentarily, he dropped a few feet and glided, he flapped frantically to avoid a tree, he peeled off listlessly to the right, falling, and crashed into the branches of another tree. He pinwheeled downward, still trying to fly. We heard a splash. Somewhere in the middle of this, Dave Hall had calmly said, "He's a head-shot." And I had asked, "How can you tell?" And he had said, "You just can."

The duck's small form was on the water about forty yards away. It was trying to swim away. "Blast it again!" Sam whined. Tullos aimed at it and fired. The shot must have gone right under the duck's feet because he went out of the water. A ring of ripples came at us; we could hear them splashing against the trees. The little duck was still alive and still trying to swim away.

Tullos grabbed the oar and began poling and paddling toward the duck while he stood in the middle of the boat. He switched from one side to the other with the effortless skill of a river pilot. We came within twenty feet of the duck, swimming in quiet little circles near a large tree. You could sense its desperation, but its brain was no longer working well and there wasn't much it could do. It was still light enough to make out the brilliant plumage. It was a wood duck, a red-eyed male, in full breeding splendor. He was beautiful.

"Smash it with the paddle!" Sam yelled.

Tullos raised the oar. The duck saw it coming and redoubled its effort to swim. It was making a strange little sound, a gurgle or a stifled quack. The oar came down, hard, and the duck disappeared. It bobbed up on its side. It righted itself feebly and kept paddling away. You could see its little webbed feet pushing air as its head sank underwater.

Tullos reached out and grabbed it. The duck squalled and flapped and for a last moment seemed fully alive.

With clinical interest, Sam said, "Twist his neck. Just twist the moth-erfucker's neck." Tullos grabbed the duck's head and twirled it like a bola. The head came off. The rest of the duck flew down into the bottom of the boat with the neck bone sticking out and its wings flapping convulsively several more times. The headless duck heaved itself halfway across the boat on its paddling wings and banged into Dave Hall's leg, where it was finally still. In Tullos's hand, the duck's head's bill still opened and closed. It was, for a moment, a creature twice dying.

The motor didn't start. Finally it did, but it died quickly. Tullos poled us toward the open bayou as Sam fiddled clumsily with the ignition in the dark. He would get it running and the boat would race a few feet and would stop. We crashed into everything in sight. We saw a light coming at us through the trees, and for a moment I thought this is where they would try to kill us, but it was only little Sam, the retarded boy, in the brothers' boat. The motor caught as if it had only wanted company, and we headed out, going too fast. We thumped violently over floating logs, and branches whipped my face and drew blood. From behind, little Sam looked like a pumpkin. Sam Ferry opened the throttle when we finally reached open water, and we were back at his landing just as the early night turned pitch-black. Tullos and Sam walked down the dirt road to his sister's house so Tullos could buy some turtle meat. The first rule of undercover wildlife-law enforcement is always to buy something, legal or not. I walked, with inexpressible relief, with Dave Hall to the car.

In the car, I still didn't dare say anything; I thought I might violate some cardinal rule. But finally he spoke. His whole manner had changed drastically. He sounded very weary.

"Real outlaws, aren't they?"

"God almighty!"

"If we didn't stop these kind of people, there wouldn't be anything left. They'd rape the last resource and leave the bleached bones and just shrug. They talk about these trashy country people having pride. These people ain't got pride. How do you think that boy of his got to be an idiot?"

"Incest?"

"More than probable. Happens all the time."

Dave Hall suddenly seemed so weary I thought he would collapse. He sunk his chin onto his chest and appeared ready to go to sleep. Then he gave a start.

"You know what's going to happen with this sucker? I'm gonna bust his ass, stick him in jail for a few months, and then I'm gonna turn him, just like I did Woody Dufrene."

"How do you know that?"

"I just know. There ain't many outlaws I can't turn, and this one is a prime candidate."

"Dave, do you think we were in any danger out there? I mean, with the brothers and everything? I mean, look, I'll admit to you, I still have the creeps just being here on their property—"

"It ain't their property. They're tolerated squatters. I wasn't worried out there, and I'm not worried now. If you let a little caper like this worry you, you'd go nuts in this business." He paused a second, looked in the rearview mirror to see if anyone was near the car, and said, "But don't think for a minute that old Sam Ferry and his goon brothers wouldn't blow out your chest with that long barrel and drop you in a net with four hundred pounds of old car batteries and go home and eat a squirrel dinner. You heard what he said about killin someone for the right price."

"How many laws did we break out there?"

"Shooting after sundown, but that's nothin. Someone down the bayou was using unplugged guns, his brothers probably, but that ain't worth it either. You heard what he said about jacklightin eight deer in one night and those duck nets and whatnot. And how he hasn't bought meat in years. This sucker is feeding his family off the land and probably making most of his living, his cash living, off it, too. We'll get him on something more serious than shooting after dark. But to tell you the truth, I'm really not interested in this asshole."

"Why not?"

"I want the big boys. I want the local politicians he sells his fish and deer meat to. I want the ones who ship tens of thousands of pounds of fish and game out of here every year. I want the ones who buy off the sheriff, the judges, the D.A.—and I want *them*."

"Then you don't really give a damn about arresting Sam?"

"Oh, no! I want him. I want him *bad*."

Tullos had been in the house a long time. I said, "Do you think Dave is all right?"

Dave Hall gave a little indulgent smile and said, "Well, let's go see."

Sam's sister's house was built up on cement blocks rather than stilts, which gave it a palatial air. It also had a better coat of paint. On the inside, it was surprisingly neat. A huge wood-burning stove dominated the living room, which had only a couple of cheap couches and a fake-wood coffee table, the kind that one might steal from a motel. On the porch outside was a very large freezer. On the way in the door I caught a glimpse of the bedroom—there was only one—with mattresses every-where. Unless there was another room off in the back, everyone slept together. Tullos was in the kitchen, charming Sam's sister with one of his coon-ass stories. Sam's sister was in her forties, plump but not fat, and bleached blond. She was wearing tight blue shorts and a cheap tank top, even though it was the middle of winter; the house temperature was probably eighty-five degrees. You could picture her behind the wheel of an old square-edged motor home while her husband lay drunk in the back. Dave Hall started telling her about chasing the wood duck through the darkness of the drowned woods and how the motor hadn't started.

"It's fun," Sam's sister cooed.

One of Sam's brothers seemed inordinately interested in what I did for a living in California. But before I was put on the spot, Tullos made a quick move to go, and Sam's sister took him out to the freezer and put about ten pounds of turtle meat in his arms. We put it in the back seat. I wondered whether the Ferrys might wonder why we didn't put frozen melting game in the trunk. They all stood around and stared at us: Sam, two of the vicious-looking brothers, fat, retarded Little Sam, the wall-eyed brother-in-law, the sister, the ugly daughter, and two neigh-bors who had just wandered over. This is where we get blasted, I said to myself. We drove away slowly, kicking back dirt as the LTD lumbered up onto the levee.

For three or four minutes no one said a word. Then Tullos said, "He is a *ugly* sucker. I don't mean just *ugly*; I mean big, capital *U-G-L-Y*. Every time I looked at Sam Ferry, I about had heart failure. I think we ought to draw extra pay for visual insult."

"I've seen em a lot uglier than that," said Dave Hall.

I realized that I was shaking. I wondered whether I had been visibly shaking in the house. I had no idea.

"Were you nervous out there?" I asked Tullos. "Tell the truth."

"Nah, not really."

"I'm telling you, this is routine," said Dave Hall. "Our supervisors put out press releases about how us agents stung a bunch of hoodlums after infiltrating them for months, and you get no idea what went into the case. You get no idea what we went through to do it."

"Were both of you carrying handguns?"

Dave Hall unzipped one of the many zip-up pockets on his hunting jacket and produced a small silver .38. "I don't go anywhere without this. I usually have another one, too, but I didn't this time."

Tullos said, "I wasn't carryin a pistolet, but man, I'm thinkin I ought to get me a little one like that. Ever since I started undercover work I hardly carry a piece, and someday, man . . ."

"So you weren't nervous?" I persisted.

"I ain't bragging," said Tullos, "but if you let a little caper like this get to you, you oughta be working down at the mill or putting mayonnaise on my po'boy. I tell you what, I could pull off two of these a day and go home and say, 'Hi, honey! What's new?' like I been sittin at a desk in a three-piece suit selling life insurance. I've been more scared out as a field warden stalkin at night than most times undercover. There you're a big, visible target, and some nut crazy enough to kill you can lay for you and blow you away. Here you got your wits on your side, and that's a big plus. Long as you got wits."

Back in Dave Hall's motel room, Tullos grabbed the phone and called his wife. He didn't say, "We made it, honey," or some such thing; he simply said, "Hi, darlin! What you got cookin?" He cupped the receiver, looked at us with a huge smile, and said, "Shrimp *gum*-bo!" as if his wife had just bought him a Porsche 944. Tullos was packed and gone like a secretary when the clock hits five. I kept on drinking bourbon out of my Orvis flask. Dave Hall fiddled a bit with his Nagra to make sure it had picked up our conversation in the boat (it had), then got on his favorite nemesis, the telephone. He was going to Alexandria that night; the following day, he was planning to go up to Little Rock on some other case; the day after, he had to drive all the way down to Cameron Parish to give a talk on waterfowl at the Rockefeller Refuge; later he was supposed to drive over to Texas to help plan a big sting involving illegal hunting and baiting at some of the state's most exclusive duck clubs; then he might go back home for a couple of nights. He had seen his wife and children four days in two weeks.

We ate dinner at a Western Sizzlin' steak house, where Dave Hall immediately sank into one of his self-immolating funks—first it was the Sam Ferrys of the world who chawed away at his peace of mind, then the drug problem, then the government, then the deterioration of the environment, and, finally, it seemed to me, the whole goddamned universe. I was relieved to say goodbye. I got in my car and was about seven miles out of Natchez when it hit. I don't know whether it was the cold black night, or the day's anxiety finally set free, or a wild and despairing anger at God and his bloody carnivorous universe. But I began to think about that little wood duck in his new breeding plumage being slapped out of the air by a bolt to the brain and chased through a darkening bayou by four huge creatures crashing death down on him, and when I thought of the bloody, gasping little head in Tullos's hands, I can't lie to you, I pulled off the road, set the hand brake, rolled down the window, and I just sat there, alone, and started to bawl.

False River, Louisiana, where David Tullos grew up, is neither a river nor a town. It is a long, long oxbow lake, a remnant of a recent Mississippi River that flowed thirty miles west of its modern course, and it is also the summer resort nearest Baton Rouge. Both shores are lined with what Louisianans call camps—summer cottages (there are some real palaces now, since oil made a few of the local boys rich) and fishing cabins, where legislators from the capital can escape for a nooner now and then and LSU students can hold raucous parties out of range of the campus police. Sometimes people even fish—the lake has a strain of very large bass. Like many resort communities, False River exhibits a practiced tolerance toward such activity—the Baptist Belt begins a bit farther north, so Cajun laissez-faire-ism has a pretty good hold on the place.

Even in such a relaxed milieu, however, David Tullos's reputation as the Teenager from Hell was second to none—which made his transmutation into a *game warden* in January of 1980, when he was a tender twenty-three years of age, hard for many of the local folk to reconcile.

Hadn't this grinning, scrawny, adolescent-looking *game warden* had papers served on him in every local bar—for disturbing the peace, for public drunkenness, for instigating free-for-alls? Hadn't the police arrived to break up a chair-smashing, mug-throwing, cue-swinging bar fight between the LSU hippies and the local good old boys just in time to see Tullos's hindquarters wiggling out a window? (A hippie, as far as Tullos and his redneck friends were concerned, was anyone who aspired to a college degree, even if his major was weight lifting and he answered to Bubba or Ding.) Hadn't people been awakened at two in the morning to the roar of Blue Bull—Tullos's superlevitated Chevy four-by-four with its jumbo Monster Mudder tires and wall of roof-mounted headlights—locked in a ferocious, grinding, mud-spraying chain-pull with a challenger in some poor farmer's field? Was this the same David Tullos whose idea of a date, according to gossip local daughters brought home, was for the girl to drive slowly down country roads while he shot at rabbits out the window with a .22?

One of Tullos's high-school teachers, who had come over to his mother's house just to see this apparition posing in a law-enforcement uniform, probably spoke for the entire community when she said, "Lord have mercy, they gave you a *gun*."

"Yes, ma'am," said Tullos.

"But no bullets, did they?"

Tullos can't explain why, exactly, but he had decided to become a game warden when he was eight. "Historically, some of the best game wardens have been former outlaws. It takes an outlaw to understand an outlaw, and if you understand outlaws, you can catch them. Under the wrong influence, I could have gone the other way. When I was twenty-three, I didn't give a damn about the environment. What I am today, I would have called a Communist back then. What I wanted was a job where I could be outdoors and have some adventures. Living on the edge is my style. I don't know where I got it from. My daddy repaired appliances for a living. My brother's in the oil business. They never had any interest in the out-of-doors. I was never like them, not when I was sucking on a pacifier. I was after thrills, man. The chases, the stakeouts, all that stuff. I'm undereducated. All I watch on TV is news, and all I read is *Time* and *Newsweek*, but all I've got is a high-school diploma.

I didn't want to work in a factory that puts swizzles on swizzle sticks. I didn't want to go to work in the oil patch, even if the money was good. I didn't have many options. I hated my first jobs. Maybe I've got some secret love of authority, cause I said to myself, It's gonna be game warden or the Marines. I'm probably too rebellious for the Marines. If I had the chance, I'd be an actor. I'd do good old boy monologues on the Johnny Carson show. Being a game warden, you get to work outdoors, you get to have some thrills. That's good. Going undercover, you get to act, you get to improvise, you get to live by your wits. That's a whole lot better. When I heard that you could be a covert-operations game warden, I thought, Man, this is a job that's made in heaven for me. I'm gonna prove myself at last."

Tullos had to wait five years before a game warden position opened. He had to spend four more years in the field before he was allowed to join Wildlife and Fisheries' covert-operations unit. He was lucky to survive. If you are a garden-variety game warden in, say, Massachusetts or Iowa, 95 percent of the violators you come across will have done something incredibly heinous like not buy a duck stamp. In a state full of nice blond law-abiding Scandinavians, such as Minnesota, a game warden can become suicidally bored. In states like Louisiana and Alabama and Nevada, where a lot of people have not come to terms with the twentieth century, a game warden takes his life in his hands.

Tullos wasn't sure whether he had more to fear from "the lowlife, dirtbag, scum-ball Sam Ferry types" he was chasing or from his partner, Cecil Broussard. Cecil was nearly twice his age, a stolid, curly-haired Cajun veteran of the game wars, but partnering him with Tullos was probably intentional. Cecil loves action. "From the first day we went out together," Tullos told me, "I knew I never wanted another partner. First, I could trust Cecil with my life. Second, it's not just a job to him. He wants his outlaws *bad*. Where we used to patrol a lot—up along the Mississippi in Avoyelles and Pointe Coupee parishes, and out into the Atchafalaya Basin—the number-one violation is deer spotlighting. The levees are grassy, you got woods and marshes nearby. It's a border zone, it's the best deer habitat. To patrol it, though, you got to drive the levee roads real quiet and slow, and you got to do it without lights. Then when you hear a shot, you got to get there right away because those suckers can have the deer in the truck and be gone in thirty seconds. You can't waste time. So Cecil—we'd hear a rifle shot, and suddenly old Cecil is traveling seventy miles per hour on a levee road *without headlights.* I've tried it in the daytime, and I can never get up to fifty-five before I back off the throttle. So I just let Cecil drive and I sat there and prayed. We never knew if there was a big bump or pothole ahead. We can get ten inches of rain in a day around here, and the road half dissolves. There were two nice dents in the roof of Cecil's cab with some caked blood all around, which we left there cause it kind of acted like a cushion the next time our heads hit the roof."

I have several sides of tape filled with Tullos's adventures as a game warden, but I am going to skip over nearly all of it and just relate to you one experience that occurred a couple of years after he joined the force. He and Cecil were patrolling a stretch of levee near Simmesport, up by the Corps of Engineers' old river control structure—the great squat diversion dam that is supposed to prevent the Mississippi from changing course again. It was almost pitch-dark, but Tullos and Cecil, who were walking the levee near their truck, were sure they caught a glint of gunmetal and three very dark figures walking toward them about three hundred yards away. They slinked down the side of the levee, hid in some tules, and waited until the three figures were within spitting range.

"Game wardens! Hold it!"

They were greeted by a fusillade. There is nothing more surprising, Tullos maintains, than a bullet taking fuzz off your ear. The assailant was so close when he shot—eight feet away, Tullos says—that he was sure he was hit, and he told himself, "I'm dead. I'm dead." But he felt no pain, so he told himself, "I'm alive. I'm alive," and then, when he could finally move, he had murder on the brain. One of the three poachers had frozen in his tracks, but the other two were running away fast, and when Tullos yelled for them to stop, one wheeled and fired again. Tullos was prudent enough to dive face-first when he saw the man aim. He heard the bullet go over his head, about where his crotch had been a split second earlier. He had his gun out by then and was firing back, and one of the poachers dropped. He fired again and the other one dropped, too. My goodness Lord, Tullos remembers thinking, I just killed two people! But then one of the poachers leaped up and was running off again, and the other one was jumping into the bayou.

So much had happened so fast that Tullos just stood there, stunned. It was then that he noticed the paralyzed poacher nailed to the ground right next to him. As he had expected, the man was black.

"*Who tried to kill me!?*" Tullos blubbered at him. "You tell me or I'll shoot you!"

He didn't know whether he meant it or didn't mean it, but the poacher was sure he meant it, and he sank to his knees. "Please, white folks, don't kill me," he begged.

"*Talk!*" Tullos bellowed.

The black man was big, but his wavering voice was in the high upper register, an ululating falsetto croak. "Ellis," he prayed. "Ellis, oh Ellis, please come on out. They gonna *kill* me, Ellis!"

There was no movement at all from the bayou. Cecil was gone, too—he had taken off after the third one. Tullos hadn't even noticed him run off.

"Ellis!"

"Who's Ellis?!"

"Ellis Bibbins. Ellis be Ellis Bibbins. Ellis, *please* come out! Is you there, Ellis?"

Ellis Bibbins finally came out of the bayou a little bit at a time, like a bullfrog. His upper body was completely covered with pondweed. He looked like a plant. Tullos caught him with his flashlight beam, but he was trembling so violently now that the beam vibrated like a strobe light and Ellis worked his way toward him in slow motion, a sleep-walking ghoul.

A couple of minutes later Cecil came back empty-handed and furious. ("Cecil was old, but he was *fast*. He hated to be outrun.") Tullos began to handcuff the one who had given up Ellis Bibbins, but he was trembling almost as violently as Tullos, and since a shaking man cannot easily cuff a shaking man, they stood there doing a flat-footed rendition of a boogaloo.

Tullos and Cecil barely had Bibbins and his partner handcuffed when they heard a car slowly crunching gravel as it crept down the levee toward them. Cecil said, "This don't look good to me at *all.*" He hissed a bloodcurdling threat at the two poachers and told them to sit at the side of the road, as if they were having a typical quiet conversation atop a levee in the middle of the night. Then he and Tullos slid back down into the bulrushes and crouched on all fours.

The sound of the car was right above them. A voice cried into the night.

"Ellis?"

Nothing.

"Ellis!"

"Game wardens! Hold it!"

The huge old car went off the line like a dragster, its rear end fishtailing sloppily. Cecil and Tullos caught faces full of rocks and flying dirt as they scrambled back up the embankment. Tullos, who had just fired at two men from thirty feet away and missed, was convinced he could at least hit a car. He dropped to his knees and emptied his revolver into the side and rear fender as it roared away. The two handcuffed poachers were watching openmouthed. Cecil ran to their pickup truck and called in an all-points bulletin. Tullos wanted to go after the car, but they had two suspects in hand, and if they left them, they were going to escape. The others in the car, and the third poacher who had outrun Cecil, were all captured the next morning anyway. When the game wardens searched the field next to where the shootout took place, they found the prize that might have gotten two or three people killed. It was a rabbit.

David Tullos liked everything there was to like about being a game warden. He was outdoors most of the time. His bosses were usually asleep when he was on the job. The day's events were utterly unpredictable. Although his paychecks were so lean—his starting salary was eleven thousand dollars a year—that Doreena, his wife, had to go to work at the local post office after their first son, Chaney, was born, he was rarely bored—Tullos's greatest dread was *ennui*. Even so, he felt that chasing after outlaws poaching rabbits was beneath him. He had splendid faith in his native abilities, and, like a lot of reformed miscreants, he has a peculiarly tender sense of justice, which was being rubbed raw. "The oldest tradition we have in this state is that the rich land puts food on the poor man's table. During the Depression, if it hadn't been for all the wildlife and wilderness in Louisiana, people would have starved. I mean *starved*—there was no welfare, and a lot of our people were sharecroppers with nothing to eat. Just since I was a kid, I've seen so many of the resources raped that sometimes I wonder if I'm living in the same state. Who's doing the raping? Not the ordinary hardworking Cajuns, by and large. Most of the poachers I've arrested all hate the Corps of Engineers and the oil companies for what they did to our wilderness here. We've got less and less. Less deer, less nutria, less fish. We've got enough oysters to feed the world, and half of them are unsafe to eat. The duck habitat's going fast. But who gets greased when the wildlife starts to run out? Not the big boys. They all belong to duck clubs, and they're puttin out bait and taking big-time overlimits, and rarely does something happen to them. Before I ever met Dave Hall, just from what I'd heard, I knew I had one thing in common with him—it always gave me the red ass to be arresting all these little fish. There's no way in hell a regular old game warden is ever gonna get the top-dog outlaws by sneaking around in the brush, man. Plus, I got to admit, I've got an ego at least half the size of Hall's. Being a regular old game warden in Louisiana means you arrest the Sam Ferrys and the Ellis Bibbinses, and after twenty-five years you get put out to pasture on a little bitty pension and you say, 'Well, that was my life.' Shit . . . if they hadn't let me go undercover, I think eventually I would have quit. Part of it was an ego thing, part of it was proving myself, but a lot of it was just being fed up with how corrupt things can get down here."

Tullos's mistake was underestimating how the corruption of which he spoke had seeped into the Louisiana Department of Wildlife and Fisheries itself.

When I set out to write this book, Dave Hall said I would hear plenty of stories about corruption at Wildlife and Fisheries. "You won't be able to prove anything," he admonished. "Reporters for local papers have tried for years, and all they really managed to put together was some circumstantial evidence. Just because thousands and thousands of illegal alligator hides were going into the Mares brothers' tannery a block away from Wildlife and Fisheries' headquarters—*in daylight hours*—doesn't *prove* collusion. I believe absolutely in innocent until proven guilty. Something that looks suspicious is *not* proof." Several years later, as I am writing this, he is giving me the same advice. He is saying that after two and a half decades of observing Louisiana game-law enforcement, during which period he collaborated closely with a number of disgruntled state game wardens and reformed outlaws, he is satisfied that "there have been bad, bad elements in the department"; but he refused to speculate how high corruption has gone, or how deep. "All you'll be able to do is repeat what someone told you. A lot of the stories are old history. They've cleaned out a bunch of the bad apples. If you try to take on corruption at Wildlife and Fisheries, you'll just get burned."

When it comes to corruption, Louisiana has an extravagant history. Louisiana is the state that spawned and elected and deified Huey Long, a jocular tyrant and razor-sharp buffoon, who raised his own army, almost went to war against New Orleans, and made graft (the "dee-duct system," he called it) as much of an institution as death and taxes. However, Louisianans still regard Huey with the kind of awe and affection Third World countries reserve for their national liberators and *caudillos* because he took on Standard Oil and the entrenched old money that had previously ruled the state, because he built roads and bridges when they had none, and because he thundered about sharing the wealth, which they had none of either—most of them. Thirty years ago A. J. Liebling described the state as an outpost of the Levant astride the Gulf of Mexico, looking not northward toward its companion states but southward toward the steamy, languid banana republics with which it still has much in common. Ruling families tend to dominate banana republics; Louisiana was dominated by Longs for half a century. Four years after Huey was assassinated, his younger brother, Earl, landed in the statehouse; Earl's most famous exploits as a three-term, on-and-off-again governor involved racehorses, the stripper Blaze Starr, and his repeated incarceration in institutions. Later, Louisianans sent Huey's son, Russell, to Washington, where he became known as "the Senator from Oil." ("Louisianans who make money in oil buy politicians, or pieces of politicians, as Kentuckians in the same happy situation buy racehorses," Liebling wrote in *The Earl of Louisiana.* "Oil gets into politics, and politicians, making money in office, get into oil. The state slithers around in it.") In 1986, the year the Senator from Oil finally retired, Louisiana sent to Washington John Breaux, who became known as the Senator from Public Works—these being the federally financed dams and levees that keep nether Louisiana from drowning and the federally financed saltwater navigation canals that let the Gulf of Mexico eat up the land thus protected. Breaux once boasted that his vote wasn't for sale, "but it is available for rent." Meanwhile, the statehouse had become the fiefdom of Edwin Edwards, another compulsive (and unlucky) gambler and the most indicted American governor in the twentieth century, who, after being elected, was deposed but then reelected and then deposed again; some people think he could be reelected any day. The father of the current governor, Buddy Roemer, was a majordomo for Edwards, and was recently convicted of bribery and conspiracy in federal court, along with the state's preeminent underworld figure, Carlos Marcello.

In Louisiana, a parish sheriff was once reelected while he was a prisoner in his own jail.

But Dave Hall was right. I have not been able to prove anything to the satisfaction of due process. All I can do is repeat what others told me. Willie Disch told me that his corrupt superiors at Wildlife and Fisheries ran him out of the department for enforcing the law. A. J. Caro told me that state game wardens and department higher-ups met with him at the estate of Carlos Marcello because they were taking bribes or, in some cases, buying and selling illegal alligator hides themselves. He says that he sat with some of them at Jack Kelly's dinner table in Breezy Point, New York. And David Tullos told me that until he became an undercover agent for Wildlife and Fisheries, he didn't know what it was to feel vulnerable. Infiltrating gangs of outlaws was one thing; hearing them talk about how they were being protected by people in his own agency was something else. That was why, after two years with the covert-operations unit, he had half a dozen guns concealed around his home and in his cars, none more than five seconds from his grasp.

Tullos says he was exposed to corruption almost from the moment he joined the force. At first he participated in it. One of his superiors, a former Cajun cook who had outlandish political aspirations—he wasn't sure whether he ought to be president or merely governor— liked to throw Cajun suppers for his colleagues and various politicians and bigwigs. (Political aspirants in Louisiana have to eat like hogs, but at least the food is good.) Since he couldn't afford to do it on his salary, he had Tullos and other game wardens seine-net fish for him on state time, using state vehicles. When the official was asking him to do it twice a week, Tullos began to wonder whether he wasn't just selling the fish to restaurants, since each load usually weighed hundreds of pounds. He says he tried to distance himself from such petty corruption, but it was so common that any warden who did felt like a thirty-year-old virgin. Later, on one of his first undercover cases, Tullos was trying to make a buy from two brothers in Pine Prairie—one of them was a town councilman—who for years had been suspected of selling illegal wild venison and game fish through the meat market they owned. The second time he visited their store he saw the local game warden's truck parked outside; he had to hide because the warden knew him by sight. Tullos went ahead with the case anyway and eventually made an illegal buy; he also managed to sneak a look in the walk-in cooler, where he saw piles of white perch (illegal) and a dead fawn hanging from a rope (very illegal). One of the brothers ("a superduper bad-ass coon-ass") told Tullos that he poached his deer at night with a pit bull, and if a game warden gave him any trouble, he would let the dog tear the warden apart—but he didn't expect much trouble, he said, because they were friends with "our big man" at Wildlife and Fisheries. The "big man" was the same supervisor who had sent Tullos out to net fish and who was rising rapidly through the ranks in the department. Even though he had been fanatical about maintaining his cover, Tullos ended up burned on that case. He and Vincent Darby, the head of the covert-operations unit, had gone over together to make a final buy before arresting the two; Darby was nervous about letting Tullos do it alone, mainly because the "big man" had developed an inordinate interest in the investigation. When they got there, they saw both local game wardens' trucks parked out front; they had to wait two hours for them to leave. With the local wardens gone, Tullos and Darby reckoned, they would have a clear shot at a buy and an arrest. They were wrong. The brothers were waiting for them. "We ain't got nothing to sell you," said one. "We know who you are." And then he addressed them by their real names.

Vincent Darby, one of the first undercover game wardens Wildlife and Fisheries had hired, had been burned before. It was Darby who had his camp shot up by Noah Cross's deputies and who was warned away from Concordia Parish forever by Cross himself. Nonetheless, Darby was utterly stunned that they had been found out. He had told the "big man" nothing because he thought he was a snake. If it wasn't just a lucky guess, then someone had to be snooping through his active files. But it couldn't have been a lucky guess. *The outlaws knew their names.*

"Don't let anyone in the department know what you're up to anymore," Darby admonished Tullos on the way back to Baton Rouge. "Work your cases to the point where it's too late for them to do anything, and then we'll let them know. If they ask what you're doing, make something up. I'll take the files home. I'll lie for you as much as I have to. We got a serious problem here."

On his next big case—the biggest one of his career—Tullos had more than his own agency to worry about. He also had to worry about the local sheriff, the district attorney, and the judge.

Emmett Bonner, the senior resident game warden in Concordia and Catahoula parishes, was relatively new to the territory, but he had some idea who David Paulk was. Paulk was one of Catahoula's solid citizens— a police juror (which, in Louisiana, is the same as a county commissioner), a member of the Larto Lake commission, a brother of the deputy sheriff, a farmer who had plowed the profits from a few hundred acres of soybeans and milo into a meat market in Jonesville and a duck-hunting guide service he operated in the fall. Paulk was a well-off old boy; he had built himself a slick new ranch house, garishly furnished in Greco-Roman–Texas style, and he owned a couple of nice motorboats and a brand-new eighteen-thousand-dollar brown-and-cream Chevrolet Suburban, which Bonner was in the process of pursuing like mad across the Mississippi River Bridge at Natchez on the afternoon of June 25, 1985.

It had begun with a tip that was called in to Bonner earlier that day, a cigarette croak of a voice muttering something about David Paulk about to make a run into Mississippi later that day with a huge load of illegal game fish. Bonner had heard all the stories and rumors about the Larto Lake gang; he had arrested a few members himself. But he had never heard of someone as prominent as Paulk being tied in with that bunch. He called one of his trusted wardens, Charles Tarver, and they parked themselves near the bridge, poured out some coffee, and decided to give it a couple of hours. Paulk came by right on schedule. A Suburban has truck-size springs and shock absorbers, but Paulk's was obviously laboring under a big load. They took off after it. At first, it seemed to them that Paulk wanted to make a smoking U-turn back into Louisiana, but he decided against it and flew off toward Natchez. It took Bonner five minutes to run him down. There were enough frozen sacalait in the back of Paulk's oversized jeep to feed a congregation.

Bonner already had it figured out. Paulk was carrying Larto Lake game fish across state lines for commercial sale, which is a federal offense. That was why he tried to double back into Louisiana. When he couldn't make the U-turn, he figured he might as well try to outrun them.

If they had him dead to rights, though, what was Paulk doing with a grin on his face?

He was digging out of his pocket Arkansas Fish Farm Permit number 0239 and receipt number 457 from the Bo Hill Minnow Farm near Winchester, Arkansas.

"I buy em from Mr. Hill, take em home, freeze em, and resell em to clubs and restaurants," Paulk was explaining to Bonner and Tarver. "The profit ain't more than a few cents a fish, but my milo crop's on its own now and my meat market sort of runs itself, and I'm a boy who's always trying to make a little extra buck."

"If these here are legal farm-raised," said Bonner, who can best be described as erect, correct-looking, and vastly oversized, "then how come you were trying like hell to outrace us?"

"To be honest, now, I had no idea who you was. I'm a police juror, you know, and some of the parish business we do upsets people. I thought you were a couple of nuts."

"Your brother's the deputy, right?"

"That's right."

"And these fish weren't caught in Larto Lake?"

"No, sir. These here are farm-raised."

"They look awful big for farm-raised."

"That's what they are."

"Would you mind telling us where you're taking these fish?"

"No, sir, I won't do that. I got the license and the permits, that's all you need. If you don't let me go now, I'm gonna call my lawyer."

"We're just asking."

"Well, I'm not answering."

The following day, at Bonner's request, agent Joe Oliveros of the U.S. Fish and Wildlife Service and a carload of Arkansas game wardens paid a visit to the Jamir Hills, Senior and Junior, proprietors of one of the largest fish-farming operations in the world. Jamir Hill, Senior, also known as Bo, insisted that he had sold the fish to Paulk. When the wardens asked to see his receipt book, however, they found that the originals of numbers 457, 458, and 459 were missing, and the copies were blank.

When Oliveros asked Bo Hill whether he was selling permits and blank receipts to commercial-scale fish poachers, he said that was absolutely untrue.

The following day, Oliveros and Bonner searched out the informant who had called in the tip and interviewed him in person. He rattled off a list of local boys who, he said, were all netting fish for David Paulk. Bonner recognized some of the names. There were a bunch of Adamses and Joneses who were all rumored to be outlaws of various stripes. There were also Beetle and Randy and Darwin Book. Paulk, according to the informant, was paying his men twenty-five to fifty cents a pound and selling the fish for three times that price. He heard that Paulk had made thirty-five thousand dollars the previous year on illegal fish alone, tax-free of course, but then again he probably made a lot more than that. It wasn't milos and soybeans that built his new house; it was game fish. He bought the Suburban because he needed an oversized vehicle to haul big loads of white perch out of state, as far away as Saint Louis and Chicago; sometimes he moved so many that he hitched on a U-Haul trailer. The informant said he couldn't imagine how there could be such demand in those cities, but he'd heard that Paulk sold to markets in the black neighborhoods, and "there's a hell of a lot of niggers in them places that love these fish."

At that point in the interview, the informant became agitated. These were rough old boys they were dealing with, he said; what they were doing was common knowledge up and down Larto Lake, but everyone kept mum about it; they were afraid they'd be hurt because illegal sacalait was letting them boys taste more money than they had seen in their lives.

Confidential Informant T-1 then refused to say another word, except that Paulk had a walk-in freezer camouflaged in a large shed on his property that could solidify seven thousand pounds of fish overnight.

Emmett Bonner was beginning to see what he had on his hands. He had a gang poaching fish on what you had to call a spectacular scale and selling them with phony permits. (He wondered how much money Bo Hill was asking for a certificate. He also wondered how many fish farmers in Arkansas made more easy money selling permits than they did selling fish.) For a gang leader he had a police juror whose brother was a deputy sheriff; he figured he'd better compare citations issued to all the people his informant had mentioned to see how many cases were being fixed. If this whole business had really been going on for years, then the local game wardens, those who had been assigned to the region before he was, ought to know all about it.

On July 17, Joe Oliveros appeared before a federal grand jury in Shreveport and obtained permission to seize and review the telephone company's records of David Paulk's calls. He had made quite a number of them to Little Rock, Saint Louis, and Chicago. The numbers were traceable, and they were all fish markets. When federal and Missouri agents paid a visit to Kram's Fish Market in Saint Louis, the proprietor, Ed Kram, said he had been doing business with Paulk for the past ten years. He always assumed Paulk was Bo Hill's man because the permits were always signed "Bo Hill." Kram said he had no idea he was buying illegal wild fish; he also said that sacalait were tremendously popular among blacks, who often bought the fish—which he usually sold for five or six dollars a pound, having bought them from Paulk for a dollar and a half—with food stamps. One of the wildlife agents discovered receipt number 457 in the pile Ed Kram had saved; Paulk, after having been released by Emmett Bonner, had moved his eleven hundred pounds of crappie straight up to Saint Louis because Kram's purchase order was dated June 26. The "Bo Hill" signature on the permit was in a slightly different shade of blue ink than the rest of the writing on the receipt.

The facts were pretty much pieced together. But there was no case.

When David Tullos first joined Wildlife and Fisheries as a field warden, he had to buy his own gun and flashlight and hat because the department's threadbare budget didn't allow for such things. When, four years later, he joined the undercover unit, he had to learn undercover police work by himself. There were four undercover wardens among a staff of two hundred fifty law-enforcement people, and there was no program to train them. Tullos absorbed what he could from Vincent Darby; he talked to some undercover people with the state police and FBI and DEA; he read every book on covert operations he could get his hands on. Then he had to come up with a good cover.

He chose oil. By the early 1980s, after the second OPEC shock—the one that had people gunning one another down in gas lines—there was so much oil exploration, so much enhanced recovery, so much drilling and canaling and poking and plumbing going on all over Louisiana that one in every five jobs in the state was oil-related. Even a marginally literate stump digger who saw a shiny black Chevrolet Blazer whiz by with GULF SOUTH RESOURCES magnetically painted on the door knew the letters spelled OIL. The Blazer was Darby's doing. He managed to sneak through a purchase order without Ray Montet, the chief of enforcement, or his deputy, Winton Vidrine, catching on until the vehicle sat glowing in Tullos's drive; in Tullos's words, "They liked to have died when they saw that thing." He waxed it until a fly couldn't grab a foothold, bought some magnesium wheels at his own expense, put on some chrome flash and pinstriping ("An oil boy wants some jewelry on his vehicle"), and then went out and bought himself some books on surveying geology and some secondhand surveying equipment, also at his own expense, to scatter prominently inside the Blazer; he got an undercover phone line and an answering service, some bogus identification in the name of David Trahan, and a set of license plates traceable only to Gulf South Resources—a post office box, no address. When investigating a promising lead, he would drive around the subject's home territory for a while, get out, make like a surveyor, drive around some more, survey again, and ultimately settle in at the local bar or cracker-barrel store, where his ears grew larger than his head. A blind undercover cop, Tullos says, would make more cases than a deaf one. "I was supposed to be a junior-grade surveyor and the boss's go-fer. I told everyone that a go-fer doesn't get paid much but gets to loaf a lot. That's how come I could hang around these places and get in on these deals. If we had a suspect in mind, I might drive over to his neighbor's place and set up to make a survey. The neighbor'd come over and I'd say, 'Hey, man, can you help me locate this benchmark that's supposed to be here?' Everybody's always looking for a benchmark in the survey business. And the neighbor'd say, 'I ain't seen no survey marker.' And I'd say, 'Well, this is a old sucker—it's been here forty years and it's probably buried,' and before long I'd have my shovel out and I'd be digging and digging, and they'd be out there lookin with me. And after an hour maybe I'd be talkin about wanting to buy some deer meat, and they'd say they could help me get some. Or if they seemed like law-abiding types, I'd be talking about how it's harder and harder to get a deer, someone must be takin em all, and they might say, 'Well, looka here, I know for a fact that last night these bad-ass dudes down the road went out and spotlighted three.' You got to be a seat-of-the-pants psychiatrist to make it at this job."

When Tullos joined the LDWF undercover force, Ray Montet told Vincent Darby that he was a smart-ass kid who "won't ever make a case; he probably won't make a single buy." Within a year Tullos had a couple dozen scalps hanging from his belt. One belonged to Jethro Anderson, a vicious, muscle-bound black deer poacher who ended up serving a life term in the penitentiary at Angola for one first-degree murder and for the rape and near-fatal stabbing of the girlfriend of his best friend, whose name was Superstud. Even though Jethro could have broken him in two, had a .45 stuck in his trouser band, and owned several pit bulls that formed a snarling circle around Tullos the moment he stepped in Jethro's yard, and even though he told Tullos that he hated game wardens so much he was dying to kill one, Tullos drove away forty-five minutes later with a poached deer in his trunk and a recording inside his pants of everything Jethro had said. It was his finesse with Jethro, as much as anything, that convinced Montet to use Tullos on the Larto Lake gang. Montet was stiff as a deacon, and Tullos's style found its antithesis in his, but he was fairly well convinced that no one else could pull off the case.

To open the investigation, Tullos essentially dropped the names supplied by Emmett Bonner's informant into a hat and picked one out. He came up with Beetle Book. Beetle was as good a target as any because his computer sheet showed a list of citations as long as his arm, none of which had put him in jail and many of which were nol-prossed. Beetle knew how to get a case fixed. With luck and Beetle's unwitting cooperation, Tullos might net a district attorney and a sheriff as well. Tullos found Beetle's home—it was a little old trailer—on Cocodrie Bayou, just outside Monterey, a town a few miles distant from Larto Lake. Beetle's wife, Zola, answered the door. Zola, Tullos was to learn, was a Scripture-quoting Pentecostal—a faith Beetle and his sons, who worshiped at the Church of Carnal Appetites, absolutely abhorred. Somehow they had remained married for thirty-odd years. Zola said Beetle wasn't in, so Tullos and John Haase, a new undercover warden who had come along with him, drove around for a while, getting the lay of the place.

When they returned and he first laid eyes on him, Tullos decided Beetle looked like an older Billy Carter gone to seed. He seemed suspicious but not exactly paranoid. He invited them inside and grilled them for about half an hour. Tullos performed well. An hour and a half later he had forty-four pounds of poached game fish in his cooler. Beetle, meanwhile, had fifty fresh bills in his pocket and three beers in his gut, and he was already giving up some of the secrets of the Larto gang. He told Tullos and Haase that, when the lake level was low and the crappie were moving around in large schools, the gang had pulled out as much as twenty-two thousand pounds of fish in a single day; they had to rent an eighteen-wheel semi-truck to take ten thousand pounds up to Chicago, where "them jigs will buy them white perch just as fast as you can get em to em." Tullos's mouth was agape and he gawd-dawgged Beetle half to death as he held forth on his outlaw exploits. Beetle also admitted that they used bogus permits not just from Arkansas, where farm-raised sacalait could be commercially bought and sold, but also from Tennessee because there was a legal commercial season at Reelfoot Lake. "None of them farm fish or them Tennessee fish is half as good as these here ones we get," Beetle pronounced. "They're spiny little pussies that's half body and half head. Them northern city niggers ain't seen a blade of grass in their lives, but they can always tell a Larto fish. They ask for them in person. 'Is these here Larto Lake fish?' they ask. Hell, yes, they are. Fat little sonabitches. Hell, yeah."

Both Tullos and Emmett Bonner, when he heard about it, were stunned by the quantities of fish Beetle talked about. If the gang could haul twenty thousand pounds of crappie out of one lake in one day, there must be dozens of people involved. How could there be any fish left? They already had enough evidence to prosecute Beetle; Tullos had his tape recorder running when he bought from him, and during the next couple of weeks, to establish Beetle's chronic criminal intent, he made a couple more buys from him. But one thing was already clear: he could get forty-four pounds of game fish from Beetle Book every single day until he retired or Beetle died. He was going to have to buy bigger to swim the other members of the gang into the net. Beetle was up there in the hierarchy, it seemed, but he wasn't the Kingfish; he wasn't David Paulk. The way to get to Paulk was to start buying hundreds of pounds; sooner or later, Tullos reasoned, Paulk would take notice, greed would vanquish his paranoia, and eventually Tullos would buy directly from him. Tullos also wanted to get at the markets and distributors in the big northern cities that were purchasing tons of illegal fish from the gang. To do that, he would have to do more than buy big. He would have to become a member.

Tullos had made his first buy on November 26. Ten days later he showed up with James Gueho posing as his uncle—Uncle Junior they decided to call him; it had a nice meatball cachet—who dealt mainly in shrimp and crayfish but could occasionally use a couple hundred pounds of sacalait. The first big buy, on December 6, amounted to two hundred and seventy pounds. Beetle Book effortlessly came up with the entire amount. They needed a cover that would let them purchase *tons* of fish and not have it look like an obvious setup. It was then that Tullos decided to bring in Dave Hall.

Actually, Vincent Darby, who retired just as the case began to take off, and Emmett Bonner had wanted to bring in the federals all along. Darby's suspicions about corruption within Wildlife and Fisheries ran deep and dark. So did Bonner's. Bonner had told Tullos that, of the seven game wardens who patrolled Concordia and Catahoula parishes with him, there were at least three whom he didn't trust. The Larto Lake gang hadn't moved semis and U-Haul trucks loaded with game fish for the past three decades without a succession of game wardens and other law-enforcement people looking the other way. Tullos trusted Ray Montet, both Bonner and Gueho, and Burton Angelle, the LDWF director, completely, but he wasn't always sure who else. "Something could happen to you," Darby had told Tullos one day. "If it does, I don't want a local grand jury investigating and a local DA prosecuting and a local judge sitting. I don't want local or state nothing. I want a *federal* grand jury and *federal* prosecutors and *federal* penalties and the goddamned FBI out here covering every inch of bayou. Some of them federal agents are better than others, but I think the one we want is Hall because he ain't cowed by anyone. If this bunch should decide to play rough with us, he'd tear up the parish with his bare hands. He's like a wolverine when he's mad."

The buy at the Redwood Inn on December 13—when a stoned Darwin Book quaked in the kitchen, a glib young redneck named Trahan prattled on, and Lonnie "Buck" Pridgen showed the California Yankee his collection of guns—was Dave Hall's first involvement with the Larto gang. He had heard plenty about them but had never gone after them himself. True to form, he began interviewing retired game wardens who had had run-ins with the gang, among them Willie Disch, whom he videotaped for hours; he unearthed half the major game-law citations written in Concordia Parish over the past two decades and compared them to the sentences meted out; he learned how Darby and Russell Landry had been threatened, how another state warden had been lured into a bayou and surrounded by a gang of outlaw fishermen and told that if he ever showed his face again he would disappear; he heard how many tons of fish were being shipped to the northern cities; and, as Darby knew he would, he got mad. "There was a lot of bad blood between him and Wildlife and Fisheries anyway," Tullos says. "With Hall it's no politics, no bullshit, big ego, and some people hate that about him. Plus, he wanted to show the big boys at LDWF that they had this mess of corruption and hadn't done much to eliminate it. Plus, his style and Ray Montet's are as opposite as you can get. Ray wears suits. Hall wears camouflage. Some of my people didn't like me working with him one bit. All I can say is, though, I felt a hell of a lot of relief with Jim Pridgen behind me."

In December Tullos decided to tell Beetle Book that he had been laid off from his job at Gulf South Resources. He'd been given a couple of weeks of severance pay, and that was that. He had no other job prospects. His only source of income now was the fish he was buying for Uncle Junior and Big Jim, and that wasn't enough. Beetle told him not to worry—he was going to make a career outlaw out of him. Beetle told him that he didn't limit himself to fish. He was a journeyman smuggler, running everything from hot goods to drugs. He was getting old, he didn't like his own sons much, and he could use some fresh help.

Tullos's strategy with a wily old hayseed who aspired to be Al Capone was pure, unadulterated, shameless flattery, and it was paying dividends. Beetle liked him, and he wasn't imagining it. So Tullos began spending more and more time with him. He stayed overnight. He spent a couple of days. Sooner or later, though, he was going to have to spend time with the other members of the gang, who would automatically suspect that he was the law, no matter how he stood with Beetle. If enough people were suspicious of him and were as friendly with Wildlife and Fisheries people—not to mention the sheriff and everyone else—as Beetle said they were, then it was just a matter of time before he would be found out. It wasn't only likely. It was inevitable.

The first time Tullos got really scared working the Larto gang was on January 2, 1986, when he made his second big buy for Uncle Junior and Jim Pridgen. He made a major move again, telling Beetle that he wanted to come with him on his rounds so he could see how the fishermen worked. At first Beetle had waved him off. "Dave, one rule these fishermen have is don't bring no strangers around. They don't trust nobody. You see, they been sending undercover game wardens around, and you can't tell who you're dealing with. This perch selling is serious business. The game wardens find out you're selling and they watch you when you run your nets, then they take your tackle—that's what hurts. Nets cost a lot of money, and you don't get that back." But then Beetle decided to relent a bit, and he drove him down to Cocodrie Landing, the bar where a lot of the outlaw fishermen and deer hunters and trappers hung out. "Dirtbag City" is how Tullos described the place. Darwin, Beetle's son, was there, looking stoned as usual. Tullos had already decided that Darwin was dangerous—much more so than Beetle, who was kind of old anyway. Darwin always carried a giant switchblade about eight inches long, and he liked to run the blade against the back of his hand. Tommy Tiffee was a Goliath—six feet six inches tall and two hundred fifty pounds. He had once stomped to a pulp a game warden who tried to arrest him, breaking several of his ribs. Tullos is five feet eleven inches tall and weighs a hundred sixty-five pounds. He was not carrying his gun, but his Nagra recorder—a gift from Dave Hall that replaced the Radio Shack model Wildlife and Fisheries had bought for him—was turning slowly under an athletic bandage he'd wrapped around his ribs. During the next several weeks, as Tullos spent more and more time with Darwin and Tommy Tiffee and the Adams boys and bad-looking Butch Cross, a white version of Jethro Anderson, who, like Jethro, carried a .45 in his trouser band, he began to feel that the Nagra would be his undoing. What would they do when Butch Cross held the gun to his temple and they stripped him and discovered it?

"We had a local warden here for a while, he always tipped us off," Beetle was saying. "When they had a raid planned, we heard about it first. We gave that old boy a lot of tubs of white perch for them tipoffs, but they done got rid of him. They was frustrated when they come in and didn't find no tackle or fish. But don't you worry none, Dave. You get caught in the parish, it ain't gonna matter none, probably. We got the sheriff, like I told you, he's on our side, he'll help us if he can. We got a good D.A. now, a real good boy. Johnny Brigman, he got caught some while back by this new agent they put here, and nothin done happened to him. The district attorney, he'll fix them tickets unless they got too much heat on him. This one's sittin on his desk, this one of Johnny Brigman is, it's coolin off there."

"Who's this new sucker?" Tullos asked.

"Big muthafucka. Real tall man, name is Bonner. He's too damn tough, he can smell out a lead net. Them local wardens is tougher now than they ever was, and this one is the toughest of all, you got to watch out for him."

"Fuckin federals, though, they're the ones'll take your ass off," said Butch Cross. "They'll tear you a new asshole."

"Them federals, right, they don't mess around," Beetle said. "And them federal judges will stick your ass right in jail. The judge we had here, I picked his crop clean when I was a boy, that's why I ain't never seen the inside of a jail. But when you and Darwin went over to Natchez, I'll be honest, I was real leery of that ride there. David Paulk, now, you know he got caught, but he had permits, so he rode it on out. But he's leery, man, he's afraid the federals are after him, he thinks his phone could be tapped, he's scareder now than I ever saw him, cause he was in the clear for years—he never got nailed for nothin. He's scared shitless. Course, now, Paulk ain't about to quit either, the money's worth it to him. Plus, he's got a lot invested in boats and equipment and that freezer. Last year he dealt in over a hundred thousand dollars' worth of white perch, all of that tax-free. When you've got a taste of that kind of money, it's hard to quit. He's got his reputation, too. Paulk'll do anything to stay out of jail."

"If Dave Hall hadn't gotten involved, hadn't gotten the federal government involved, I would have made a couple of buys from Beetle and said, 'Case closed.' They had it all fixed-up up there. Beetle didn't tell me till later that he *still* had a local game warden tipping him off. He never told me who it was either. I couldn't get it out of him. I thought I knew who the sucker was. I told Emmett who I thought it was, and he said, 'Yeah, that wouldn't surprise me.' Every time I went up there to make another buy, I called Emmett first and asked him where that boy was gonna be. I got his work schedule and planned mine around his. I don't even want to *think* about what I would've done to another

Wildlife and Fisheries agent who gave me up. I wouldn't have killed
him, but I'd've like to hurt him bad for about three days. This particular
one might not have known me by sight, but he might have. My picture
was around headquarters somewhere. I'll bet he knew what Gueho
looked like. I'm not saying he *would* have turned over one of the department's undercover agents, but I'm not saying he wouldn't. He might
have just told them there's an undercover warden working them right
now, this minute, if he'd found out. They'd've figured out it was me. It
could *only* be me. There were so many ways I was vulnerable. I never
realized how hard it is to get permission to work these cases the way
they have to be worked. I had to get a judge's authority just to be wired.
If I'd have had to go to the local judge, I never would have stayed with
the case either. It's all kinfolks up there. The game wardens grew up
with the poachers, the judge grew up with Beetle, he goes to suppers
with Paulk. The judge probably doesn't think they're doing anything
really *wrong*, that's why he always lets them off. But what the judge
and the D.A. don't think is so wrong, the outlaws *know* is wrong and
can get them a nice big fine and jailtime and loss of hunting and fishing
rights, and these boys—they're making five times more money than they
could at a legitimate job. Besides, it's all they know. So if they were
gonna find me out, what were they gonna do to me? Were they gonna
do nothing to me, or were they gonna warn me away, or were they
gonna kill me, or were they gonna make me disappear? Beetle I don't
know about. Basically, I think Beetle's harmless. Darwin and Butch
Cross and Tiffee looked *bad.* Darwin got in with a rough drug crowd,
he's much more violent than his daddy. Paulk . . . whatever he did, he'd
have someone do it for him. He'd keep his hands clean. One day I told
Emmett Bonner, 'If I come up missing on this thing, I want you to swear
that you'll leave no stone unturned until you find out what happened
to me. Promise me that. It's not so much for my sake as for my family's
sake.' Emmett said, 'If anything ever happens to you, I'm gonna turn
this parish over and over until I die.' Small comfort to me, though, cause
I was already gonna be dead. Time was not on my side with this case.
Every day that came and went and I hadn't got to Paulk and the others,
I wondered whether I should cut the cards or call for a new hand. It
was pride versus fear, pride versus fear. I'm not gonna say I wasn't

scared. Toward the end I had to conk myself on the head with a two-by-four to get to sleep."

On February 2, Tullos called Beetle and arranged to buy another couple of hundred pounds for Uncle Junior. Gueho decided to go with him the next night to pick up the fish. When they arrived, they noticed that Beetle had a huge load of crappie—much more than they had asked for—in the back of his truck, all dressed and bagged in plastic.

"Look here," Beetle said, "y'all want to move twenty-five hundred or three thousand pounds?"

"Hell, yeah," said Gueho.

"Double back and I can line you up with a market, and this is a step toward getting some permits. Now this will be to Arkansas at a dollar and a quarter a pound or Saint Louis at a dollar and a half. This fella in Arkansas, Junior, we may ought to start with him cause he's the one that can lead to the permits. You got to buy at a dollar a pound, though, and they won't budge off that price cause they're used to haulin up there themselves, they're used to them there profits."

"Whose fish are these?"

"It's mainly a local fella I've hauled for before."

"The one that got caught?" Tullos asked.

"Yeah, right."

"Paulk?"

"Yeah, right. I'd haul this load myself, but my eyes is gettin bad. I think we can make y'all some money on this deal."

"We'll do it, you think, Uncle Junior?"

"Are these all the fish?"

"No, these is some. Paulk's boys has got to run his nets a few more times to come up with the rest. Now, one thing is, is, you can't go to his place to pick em up. He's scared to death of undercover agents, he's scared of y'all. He thinks the federals are after him, he's afraid his phone's tapped. He told me never to bring anyone around he don't know. I'm gonna have to take your truck and load it myself."

Tullos was furious. He suddenly had it figured out—why Beetle was going on *ad nauseam* about Paulk's fear of being caught and not letting him near the man. Paulk was probably as paranoid as Beetle said, and if *Darwin* was physically afraid of him—sinister, wolfish Darwin, who hung around with the local drug crowd (which meant bikers) and carried a blade that could skewer an elephant—then Beetle had every reason to be, too. But what a convenient setup it was for his little scam. Beetle was treating him like a son, he was talking about breaking him into his new outlaw career, he was saying he only asked 15 percent of Tullos's profits after he unloaded a batch of fish—and he was lying like Nixon. For every hundred dollars Tullos gave him to buy white perch from Paulk and his fishermen, Beetle must be pocketing . . . what? . . . twenty? . . . twenty-five? Nobody who was flirting with a jail sentence was going to settle for a 15 percent profit. And the bad thing was, if Tullos let him get away with it and began buying really big loads—two thousand pounds, three thousand—Beetle would make five hundred dollars upfront and another three or four hundred out the back door. To him, that was real money. Four or five hundred dollars just to drive his truck over to Paulk's and load it up with fish. Meanwhile, he and Gueho would hardly clear any more profit than Beetle did by running the fish to Chicago or Saint Louis, taking all the risks, spending two or three days on the road . . .

Tullos stopped himself. He was thinking just like an outlaw. There weren't any risks delivering the fish. They were *law officers*, for God's sake. All the money in his pockets belonged to the republic of Louisiana anyway.

But he had no idea what to do next. His whole strategy had backfired on him.

Chicago. February 20. Seven o'clock at night. The Louisiana Fish Market is on Kedzie Street, on the South Side, planted right in the middle of the second-largest black ghetto in the United States. Tullos told me that the only things he saw that were white, besides himself and Gueho, were the snowflakes blowing like confetti through the ice-entombed streets. Beetle Book had told Tullos that in 1973 he had delivered three hundred thousand pounds of Larto Lake crappie to the South Side all by himself.

Tullos and Gueho left Jonesville at one in the morning, after Beetle brought them back their loaded truck. The half-ton pickup they were driving had been borrowed from the state police. Just in case Paulk, through his brother, decided to have the sheriff's office run a trace on the license plates, Tullos had to go to the license branch himself and work up a phony registration that led to Uncle Junior's shrimp business at a bogus address in New Orleans. "Wildlife and Fisheries will get you funny plates, but they don't create an address they're traceable to. The computer just brings up 'no record of address.' Well, that's just *genius*. Any outlaw sees 'no record of address' and he smells the law. What a silly old scam, he'll say. I had to do all this stuff myself or get Dave Hall to help me, or they would have been onto me in no time." In the well of the pickup sat a camper shell. Inside the camper shell were two thousand three hundred and eighty-four pounds of sacalait and eighty pounds of bream. "You couldn't have squeezed another thing in there," says Tullos. "Not a toothpick."

Tullos had seen snow once. Gueho had never seen it in his life. From the tristate line on north, they drove through a blizzard that became so intense they couldn't even see the twenty solid blocks of twenty-story public housing they passed on the interstate before they exited onto Kedzie Street. "I don't know how those people can live like that," Dave Hall said after he saw the South Side himself. "I don't care what you say about racist, those people had it a lot better in the old segregated South."

One of the things that made life in the South Side ghetto slightly more tolerable was Donald Clayton's fish store. He was—he may still be—the largest retail fish dealer in the city, even if much of what he sold was contraband. He told the agents that whatever they brought him, he could sell—two thousand pounds, five thousand, he could get rid of it. His price for Larto Lake crappie was six dollars a pound. He paid Tullos and Gueho a dollar seventy-five. The big-city dealers were making the most money on these fish, and the taxpayers paid the bill. Most of Clayton's customers bought their illegal game fish with food stamps. "I come up from Greenville, Mississippi," he told them, and his accent was such that he could have left there the day before. "I still remember them big fish suppers. The older folks here, they pine for them fish, but the younger ones, they be liking em, too. Larto's the best. Them Reelfoot

Lake fish, they ain't nothin but minnows, what you gonna do with a minnow? Farm fish the same. Damn little old fish ain't that big.

"This ain't no wrong thing we're doin with these crappies," Clayton said. "You gotta make a livin. They pick up all that money for fishin license and shit, talkin about how they gonna stock de river and they never stock it, talkin about how they gonna stock de place so you can catch crappie, they never stock. The only thing my fishin license do is make it so dat game warden, he can just worry the hell out of you."

Donald Clayton was a huge man, nearly as tall as his safe, which was almost the height of the wall in his office. After he took four thousand dollars in bills out of there to pay for the ton and a quarter of crappie, it looked like nothing was missing. "He must have had a hundred thousand dollars cash in there," Tullos says. "He told us that besides fish he sold a lot of television sets and guns. I wish I'd've seen old racist Beetle deliver five tons of fish up there in the middle of the night."

The run to Chicago was a revelation. Tullos hadn't believed Beetle when he bragged to him that he trucked three hundred thousand pounds of fish up there in a single year. Now he did. Then there was Saint Louis, there was Memphis, there was Jackson—those were all big markets; Beetle had told him so. The gang had to be selling in other cities, too. Concordia and Catahoula could swallow a lot of illegal game fish themselves. Down-on-their-luck sportsmen probably bought a couple dozen pounds from time to time to take home. These weren't drug-size profits the Larto gang was making, but they were big-time country boy profits. Someone might go to some extreme lengths not to lose such business.

At first Tullos had thought, No one gets killed over a bunch of fish—even when he was looking at Butch Cross's .45 and Darwin's huge knife. But now he felt like a circus acrobat walking over an alligator pit, which had two types of alligators in it. On the one side were the Beetle Books and David Paulks and Butch Crosses; on the other were his own people—the game wardens on the take, the sheriff, the D.A., and the local judge who had delicately tapped the outlaws on the knuckles all these years. Except for Dave Hall and Emmett Bonner, he was alone behind enemy lines. The corrupt wardens, whoever they were, would *not* want to see him take down this case, because a David Paulk in custody was a David Paulk who would sing—he would try to plea-bargain his way out of a felony offense because such an offense would bar him from ever seeking public office again, and without his political power base, his outlaw career was sunk. As for the law-enforcement people who were protecting him, they could be regarded by a tough federal judge as co-conspirators in a Lacey Act offense. (The Lacey Act prohibits interstate commerce in protected species; violators can face five years in the penitentiary and a twenty-thousand-dollar fine.) The game wardens might not just lose their jobs and pensions; they could end up ruined for life. Tullos was beginning to see respectable odds that, at some point, he was going to have to shoot his way out of this one or at least lay his badge and gun on the table and dare someone to shoot him. Only he wasn't carrying his badge most of the time. He usually wasn't carrying his gun. That was the grim little irony of undercover police work—a lot of the time you couldn't risk carrying a gun. You depended on backup. But he had none.

The case was consuming him. The astronomical divorce rate among undercover agents began to make plenty of sense. He was Dave Trahan now from morning to night; it was as if he no longer knew who David Tullos was. In the early morning, when he ate breakfast and played with Chaney, he was Tullos; but the moment he kissed Doreena goodbye he metamorphosed. During the drive from his house to Concordia parish, which took a couple of hours, he played with lines, lies—everything he said was a lie, anyway—with excuses, alibis, right moves versus wrong moves. By the time he hit Ferriday, it was all clattering around randomly in his head and he had to force himself to stop. And that drive was the time he *relaxed*. The rest of the day—when he was acting out his nineteen-year-old coon-ass role—demanded a state of total concentration, as if he were playing pool for five thousand dollars a game. He had to lose himself completely in the role. He couldn't remind himself—not for a *second*—that he was an undercover agent in the midst of a bunch of outlaws, any more than a pool hustler lining up the eight ball can remind himself that if he misses, it is going to cost him a fortune. Pure concentration requires *serenity*. But when the performance was over he was still acting it out in his head, anything but serene. What had he said that was wrong? What compromising little remark had he uttered that he would have to do something about? As he drove home, he thought strategy. How *was* he going to trick David Paulk? What about the sheriff and the D.A.? What a coup it would be if he could rake them up with the rest of them! What if a *game warden* managed to put together an ironclad case against a corrupt local judge? The possibilities made him giddy.

But then, when he was finally back at False River and saw a fat moon reflected beyond the huge swamp oak by the side of the road where the lake first comes into view, he suddenly wanted to break down. Emotionally, the case was destabilizing him.

Why had he taken this job? Why had he taken this case? Was he really taking all these risks for a *fish?* His brother's friends had just opened a fancy new discotheque and restaurant; why didn't he just tend bar there? He could make twice as much money. Why didn't he go back on patrol with Cecil again? Why didn't he just *drop the goddamned case?!*

When he got home he was exhausted, moody—and he still wasn't ready to become Tullos again. He sat down in his BarcaLounger, underneath the stuffed squirrel mounted on his wall, and brooded. He came out of Dave Trahan bit by bit, as a snake slowly wriggles out of its skin. Some nights he never did.

It was damaging his marriage, he could see that. Doreena was a Cajun Catholic southern belle—she had graduated from the school of sweet, passive southern womanhood—but when Tullos walked in the door and just sat down and tuned out, he could feel her resentment . . . when he was paying attention anyway. And when they went out for an evening and he had a couple of drinks and became fun-loving, wonderfully entertaining David Tullos again, it hurt her how he held their friends spellbound; everyone's attention cascaded over him while she sat there like a beached little fish. After all, he was an undercover game warden, and she was a postal clerk; her ego wasn't strong enough to handle him *or* his career. Even when he tried to draw her in, she sulked, and now there was something almost explosive about her sullen repose.

Tullos wasn't blind. He saw how things were going between them, at least sometimes. But he couldn't make enough time for Doreena. He was obsessed. He hated himself for doing it, but he was becoming a little like Dave Hall. On the other hand, he didn't have an ordinary job.

To do it right, he *had* to be obsessed and consumed. And he *was* going to do it right. Tullos has very little patience for a lot of things, but he found he had enormous patience playing this undercover game. It was something he just couldn't rush. Nothing was likelier to bring the edifice down around his ears than a hurried or off-balance move.

Gueho, who was playing an ever-larger role himself, had a different take on the entire thing. Gueho's attitude toward undercover work was that of a whore in a hurry. He didn't like cases that went on for too long—in part because he was almost as scared as Tullos of being betrayed by someone at Wildlife and Fisheries, but mainly because he simply had a lower tolerance for irresolution . . . or for complexity anyway. Perhaps he was just less patient. They *had* Beetle. He was enough of a prize. When they prosecuted him, it would scare the daylights out of all the others. They could still make a run at Paulk, but there was no point in putting months into this thing, and thousands and thousands of dollars. It wasn't necessary. Besides, how many more trips to Chicago was he going to have to make? How many more times was he going to have to play silly old Uncle Junior and drive through that sprawling ghetto in a truck with Louisiana plates wheezing under a camper shell crammed with illegal fish? God knew what those Negroes thought was in the camper shell, but he was willing to bet they thought it was something more tantalizing than fish, and if they heard a Louisiana accent chirping, those coons would probably *massacre* them.

Tullos ought to have seen it coming, knowing Gueho, but still he wasn't quite ready when he jumped the gun.

"You know," Gueho told Beetle when they were back at his house after the Chicago run, "we got to be more efficient about this."

"Efficient?"

"It was a hell of a long trip up there. We got to be more efficient. Maybe next time we should load directly at his house instead of do the vehicle transfer and all that."

"Paulk don't want no strangers brought around. I told you."

"Well, we're doin good business with him. We ain't really strangers."

Tullos was frantic. "Uncle Junior, goddamn, if he ain't willin he's not . . ." Gueho was out of his mind! Why would Uncle Junior want to run the extra risk of loading up at Paulk's house—Paulk, who was convinced he was being watched by the feds—when he had an expendable nephew to do it for him? Beetle would smell a rat!

"Well, it's a *long* ride up there."

Tullos saw Beetle's antennae uncurl and go up. He thought he saw a grim gray light of recognition begin to glow across his face. Beetle had them figured out! Why else would they want to deal directly with Paulk? He had to cut this conversation's throat.

"Like I was thinking, Mister Beetle, maybe we should have one driver with the fish and the other of us in another car, that way we don't all of us get arrested if the game wardens come around. We could use CBs to communicate." He just pulled it out of thin air.

Beetle grunted. Tullos was already contemplating an immediate takedown. He was sure Beetle knew who they were now.

"Them CBs—can the game wardens hear in on them?" Beetle asked.

Now Tullos wasn't so sure.

"No. Unh-unh."

Shit! Tullos chomped down on his tongue. How was he supposed to know that?

"That's a sure fact?"

Tullos began jabbering like a lunatic, making up stories about using citizen-band radios in the oil business, communicating by CBs from oil platforms, from helicopters, lockout channels.

"Damn!" said Beetle, "I guess you know that shit."

Tullos shucked and jived, as if he had been paid the greatest compliment imaginable. "I'm just startin out, Mister Beetle, but a boy got to know *somethin.*" He suddenly had the vaguest of ideas about how to get to David Paulk.

Beetle was now calling every couple of days. He always had more fish to sell. One night Darwin had gone out and jacked three deer; did Big Jim want to buy a couple? He had crayfish. He had catfish. He had bream. He had gasper gou. Some of it was legal and most of it was not. Even though Beetle was scamming him, he also treated him like a son—better than he treated Darwin, although Darwin didn't deserve to be treated better than a crocodile. Gueho's dumb remark apparently hadn't jeopardized the operation after all. Beetle needed their money so much he wasn't as suspicious as he ought to be. Tullos figured that Beetle was probably making two, three, or maybe four times as much money as he was, but he had nothing to show for it except his trailer and truck and monofilament nets. There was mildew on the walls of the trailer, and its aluminum skin was peeling off. Beetle didn't even have a telephone. Tullos wondered how he spent it all. Sometimes he would go on a drunk, but liquor is cheap, and Beetle spent money as if he were hooked on coke. He either gambled it away or dropped it on women or had made some woebegone business deals (he had alluded to a couple of those). However he spent it, it went through his fingers like sand. Tullos was sure he didn't let Zola and the girls give it all to the Pentecostal church. One Sunday evening, when he had gone over and found Beetle in a lazy mood, just lying on the couch drinking a beer, Zola and the daughters had shown up in frilly dress, saying they were going to church; when Tullos said he wanted to come along, Beetle almost leaped off the couch. "No you ain't!" He meant it, too. They went out and drank instead. The Books were not so much a family as they were a juxtaposition of holy and profane.

The next trip to Chicago was scheduled for February 19. Beetle told Tullos that he would probably put together another three thousand pounds. Tullos called Dave Hall, who said he wanted to join in the run this time. He would meet him along the route somewhere. Tullos told him that he was going to get to Paulk's house that night—he didn't know how he would do it, but he was going to be there and his recorder would be running. Dave Hall said if he was that sure, he would send a couple of federal agents over to stake out the place in case something went wrong. They would have night scopes and rifles. Emmett Bonner would be there, too, but he wouldn't tell any of the other local game wardens where he was going.

Tullos and Beetle left the trailer just after eight o'clock on the evening of the nineteenth. For some reason, Beetle was acting much less hincky. It sounded as if he were going to take Tullos with him to Paulk's. He was even telling Tullos not to call Paulk by his name when he met him because Paulk would have a fit. He told him again how Paulk's best fishing buddy had worked with some federal agents to try to arrest him—that was why he was more paranoid than anyone else, that and his standing in the community. He was scared of this and scared of that. He thought his phone was bugged. The more Beetle let himself go on, the more bothered he became by a vision of Paulk greeting him and Tullos with a shotgun. Maybe he *was* scared of this Paulk. When they were half a mile shy of the Monterey Coop, Beetle pulled to the side of the road. Tullos knew he had chickened out.

"You better give me the money and let me go," he said.

"You for real, Mister Beetle?"

"It got to worryin me, Dave. I really don't think Dave Paulk's gonna like me bringin you."

Tullos had to do something fast. He was stumped. No! He had to think of something. But what? He had to!

He decided to cry. He had never tried to cry in his life. He had no idea whether any undercover agent in history had ever tried crying to get out of a jam, but he was in one now and he had to get out of it fast.

He didn't just cry. He bawled. He yammered like a baby!

"Don't nobody trust me," he burbled through a pair of tears he managed to wring out of an eye.

Beetle said, "Hunh?"

"My daddy didn't trust me, my granddaddy didn't trust me, Uncle Junior don't trust me. Nobody gives me no responsibility. Haul a few fish, Dave. Find us a little deer meat, Trahan. All I am is a go-fer, is what I am. How am I gonna make anything of myself?"

"Hell, Dave . . . you know how to survey—"

"That don't mean shit to me."

"Hunh . . ."

"I don't mean to go on"—Jesus! It all sounded like a ground-down cliché, but it seemed that he had Beetle on treble hooks—"but it's the Lord's truth. And now it's you, too, Mister Beetle." The tears were pouring from his eyes.

Beetle got out of the truck. He slowly walked around the back end and came up to Tullos's door and opened it. He yanked him out of the truck as if he had seen through it all and was going to slit his throat. Instead, he gave Tullos a great big hug.

"Well, I tell you what. We're gonna go over to his house together, me and you, and if he don't like it, well, then, *fuck him!*"

Tullos managed a weak, slobbery smile. Beneath it, he was grinning from ear to ear. When they got to Paulk's house and Beetle went inside to explain things to him first, he sat in the truck and began to laugh out of control. He couldn't help himself.

"*Sucker!*" he said aloud. "You *sucker!*"

Later that night, while Tullos and Beetle were doing business inside Paulk's house, Frank Simms, one of the federal game wardens watching from the woods across the road, was chased up a tree by Paulk's dog. Neither Tullos nor Beetle nor Paulk heard the dog bark. But Tullos's Nagra did.

Paulk had not taken his sudden appearance badly at all. He looked him over very carefully, but Beetle had softened him up and Tullos was ready for him—he got out of the truck with a huge grin plastered across his face and his hand extended and his coon-ass babble bubbling like a squirrel gumbo. He was acting like a fifteen-year-old getting his first big-time kicks, and he probably looked it, too. Beetle had mainly been scared that Tullos would find out about his skimming twenty cents off every dollar he paid him—that was what Paulk's so-called paranoia was really about. Or half of it. Tullos had guessed that one right, too, and he got Beetle to confess it to him in the truck on the way to Paulk's.

It was downright miraculous what those three minutes of bawling had wrought. They were on the level with each other now! Tullos said it was Big Jim's and Uncle Junior's money, not his, and he didn't care if Beetle skimmed a little extra profit; he would never tell them about it. Big Jim was a hell of a con artist anyway; he had a dozen scams going at once. Beetle was aglow. They were partners! They were going to screw Paulk by understating Chicago's price so he would sell to them for less money; they were going to siphon a bit of profit—together now!—from Uncle Junior and Jim Pridgen; they were going to branch out into alligator skins and dope and women. Maybe Beetle wasn't too old to become a pimp. Big Jim could supply the girls from Jackson— if they were sixteen or seventeen years old, that would be ideal—and he could dole them out to the politicians who were helping them. Then they would *really* be safe. Women meant even more to them boys than votes and payoffs because pretty young girls were hard to find out in these boonies; they were usually over the hill by the time they were fifteen. And if the *politicians* knew that *they* knew they were fucking underage girls . . . well, what could they do? *They had them!* . . . This was how you lived!

Dave Trahan was beginning to feel that way, too, which was why he decided to screw Beetle back. He was supposed to be an outlaw now, and any outlaw with two brain cells in his head would drop Beetle Book like a lump of *merde* once he could do business directly with Paulk. Paulk would expect him to do that anyway; so he did. He didn't exactly screw Beetle; he just bought independently from Paulk without telling Beetle about it. Beetle probably sensed it, though, and Trahan had them climbing over each other just to get at him and the inexhaustible demand from Uncle Junior and Big Jim. Not that Paulk wasn't still leery. Once, when Tullos walked into his house, he greeted him with "I *know* who you are," and it was a good thing Tullos managed to stay cool because Paulk was only talking about the license plate check the sheriff had run on Uncle Junior's truck; it had led right to Tullos's make-believe brother in New Orleans. They had run a check on his telephone, too, which was in Dave Hall's office in Slidell, but Tullos had run the phone through an exchange in New Orleans, so he came up clean again. Tullos sat at home evenings with a big grin on his face, replaying conversations where Paulk and Beetle badmouthed each other. "Beetle ain't cautious enough," Paulk told him one day. "Look at all the times he's been caught. Me, I never got caught. I been doing this for years and years and I only got stopped once. I'd be extra careful about doing business with Book. He's got things all stirred up around here. The game warden's been watchin him." And Beetle said, "Paulk's not predictable. I don't trust him and them boys of his, and hell, look at how he's got it stirred up around here since they caught him with them funny permits of his. It's them permits got them mad cause they knew they was being conned and couldn't do nuthin about it. I don't use them damned things, Dave, they ain't worth all the bother. And now Paulk, he's paying twenty-five cents a pound on them permits, so you buy from him and he's gotta cover that. He used to just pay a nickel a pound until he got em stirred up there in Arkansas."

The only bad thing was that Tullos had really heated up the market for sacalait. Not that the market didn't already exist, but he was now shopping for used freezers in Beetle's behalf because Beetle was tired of using everyone else's, and now that he was doing regular business with Junior and Big Jim, he needed more reliable storage. Every time they bought another couple hundred pounds, a collective groan arose from the hospitals and schools for troubled youth in the region because they were the ones who were being force-fed all the fish. Tullos wondered whether there would be a crappie left in Larto Lake by the time they brought down the case. "It's an amazing resource, though, that lake is. You can almost understand how these outlaws felt they'd never run out of fish. And it isn't half what it used to be because Larto Lake is part of Saline Basin, which got all messed up by the Corps of Engineers. The one thing we had in common was, we all ragged on the old Corps. Those dirtbags could sound like the Sierra Club at times."

Dave Hall, whose enthusiasm for techno-gimcrackery is nearly boundless, decided they had to get some of it on film. On the evening of February 26, after the second Chicago run (Donald Clayton had told them he would probably sell out the two and a half thousand pounds in three days), Tullos drove Beetle to the Ramada Hilltop Inn at Natchez, where Dave Hall and two concealed video cameras were waiting for them. One was in a Kleenex dispenser in the bathroom; the other, a tiny cylindrical thing, was in a coat sleeve. Tullos had watched Dave Hall and an agent from the Bureau of Alcohol, Tobacco, and Firearms spend most of the day setting up the surveillance; they had practically torn up the room. With a good bottle of bourbon and a twelve-pack of beer on the table, Beetle felt quite relaxed. For two hours he told them about forty years of poaching game fish and how he had gotten away with it—about his uncle, Julius Book, who had run interference for him when he was chief of enforcement for Wildlife and Fisheries; about two generations of purchasable game wardens ("Some of the high-ups are workin on transferrin this new one. The way they do it sometime is they promote them out of there"); about the cooperative sheriff and the district attorney and the judge whose crop he used to keep beetle-free. Dave Hall showed me the video once, at his home. We were sitting on a couch that felt mushier than a waterbed, and Dave Hall sank into it and immediately went to sleep. After about twenty minutes the video showed Tullos reaching into a bag of potato chips, and a hypersensitive microphone picked up the sound of a granite quarry where huge rocks were being crushed. Dave Hall woke with a vengeance. "Goddamn Tullos," he snarled. "All that crunchin and munchin! We could of lost this whole tape! I couldn't kick him under the table, but I felt like knocking his head off!" When Tullos finally stopped eating, he went right back to sleep.

2/26/86 (the same night as the videotaping): Tullos buys six hundred eighty-one pounds of game fish from Johnny Brigman and two hundred twenty-five pounds from Charles Lee Ellard, mainly to nail the Lacey Act to their door.

3/3/86: Beetle Book calls Buck Pridgen at the Redwood Inn and asks again whether Big Jim is interested in five hundred pounds of fresh deer meat. Deer season is seven months away.

3/3/86: Tullos calls Beetle Book about a freezer he has located. Beetle says he has another five hundred pounds of sacalait for sale.

3/4/86: Tullos, in Beetle's company, buys crappie from W. L. Adams and Dellard Watney, more of Paulk's boys, again to apply the Lacey Act. For the recorder's sake, and that of the judge and jury who will try the case, Tullos makes a point of mentioning that the fish are going to cross state lines and that they are all involved in a federal felony offense. He has the right measure of fear and pride in his voice. They say they are well aware of this. Later that night, Tullos sneaks over to Paulk's to buy more fish and to get him to explain how he obtains phony fish-farm permits from Arkansas. He does. He also shows Tullos his gigantic walk-in freezer, camouflaged in a building out back. Still later that night, Tullos goes back to Beetle Book's and meets up with Tommy Tiffee, the goliath who stomped a game warden senseless with his cowboy boots. Tullos learns that Tiffee's leg was broken at the time.

3/8/86: Tullos calls Paulk to ask about obtaining phony fish-farm permits. Paulk says he isn't sure he can get some because he hasn't got everything straightened out there yet.

3/17/86: Tullos arranges to buy five hundred more pounds of crappie from David Paulk and at least that much from the others. He plans to arrive on the following night and spend a couple of days.

3/20/86: About fifty federal and state game wardens gather at the Days Inn in Natchez to split into teams for a massive raid on Larto Lake and environs.

On the night before the takedown, Tullos developed an awful feeling about the case. He had worked it for nearly six months, and everything had gone flawlessly—too flawlessly. Now he began to wonder why. He tried to be rational about it. Before any great event in your life—marriage, the birth of a child, the publication of a book—you always worry that you are going to be hit by a runaway locomotive or a meteorite. The waiting becomes unbearable, and you know that the Evil Gods Who Plot Fuck-ups are sitting up there somewhere in the sky, drinking mead, convulsed in cruel laughter, making diabolical plans. How could he have been on the case for six months, dodging an allegedly corrupt sheriff, an allegedly corrupt district attorney, an allegedly corrupt local judge, and God knows how many corrupt wardens and officials at Wildlife and Fisheries and have his cover remain intact? On one of the nights when he went out drinking with Beetle and some of the others in the gang, why hadn't one of the local wardens joined in and recognized him? Why hadn't someone as spooky as David Paulk figured out who he was? If he had been burned on a previous case—and he was—when he *knew* his cover was solid—and it wasn't—then why not on this one, when he was tortured by doubt all the time? What last-second apocalypse awaited him?

He told himself that it was all nonsense, that his imagination was taking advantage of his chronic exhaustion and exercising a perverse will of its own. But the last night was turning into an Indian gauntlet run. When he arrived at Beetle's at nine in the evening, he found him in a foul mood—the worst he had seen—because of a few hundred dollars he owed him. Tullos hadn't paid him for a couple of recent buys because, as far as Wildlife and Fisheries was concerned, the case was costing a fortune, and if he gave Beetle another thousand dollars, even on the last night before the takedown, he would make it disappear before they busted him. But now Beetle was demanding that he pay up—and quickly. Was Beetle suspicious or smart enough to figure out why he hadn't been paid? Probably not. But then again . . .

In any event, he had planned another big buy for the final night, mainly to keep all the suspects busy as the strike force came at them like Napoleon's army. He wanted everyone there because the gang had safe houses all over the place where they could hide out if for any reason they managed to escape the bust. He wanted these people in jail, not out looking for revenge. (He also wanted a mountain of poached fish to show off to the press. Saying that he had bought five tons over the course of several months would mean nothing to a television camera.) That meant he was going to have to deal with all of the outlaws once more, even while knowing that they were hours away from handcuffs and their imminent fate would be all his doing. What slip of the tongue, what facial tic would give him away? For the first time, he didn't trust his own nerves. It was one thing to work a case when the takedown was weeks away. But when fifty agents were getting ready to climb into their cars, when they were checking shotgun casings and tear-gas canisters, and when he knew that and the people he was drinking with didn't—they would be laughing and bragging and talking outlaw talk, utterly oblivious . . . He couldn't let himself think about it, but he hadn't imagined how much pure will that required. It was all he could manage not to seem distracted.

At a few minutes before ten, Tullos and Beetle got in Beetle's truck and drove over to Butch Cross's place. Beetle drove the roads back and forth for almost half an hour before they went in; he said he had a feeling there were game wardens around. His antennae were fully erect—Tullos had never seen him quite that way before.

Tommy Tiffee was at Butch Cross's house that night, and seemed a little too interested in where Tullos was taking the fish later that night. Tullos told him they were going to Memphis. Tiffee wanted to know where in Memphis. Tullos figured that a real outlaw doesn't reveal his buyers any more than a cop identifies his informants, so he played coy with him. Tullos also complained about a sour smell coming from a few bags of fish, and he said some of the others were too small. Tiffee didn't like that a bit, but Tullos thought to himself that it was a good move; if he accepted some spoiled and undersized fish without a peep of complaint, it could get someone to wondering.

To his inexpressible relief, Tullos got out of there without incident and with twelve hundred pounds of crappie in the camper shell in the back of Beetle's truck. At midnight they drove up to W. L. Adams's trailer to add a few hundred pounds to the load. They ended up spending two hours there. For some reason everyone was bragging about his law-enforcement connections that night. Dellard Watney said the sheriff, Hubert McGlothin, was as big an outlaw as the rest of them; that was the reason he rarely arrested anyone—because everyone had the goods on him, too. Adams talked about all the times he had plea-bargained his way down to an inconsequential misdemeanor, no matter what the offense. Watney's cousin was an assistant district attorney in the parish—that was how he always got off. Were they setting him up? Were they trying to smoke him out? Tullos couldn't figure out what was going on. The wait was excruciating now. He tried to imagine where the strike force was. Were they still in Natchez? Were they at the local LDWF headquarters in Ferriday? Tullos knew they were going to reconnoiter there, and that had him badly scared. None of the local wardens was supposed to be told what was going on, but when fifty wildlife agents suddenly descended on the place and began laying in guns, anyone with an IQ in the high two digits ought to be able to figure out that the Larto Lake gang was about to be taken down. They were the only outlaws in the area who deserved to be treated with such respect. All it would take was one last-minute telephone call . . .

Tullos decided that he had to get back to Beetle's trailer because Beetle was the one person who didn't have a phone. It was the safest place to be. Here, at Adams's, if the phone rang, it could be bad, bad news for him, and he would never know.

The problem was Beetle had gone to sleep in the back of Adams's trailer. Beetle lived like an animal, an opportunistic animal—a coyote or a raccoon—and he had developed sleeping habits in kind. He never slept long, but he took snoozes all the time. His whole life had been a succession of deals, drinking, fishing, women, and naps.

Tullos didn't know what to do. If he seemed anxious to leave and woke him up, how would that look? Uncle Junior wasn't due at his place until four or five in the morning. He decided to let him sleep. He sat around with Adams and Watney for another hour and a half, listening to outlaw stories. Watney was on probation for half a dozen offenses, but none was particularly serious. It was better to be here than with serious outlaws like Tiffee and Butch Cross. But they were just down the road.

Finally, at a few minutes after two, Beetle woke up. Tullos all but hustled him out of there and got him back to his trailer, where Beetle promptly went to sleep again. In another hour and a half, it would be over. Tullos sneaked out and got his gun and his badge out of his own truck. Then, for lack of anything better to do, he sat down and began updating his case report. If Beetle woke up, he would show it to him. It was as good a way as any to introduce himself.

At four-thirty, he heard a vehicle pull up to the house. He almost didn't dare look. It was Gueho. There were four uniformed state game wardens with him. He hoped they were the right kind.

Beetle took it hard. When Tullos and Gueho showed him their badges, he went numb. He didn't appear mad; his eyes just expressed the deep hollowness of someone who returns home after a tornado has come through. He sat there, wordless, for a good while longer. Then he began to tremble. Tullos had brewed him a pot of coffee while he was asleep, but Beetle couldn't raise the cup to his lips. Finally he said, "I don't know how anyone can lie like you did." Tullos wasn't sure he knew the answer himself.

At three in the morning, we finally left Natchez. We didn't so much leave as explode out of there—nothing was going to be left to chance. We stopped briefly at Wildlife and Fisheries' regional office in Ferriday to pick up a few local game wardens, who had been roused out of bed an hour earlier. For obvious reasons, they weren't given the faintest idea what was going on, but it would have looked bad if Emmett Bonner had been the only local agent allowed to help bring down the biggest ring of wildlife outlaws operating in the state. I did notice that the federal wardens appeared to occupy all the telephones.

Dave Hall and Ray Montet, erstwhile buddies whose relationship had long since gone sour, but who were finally cooperating on a case again, were in the lead cars. (In a talk to the invited press—Dave Hall's doing—back at the Days Inn, Montet had made a big deal of how the feds and state had cooperated magnificently on the case.) I brought up the rear, not so much by choice as by necessity; I had rented a four-cylinder Mustang in New Orleans, which had a top end of ninety-three miles per hour, and the thing couldn't keep up with the other nineteen vehicles in the whizzing caravan. A few miles shy of Larto Lake, we had first light. A couple of farmers were already pulling out of their drives. I remember how their eyes bugged out and their jaws appeared to drop into their laps. In the rearview mirror I could see one running back to his house. I remember how sweet-scented the morning air was in the effulgence of spring. There were blossoming shrubs everywhere back in the woods, and the live oaks lining the road were burdened with ripe Spanish moss. It was a good life these Larto Lake outlaws had. It seemed a shame that it wasn't legal. If they had left Louisiana alone, instead of civilizing the place half to death, it might still be.

David Paulk lived in a big brick ranch house right across the road from the endless semicircular lake, which sat there rippling quietly and exhaling morning mist. Dave Hall went up and rang the bell, and I saw a light go on and a large pale blond man in an undershirt look out the window to see a bunch of people carrying weapons on his lawn. Paulk must have thought he could still get out of this one because his reaction seemed to me one of forced equanimity. When we reporters crowded close around his house and began peering in the window, Dave Hall came out in a fury and chased us all away, yelling something about respect for privacy and the Bill of Rights. I walked over toward the lake and played with Paulk's oaf of a dog, the one that had chased the game warden up a tree on the night Tullos ensured Paulk's demise. The dog knew something was going on because he let forth a series of low, whimpering whines.

A couple of the federal wardens took a call on the radio from Gueho, who said that he and Tullos were going to round up the others and wanted some reinforcements. I jumped into their truck. As we passed the store and bar at Cocodrie Landing, we saw Tullos's vehicle parked outside. He had noticed Watney and Adams's truck on the way by and decided he might as well arrest them then and there. When we pulled in, he decided to let the federals do it instead. I sat in their truck and watched. Tullos had gone into the store, as if he were pretending not to know Adams and Watney from the gehkwar of Baroodi. I suppose it was his last opportunity to play a role that he was going to find very difficult to give up. When Tullos sauntered out, Adams and Watney, who had been read their rights, charged, and released on personal recognizance, came skulking over to him. They were both short and wiry and had long, greasy hair.

"Dave," I heard one of them hiss under his breath, "get the fuck out of here! It's the fucking law!"

You should have seen their expressions when he told them who he was.

Tullos visited Beetle a couple of times in the penitentiary. Beetle was deeply fearful that David Paulk was going to hurt him because it was he who had given Tullos his opportunity to nail him. He ended up sharing a cell with him anyway because everyone else in the place looked a lot more worrisome than Paulk. They spent their six months there arguing about whose fault everything was. Paulk wouldn't talk to Tullos when he visited, but Beetle held him in such awe that he wasn't even able to get mad; he just wanted to know how Tullos had outsmarted him. Darwin, on the other hand, who, like most of the others, wasn't sentenced to jail by the federal judge who tried the case but was fined for almost all he was worth and lost his hunting and fishing privileges for several years, sank into a miasmic rage that will bother him until he dies. It was Darwin, ironically, whom Tullos ran into a few months later at a gas station a few miles down the road from his house. There was so much hate in Darwin's eyes that Tullos didn't bother to try to talk to him. Instead, he went out and bought himself another gun.

The sheriff, Hubert Lee McGlothin, the district attorney, Johnny Johnson, and the presiding local judge, who were all reputed to have fixed and thrown cases for the Larto Lake gang, were never tried or prosecuted or even investigated for game-law violations, despite some fairly strong circumstantial evidence. However, the case was one of the things that made the FBI pay closer attention to McGlothin; he finally became the target of an involved investigation and, in September of 1990, pled guilty to charges of mail fraud. ("That's what they get all these gyppo politicians on," Tullos said when he called me up and gleefully told me the news. "If someone sent a body through the mail, they'd still go after him for mail fraud.") Johnny Johnson has come under savage criticism in the local press for not mounting the investigation itself, and the entire Concordia Parish police jury is being investigated and audited. Meanwhile, McGlothin's regime as sheriff of Concordia Parish is being compared to the reign of his predecessor, Noah Cross. In Louisiana, that could be taken as a compliment.

For what all this may be worth, though, it is entirely possible that the Larto Lake gang—minus Beetle Book (who migrated away somewhere, reportedly to Alabama) and David Paulk (who lost his police juror's seat, his vehicles and boats, a lot of his money, and, most likely, his ability to fix things)—is operating again today.

"If I could find me a good makeup artist," David Tullos says, "and change my voice and grow or shrink about four inches, I'd be tempted to make another run at that bunch."

About a year and a half after he brought down the Larto gang, I flew back to Louisiana and saw Tullos again.

His life had taken some interesting turns. He hadn't been able to work any cases for several months afterward—not seriously anyway. Everything was too insignificant or mundane. He was suffering from undercover malaise, the profound depression and ennui that follow the adventure high. Finally, he managed to make one more big case on an Arkansas fish farmer who was making a 3,000 percent profit selling white amur—a giant, gluttonous, horribly destructive bottom-feeding fish, worse even than carp, and, like carp, an import from China—which is banned absolutely in forty-nine of the fifty states even though it can't survive in some of them. The amur is used in China for pondweed control (the fish farmer was advertising it as the "environmentally sound answer" to pondweed), but, like carp, it is utter hell on game fish and waterfowl habitat; it's a vertebrate version of water hyacinth or Russian thistle or kudzu. At first it seemed that Tullos busted up the operation before many amur managed to ride the overflow from farm and golf course ponds and spread through the South's aquatic habitat, but more and more of the fish have been netted lately in rivers and large lakes and streams, so it's quite possible the region is now host to yet another horrendous ecological pest, courtesy of greed. "If I'd brought him down just a few months earlier," Tullos told me, "I might have stopped it. He may have been the only bastard in the whole country selling those monsters big-time."

As Tullos was wrapping up that case, Doreena left him. He might have taken it better if she hadn't run off with the postmaster from Jackson, or if he had seen it coming. Their new baby, Seth, was four months old when Doreena said she was leaving, and he decided to fight her for custody of the children. Fight is what he did. Once, in the office of Doreena's lawyer, the lawyer paid him an insult that Tullos, whose nerves were completely shot by everything that had happened within a few months, simply couldn't brush off, so he went after him and wrestled him to the floor and bit him clean through the cheek as the lawyer had a clutch hold on a sensitive part of his anatomy.

Tullos won custody anyway: Doreena was as tired of being a mother as she was of being Tullos's wife, so she conceded to his demands before the trial. Until he could work out day-care arrangements, however, it was impossible for him to work an ordinary undercover caseload. He begged to be temporarily transferred back to uniformed patrol. Instead, he was permanently moved out of the covert-operations unit by the same superior for whom he was forced to poach fish when he joined the force. Mainly for the sake of his children, Tullos caught himself before he broke his superior's jaw when he served him the news—his fist was clenched, his arm coiled—but despite his formal protest the demotion went through; he went back on mundane patrol—mundane for Louisiana anyway—and had to take a salary cut.

Then Doreena was assaulted. She was grabbed by a young black burglar as she returned with a load of groceries to her mother's house. The youth attempted to rape her, she resisted fiercely, and he strangled her and left her for dead. She survived. Tullos knew they could never be man and wife again, but he was torn to pieces over the incident; he has the strongest feelings imaginable about the crime of rape. Rage and raw hurt and despair suffocated him for weeks, and he nearly came unhinged.

A few months later, while patrolling some difficult terrain in an off-road vehicle, he flipped the machine, landed hard, and ripped apart some ligaments in his left knee. He underwent an expensive and extremely painful operation but months afterward could barely extend his leg halfway. "You take a southern outdoor boy and mess up his mind and then mess up his leg, and you've messed him up about as bad as you can," he says. He hit bottom, fell through it, and landed on the next level down. As I write this, he is still on disability leave, his future beyond his imagination or grasp. He has been recognized by several conservation and outdoor organizations for extraordinary contributions to wildlife and fisheries, but he remains quite convinced that Wildlife and Fisheries will never again let him work as an undercover game warden. He was far too successful and, by telling me his story, he violated bureaucracy's cardinal rule.

But then the girl in the ponytail came along. Actually, she came along just before Tullos's accident. He was walking down Bourbon Street in the French Quarter when he saw her sitting at the window of a Cajun music bar. Something about her made him stop, walk in the door, introduce himself, and ask her to dance. Less than a year later, they were married. "Lord, can he lie!" was Kathy Tullos's answer when I asked her why she married him. She is a physician and former beauty queen from Texas with three children of her own; she was going through a bitter divorce herself when Tullos saw her in the window and asked her to dance. She has a practice now near False River, and Tullos has five young boys on his hands, besides Kathy's horse and Jethro the dog, an eleven-month-old German shepherd who, like his namesake, is big and black and mean. In one sense, Tullos is dismally frustrated; he knows the amplitude of his talent at undercover work, and he has metamorphosed from a redneck into a rabid conservationist with no outlet for his passion and no venue for his skills. But in another sense David Tullos—unlike Dave Hall, who is still running himself to physical ruin, trying to save the world before he dies—is as happy as he could ever be. He has found and embraced a measure of calm inside a disintegrating world.

Part IV

LOSS

I N THE improvised economy of the American frontier, beavers were the most valuable thing around. Compulsory, by kingly decree, in the manufacture of English gentlemen's hats since 1638, beaver pelts were a paradigm of fashion by edict; the style caught on in mainland Europe, then in the American colonies, then as far away as China. The result was a beaver holocaust. Beavers were virtually extinct in the original thirteen colonies by the time of the Revolutionary War. They were gone from the territory west of the Appalachian Mountains by the War of 1812. Trappers were scouting for beaver in the Rocky Mountains and the Great Basin four decades before the first Mormons looked down on Great Salt Lake. Since a person could earn six to ten dollars from a single good pelt—several days' wages at the time—the beaver business, by the 1820s and 1830s, had a lot in common with the contemporary cocaine trade: the entry-level traffickers (the trappers) scrambled for virgin beaver territory to exploit and bickered among themselves and killed each other off—they were, by and large, sociopaths—while the top-level traffickers (the Hudson's Bay Company, the American Fur Company, and others) merged and purged themselves into a shadowy, shifting cartel. The first great American fortune—John Jacob Astor's— was made from beaver pelts. Between 1853 and 1877, the Canadian counterpart of Astor's American Fur Company, the Hudson's Bay Company, processed more than three million skins.

For a long time, beavers were the standard of currency on the frontier:

a single pelt bought a pound of tobacco, two axes, or a kettle; four bought a gallon of whiskey. The animals were an endlessly renewable resource—by one estimate, sixty million inhabited the virgin United States alone, with tens of millions more in Canada—but by the 1880s, after two and a half centuries of relentless trapping and hunting, the species was commercially extinct. Ninety-nine point nine percent of the original numbers were gone. Only since the Second World War, in fact, have beavers become fairly common again.

A swimmer, a recluse, an animal at home in subtropical swamps and in Canadian winters, the beaver was tough to exterminate. Other species were easier, like the great auk. A diving seabird about the size of a goose, it formed spectacular penguin-like colonies on the rocky islands and headlands of the North Atlantic, where it was usually so safe from predation that it evolved a disposition somewhat like a dodo's: on land, it feared nothing. "These Penguins are as big as Geese, and fly not," wrote one seaman in 1618, ". . . and they multiply so infinitely upon a certain flat Island that men drive them from thence a boord into their Boates by hundreds at a time; as if God had made the innocence of so poore a creature to become an admirable instrument for the sustenation of man." When European ships began making regular trading voyages across the North Atlantic, the great auk metamorphosed from a curiosity into a free and convenient source of food. Hundreds of thousands were herded onto ships like sheep; their eggs were boiled and packed in barrels. A rendered auk, like most cold-water seabirds and mammals, also produced a valuable oil, and its down feathers made a respectable quilt. In early June of 1844, the last living pair on earth was captured on a small rocky skerry called Eldey, a few miles off the Icelandic coast, and the great auk owned the distinction, as far as we know, of being the first North American animal to go extinct entirely by the hand of man.

The heath hen, or pinnated grouse, was a large upland game bird found mainly along the Atlantic coast from Philadelphia on north. A close relative of the midwestern prairie chicken—it was hard to tell the two apart—heath hens were reported in the early colonies in such prodigious numbers that one wonders how anyone could have starved. According to John Winthrop, the twelve-time governor of Massachusetts colony, the birds were "so common on the ancient busky site of the city of Boston, that laboring people or servants stipulated with their employers, not to have the Heath Hen brought to the table oftener than a few times in a week." But it was also hunted so efficiently that, as early as 1791, when there were still a fair number of moose and bears inhabiting Long Island, any islander found in possession of a pinnated grouse was made to pay a draconian fine of two dollars and fifty cents. It wasn't enough. Henry William Herbert, a sportsman and naturalist who wrote under the pen name Frank Forester, complained bitterly in 1848 that "the destruction of the pinnated grouse, which is total on Long Island, and all but total in New Jersey, and the Pennsylvania oak-barrens, is ascribable to the total and brutally wanton havoc committed among them by the charcoal burners, who frequent those wooded districts; and who, not content with destroying the parent birds, at all seasons, even while hatching and hovering their broods; shooting the half-fledged *cheepers* in whole hatchings at a shot, and trapping them in deep snows—with a degree of wantonness equally barbarous, and unmeaning, steal all the eggs they can find." (Forester was so obviously upset by all this that he lost control of his syntax.) The heath hen was extinct on the mainland by 1869, and at the turn of the century only about a hundred were still alive, scattered across Martha's Vineyard. In the early years of the twentieth century the Vineyard flock, which was fully protected, grew to six or seven hundred, but a fire in the spring of 1916 destroyed a lot of their habitat and killed quite a number of birds. Hawks, poachers, and feral cats stole diligently from among the survivors, none of which was safe in captivity, and the last member of the race, a desolate, threadbare old male, was unofficially sighted for the last time on the eleventh of March, 1932.

Birds fared poorly in nineteenth-century America. By coincidence, the most striking and the most populous of all American birds were both sucked down the vortex of extinction in the same decade. The Carolina parakeet was striking not just because of its brilliant coloration, but because one wouldn't expect to find a parrot in such a cold climate. The northernmost of all the world's true parrots, it was similar in size and appearance to its tropical relatives and distributed throughout the eastern hardwood forest from Florida to New York to the Mississippi Valley. Occasionally, one was reported as far west as the Dakotas. Like parrots everywhere, the Carolina parakeet was gregarious and fond not just of fruit but of pecking at fruit, and those characteristics were its downfall. Alexander Wilson, who was, after Audubon, the most famous of the early American ornithologists, once shot a large number of them— that was what ornithologists did in those days, sometimes to gather specimens and sometimes for the sheer hell of it—observing that "the whole flock swept repeatedly around their prostrate companions, and again settled in a low tree, within twenty yards of the spot where I stood. At each successive discharge, though showers of them fell, yet the affection of the survivors seemed rather to increase; for, after a few circuits around the place, they again alighted near me, looking down on their slaughtered companions with such manifest symptoms of sympathy and concern, as entirely disarmed me." Wilson, like most naturalists of his time, may have let anthropocentrism short-circuit his scientific rationality, but other species of parrots that have survived into modern times display social behavior similar to that of which Wilson wrote—they refuse to leave their slaughtered mates.

The population of Carolina parakeets may have briefly increased in the early 1700s, as orchards and corn rows were planted up and down the Eastern Seaboard, but the parakeets' depredations infuriated colonial farmers, who shot them on sight. According to the nineteenth-century naturalist Frank M. Chapman, parakeets were also "trapped and bagged in enormous numbers by professional bird-catchers," presumably to be eaten or sold as pets; the bird was also "killed in myriads for its plumage and . . . wantonly slaughtered by so-called sportsmen." Audubon was apparently the first to warn of total extermination, and by the latter part of the nineteenth century any naturalist might have offered the same prediction, though it wouldn't have done any good; wildlife-protection laws were still hotly resented, especially in the case of animals perceived as pests. The surviving population of parakeets took a terrible beating during the Civil War, when a couple of million armed and starving men tramped through the heart of its habitat. It was Frank Chapman himself who saw the last known wild band, in April of

1904, in the wilderness that was southern Florida, fluttering through a canopy of cypress trees near Lake Okeechobee. He counted thirteen. The last known Carolina parakeet died in captivity in 1918.

Ever since grade school—before I developed much interest in natural history—I have associated the year 1914 with two things: the First World War and Martha's death. I have carried her image with me all these years: Martha, the last survivor of what was likely the most abundant warm-blooded species that ever lived, falling off her perch at the Cincinnati Zoo, stone-dead. What was it like for the keepers to discover her there on the floor of her cage? Did they find significance in her mortified form—a sense, perhaps, that evolution had taken a drastically wrong turn with the emergence of the thinking ape with opposable thumbs?

How do you compare the continent today with the continent when the passenger pigeons were still here? They were the golf balls of gold gleaming in the gravel bars of Sierra streams. They were the lobsters crawling on Atlantic beaches at low tide. They were the salmon crowding themselves out of spawning creeks and flopping into the woods. They were abundance and superabundance in nature that could never end. In the fall of 1813, when Audubon was riding a keelboat down the Ohio River from Hardensburgh to Louisville, one of the largest flocks anyone ever saw—though it was not *the* largest by any means; Alexander Wilson saw a much larger one—came streaming out of the eastern sky, following the river to some distant roosting place. "The light of the noonday sun," he wrote, "was obscured, as if by an eclipse." The boat drifted on and the flock kept wavering overhead, its dimensions beyond sight. By the time he got to Louisville, Audubon, who should have been fairly good at estimating bird numbers, was willing to venture that a billion one hundred fifteen million pigeons had passed over his head— and as he sat in his lodging house, hour by hour, the horizon was still expelling millions of birds. He chucked his immediate plans, got a horse, and went overland until, in northern Kentucky, around the Green River, he found the swath of forest, miles square, where the birds were laying in:

The dung lay several inches deep, covering the whole extent of the roosting place, like a bed of snow. Many trees, two feet in diameter, I observed, were broken off at no great distance from the ground, and the branches of many of the largest and tallest had given way, as if the forest had been swept by a tornado. Every thing proved to me, that the number of birds resorting to this part of the forest, must be immense beyond conception. As the period of their arrival approached, their foes anxiously prepared to seize them. Some were furnished with iron pots, containing sulphur, others with torches of pine-knots, many with poles, and the rest with guns. The sun was lost to our view; yet not a Pigeon had arrived. [The flock had flown some miles away in search of more food, but passenger pigeons always returned to the roost by nightfall.] Every thing was ready, and all eyes were gazing on the clear sky, which appeared in glimpses amidst the tall trees. Suddenly, there burst forth a general cry of "*Here they come!*" The noise which they made, though yet distant, reminded me of a hard gale at sea, passing through the rigging of a close-reefed vessel. As the birds arrived, and passed over me, I felt a current of air that surprised me. Thousands were soon knocked down by polemen. The current of birds, however, still kept increasing. The fires were lighted, and a most magnificent, as well as a wonderful and terrifying sight, presented itself. The Pigeons, coming in by thousands, alighted everywhere, one above another, until solid masses, as large as hogsheads, were formed on every tree, in all directions. Here and there the perches gave way under the weight with a crash, and, falling to the ground, destroyed hundreds of the birds beneath, forcing down the dense groups with which every stick was loaded. It was a scene of uproar and confusion. I found it quite useless to speak, or even to shout, to those persons who were nearest me. The reports, even, of the nearest guns, were seldom heard; and I knew of the firing, only by seeing the shooters reloading. No one dared venture within the line of devastation; the hogs had been penned up in due time, the picking up of the dead and wounded being left for the next morning's employment. The Pigeons were constantly coming; and it was past midnight before I perceived a decrease in the number of those that arrived. The uproar continued, however, the whole night; and, as I was anxious to know to what distance the sound reached, I sent off a man, accustomed to perambulate the forest, who, returning two hours afterwards, informed me he had heard it distinctly when three miles from the spot. Towards the approach of day, the noise rather subsided; but long ere objects were at all distinguishable, the Pigeons began to move off, in a direction quite different from that in which they had arrived the evening before; and, at sunrise, all that were able to fly had disappeared. The howlings of the wolves now reached our ears, and the foxes, lynxes, cougars, bears, raccoons, opossums, and pole-cats, were seen sneaking off from the spot, whilst Eagles and Hawks, of different species, accompanied by a crowd of Vultures, came to supplant them, and enjoy their share of the spoil. It was then that the authors of all this devastation began their entry amongst the dead, the dying, and the mangled. The Pigeons were picked up and piled in heaps, until each had as many as he could possibly dispose of, when the hogs were let loose to feed on the remainder.

In the slaughter's aftermath, Audubon was moved to make a prediction in which, it turned out, he was wrong in every conceivable way: "Persons unacquainted with these birds might naturally conclude that such havock would soon put an end to the species. But I have satisfied myself, by long observation, that nothing but the gradual diminution of our forests can accomplish this decrease, as they not infrequently quadruple their numbers yearly, and always at least double it."

The passenger pigeons' preferred foods were acorns and beech nuts, which they managed to work down their peristaltic throats—they were only the size of mourning doves. By the 1850s, billions of virgin mast-bearing eastern hardwood trees had been cut down—oaks, chestnuts, beeches, hickories—and replaced either with second growth that produced much less food or with farms. In that sense Audubon was right—American settlement, which meant forest-clearing exactly as we see it in the Amazon today, was sure to reduce the pigeon's numbers catastrophically. But large remnants of habitat remained when the last pigeon died, and since then a lot of the eastern forest has regenerated itself. It was overhunting—unimaginable mass slaughter—that made the passenger pigeon go extinct.

It may not be the awesomeness of the killing—tens if not hundreds of millions were usually annihilated whenever a great flock came in to roost for weeks—that dazes our modern minds so much as the fact that the killing was allowed to go on without end. Every now and then some effort was made, somewhere, to control it, somehow. According to Peter Matthiessen, the naturalist, who made an exhaustive inquiry into early American game laws in the course of writing *Wildlife in America*, none ever succeeded. In 1857, the Ohio legislature commissioned a study of the birds' prospects for survival, and received for its money a splendidly ill-informed and pompous report claiming that "the passenger pigeon needs no protection. Wonderfully prolific, having the vast forests of the North as its breeding grounds, travelling hundreds of miles in search of food, it is here to-day and elsewhere to-morrow, and no ordinary destruction can lessen them or be missed from the myriads that are yearly produced."

Actually, there was nothing prolific about pigeon pairs; they usually produced a single offspring with each mating. There were billions of them only because, for the past fifteen thousand years, they had enjoyed a vast expanse of perfect habitat that nothing had disturbed, and all that habitat lacked was a predator that could kill them efficiently. Now they had an immensely disturbed habitat and a wanton, nightmarishly efficient predator. In 1882, one of the most influential sportsmen's journals of the time, *American Field*, finally brought itself to editorialize that pigeon shooting must be curtailed during the roosting season, roughly March through May. On May 13 of that very same year, the Lacrosse, Wisconsin, *Republican and Leader* carried this brief social item: "The editor of the *Field* and other sportsmen from Chicago took the evening train [to Lacrosse]. They expended a large quantity of powder and shot, and in return received all the pigeons they desired." As for the W. W. Judy Company of St. Louis, the largest pigeon processor in the nation (canned pigeon, like canned tuna today, was a nineteenth-century American staple, and pigeon prices were quoted daily in the financial pages of major newspapers), it received its last shipment of dressed pigeons in 1893, originating from Siloam Springs, Arkansas. For some years, the Judy Company answered inquiries as to why it no longer canned pigeon meat with a form letter explaining that all the flocks had migrated overseas, most likely to Australia.

"The pigeon was no mere bird, it was a biological storm," wrote Aldo Leopold. "He was the lightning that played between the two biotic poles of intolerable intensity: the fat of the land and his own zest for living. Yearly the feathered tempest roared up, down, and across the continent, sucking up the laden fruits of forest and prairie, burning them in a travelling blast of life. Like any other chain-reaction, the pigeon could survive no diminution of his own furious intensity. Once the pigeoners had subtracted from his numbers, and once the settlers had chopped gaps in the continuity of his fuel, his flame guttered out with hardly a sputter or a wisp of smoke."

The buffalo, as everyone knows, was to the American land what the pigeon was to the American sky. In *Wildlife in America*, Peter Matthiessen calls the primordial bison herds "almost certainly the greatest animal congregations that ever existed on earth"—a claim few naturalists have ever disputed. Elephants and wildebeest, springbok and gazelle, pronghorn and elk—in sheer numbers, none compared. In the 1600s, in what is now the continental United States, bison were nearly everywhere. De Soto saw bison in Florida. Spanish friars reported some in California. Cabeza de Vaca saw enormous herds in Louisiana. La Salle, scribbling in his diary somewhere near the future site of Dayton, Ohio, one of the places where I grew up, wrote that, for several days, he had seen "more wild cattle than anyone can say." (A hundred years later, George Washington shot a bison near Gallipolis, one of the last to survive east of the Mississippi River.) The explorer Alexander MacKenzie reported seeing "enormous numbers" as he crossed the Canadian prairie. As one went west and east from the heartland of the continent, the herds slowly feathered out; Jedediah Smith mentions none in Great Basin country, and John Lawson, the surveyor-general of the Carolina colony, remarked that "he [the bison] seldom appears among the English inhabitants, his chief Haunt being in the Land of Massiassippi." But twenty-two towns and cities in as many states, according to one collector of minutiae—not to mention creeks, hollows, mountains, springs, rills, meadows, clearings, and crossings—have become the animals' namesakes (including, obviously, Buffalo, New York).

The eastern bison, or woodland buffalo, was the same animal as the bison of the plains; only its coloration and habits were different. It grazed and lumbered its way single-file under the forest canopy, leaving scalloped trails that engineers transformed into routes for civilization to reach westward. The Wilderness Trail through Cumberland Gap in the

Great Smoky Mountains was one; the Great Portage connecting the Ohio and Potomac rivers was another. (George Washington, who surveyed some of these early pathways, thought that bison trails were "crooked and not well chosen," but Lewis and Clark said the animals possessed "a wonderful sagacity in the choice of routes.") Unwittingly, the eastern bison was, of course, ensuring its own demise by speeding civilization's course west. "Sir, what a wonderful difference thirty years makes in the country," Daniel Boone said to a visitor, John James Audubon, in 1810. "Why, at the time when I was caught by the Indians, you would not have walked out in any direction for more than a mile without shooting a buck or a bear. There were then tens of thousands of buffaloes on the hills of Kentucky; the land looked as if it would never become poor; and the hunt in those days was a pleasure indeed. But when I was left to myself on the banks of the Green River, I daresay for the last time in my life, a few signs only of deer were to be seen. . . ."

When Boone offered that lament, the last bison from the Appalachian ridges had been dead probably for nine years. But there were still twenty-five million on the plains.

From Nathaniel Langford, the first superintendent of Yellowstone National Park, in a letter written to his family in 1862, describing his overland trip: "I want you as a preliminary, to season [your] imaginations with a recital of your own experience with the pigeons in St. Paul in 1857. You remember that enormous flock of them. Did they not darken the air at times? . . . We thought the herds of 5,000, 10,000 or more, very large herds, until we got beyond the second crossing of the Cheyenne River, where . . . we saw a cloud of dust rising in the east, and the rumbling grew louder and I think it was about half an hour before the front of the herd came fairly into view. . . . From an observation with our field glasses, we judged the herd to be 5 or 6 (some said 8 or 10) miles wide, and the herd was more than an hour passing us at a gallop. There seemed to be no space, unoccupied by buffalos. They were running as rapidly as a horse can go at a keen gallop, about twelve miles per hour . . . the whole space, say five miles by twelve miles, as far as we could see, was a seemingly solid mass. . . . I have no doubt that there were one million buffalos in that herd."

From various others:

"There is such a quantity of them that I do not know what to compare them with, except the fish in the sea. . . ."

"[They were] numerous as the locusts of Egypt . . . they were crowded together so densely that in the distance their rounded backs presented a surface of uniform blackness. . . ."

"We could not see their limit either north or west. . . ."

"The plains were black and appeared as if in motion. . . ."

"The country was one robe. . . ."

In sheer numbers, the slaughter of the passenger pigeon eclipsed all others in the history of man and beast, but the downfall of the bison owns a couple of historic distinctions in its own right. A continental herd totaling thirty to sixty million animals—no one will ever know how many there were—was reduced to a few dozen survivors over the course of a hundred and fifty years, but the animals, those that were left, were reproducing the whole time, so many more millions were killed. And since a buffalo outweighed a passenger pigeon by a factor of two or three thousand, the buffalo massacre ranks by weight as the greatest ever. And what sets it apart even more is the fact that nearly all of this miles-high mountain of animal flesh was wasted. Theodore Roosevelt, himself a legendary buffalo killer, but one whose belated efforts helped the species survive, made a long ride across the plains when the bison were nearly gone and observed that the carcasses, which were everywhere, were mostly intact. The animals were killed for body parts—mostly tongues and hides—or they were simply killed and left. The greatest wild-animal resource on the continent, they were treated as if they had little intrinsic value except in death.

That is precisely how their worth was measured. The bison fed the Crow and the Comanche and the Blackfeet and the Sioux; it fed all the plains tribes, who, more than the others, resisted conquest and banishment with a steadfast ferocity. Bison meat, hide, and hair was almost the sum total of their economy, their entire means of subsistence and resistance. The wild and feckless herds would also compete for pasturage with the settlers' domesticable cows. The bison's value was, therefore, inversely proportionate to its numbers; it was measured by the rate at which the species could be wiped out. Left to range, its numbers merely culled, the buffalo was worth a lot to Indians and trappers and traders, who represented the wild West that most Americans, despite their glorification of it, were eager to destroy. Exterminated, it was worth plenty to a frantically aggressive westward-moving agrarian civilization. In 1874, when millions of bison were still alive but a few voices were predicting they would go extinct, General Phil Sheridan answered them before the Texas legislature: "Instead of stopping the professional hunters," he said, "we ought to give them a hearty, unanimous vote of thanks, and appropriate a sufficient sum of money to strike and present each one a medal of bronze, with a dead buffalo on one side and a discouraged Indian on the other. These men have done in the last two years, and will do in the next year, more to settle the vexed Indian question than the entire regular army has done in the last thirty years. They are destroying the Indians' commissary." In that same year, the U.S. Congress finally passed a bill "to prevent the useless slaughter of the Buffaloes within the territories of the United States," only to see it pocket-vetoed by President Grant, who was following the advice of General William Tecumseh Sherman.

Led by *comandantes* of the Sheridan and Sherman ilk, the U.S. Cavalry, of course, shot into any bison herd it saw, and the wagon trains and plains settlers killed plenty for subsistence, and the Indians—who were not always the great conservationists they are made out to have been—happily traded bison tongues for liquor and guns and fabric. But a few thousand professional hunters did most of the job. According to one published record (all of these figures come from *The Time of the Buffalo*, a book written by Tom McHugh), one small group of hunters left about a million pounds of buffalo meat to stink on a hot July day in 1875, in the Kansas Territory, and there was nothing exceptional about that particular stand. Firing a rolling-block .44-90 Remington, or perhaps a newly minted .50-110 Sharp—an ancestral elephant gun—a hunter named Wright Mooar killed ninety-six bison that day, in the span of an afternoon. His companion Kirk Jordan killed one hundred even. Charles Rath killed a hundred and seven. Vic Smith, a hundred and seven, too. Doc Zahl, a hundred and twenty. Tom Nixon, two hundred and four. Brick Bond, two hundred and fifty, or perhaps a few more. A true count was nearly impossible, since, during any such stand, bison were also wounded and stumbled off to die. On the other hand, evolution made the bison too dumb to fathom death and too big to feel an appropriate measure of fear at the sight of a scrawny, slow-moving biped with a gleaming stick, so it usually stood blankly around its dead compatriots, pathetically easy prey. "They cluster around the fallen ones," observed William Hornaday (who, while chief taxidermist for the National Museum, deserves much of the credit, along with Theodore Roosevelt, for saving the last remnant herd). "[They] sniff the warm blood, bawl aloud in wonderment, and do everything but run away."

The bison population plummeted fantastically in the 1860s and 1870s, when thousands of hidemen fanned out across the plains. The skinners followed at their heels, removing hides from flesh and extracting tongues. (The tongues, which were considered a delicacy, could be preserved better than the meat, and hides were worth much more by weight than flesh; that is why they were the only parts most hunters took.) The most famous of the professional hunters, William Frederick Cody, killed 4,280 bison in a single year, but that year was pretty much the sum total of his career; more durable hunters slaughtered many more. Wright Mooar claimed to have killed 20,500 in his nine years on the bison range. If he did indeed, then he may have singlehandedly left behind twenty-two million pounds of rotting flesh. With the railroads the killing intensified. Colonel Richard Irving Dodge, who had proclaimed the bison "limitless" in 1871, was singing a different tune two years later, in his 1873 report on the Kansas Territory. "Where there were myriads of buffalo the year before," he wrote, "there are now myriads of carcasses. The air was foul with a sickening stench, and the vast plain, which only a short twelvemonth before teemed with animal life, was a dead, solitary, putrid desert." Between 1872 and 1874, 4,150,000 buffalo were killed in the Kansas Territory. By 1877, five years after it reached Dodge City, the Santa Fe had reportedly shipped out seven million skins.

The hunters blasted a huge hole in the central portion of the bison range; then they went south; then they went north. By 1875, they were already trespassing into Oklahoma and Texas, Comanche territory protected by the Medicine Lodge treaties. The enraged Comanche killed several hunters, the cavalry decided the treaties were therefore void, and by 1876 it was open season on the southern herd. During the winter of 1877, at least fifteen hundred hidesmen were operating out of Fort Griffin, Texas, a town about one hundred miles west of Fort Worth. In the spring, one hide company (there were many) had four acres of fenced land piled waist-high with skins. Another sixty thousand or so were piled along the tracks of the Texas and Pacific terminal in Fort Worth; in an old daguerreotype, the pile looks like a caterpillar, monstrous and eyeless, longer than a train. By the summer of 1879, fewer than a dozen hunters remained at Fort Griffin.

"Most of our citizens saw the big load of buffalo skins that the *C. K. Peck* brought down," a columnist wrote in the Sioux Falls *Citizen* in 1880, "a load that hid everything about the boat below the roof of the hurricane deck. There were ten thousand hides in that load." The hidesmen must have literally raced north after they annihilated the southern herds, because by 1882 there were already five thousand hunters encamped across the northern plains—"a cordon of camps," wrote an army lieutenant, "from the upper Missouri, where it bends to the West, stretched toward the setting sun. . . ." Like the bison in the southern and central plains, the northern herds vanished almost overnight. "They *couldn't* have all been killed so quickly," a locomotive engineer for the northern Pacific wrote home. "I saw them crossing the Yellowstone River. They darkened the plains with their numbers. Some of them must be living in the north."

During the few decades the plains bison survived English-speaking civilization, when tens of thousands, then hundreds of thousands, then millions were permanently disappearing every year, those who predicted their extinction were very few. Josiah Gregg, the explorer, was probably the first, in 1833, a year after the last known surviving band east of the Mississippi River was shot in Wisconsin. "Were they killed only for food . . . their natural increase would perhaps replenish the loss," Gregg wrote. "Yet the continual and wanton slaughter of them by travellers and hunters, and the still greater havoc made among them by Indians, not only for meat, but often for the skins alone . . . must ultimately effect their total annihilation from the continent." Such warnings were rare. Tom McHugh, the author, who conducted a rather exhaustive search through the literature for more, discovered almost none. In 1843, Audubon, who was an enthusiastic participant in the slaughter for a while, was finally moved to predict (as he did not in the case of the passenger pigeon) that "before many years the Buffalo, like the Great Auk, will have disappeared." The next such vaticination unearthed by McHugh was offered by Francis Parkman, the historian who rode the Oregon Trail, but not until the 1870s, when anyone should have seen that the bison herds were doomed. Part of the problem was that those making fortunes on the bison's demise—like the Taiwanese and Japanese today with their huge, ocean-cleaning drift nets—wanted no one to fathom the extent of the killing. Colonel Dodge requested detailed statements on bison hide shipments from the three railroads that ran through his domain—the Union Pacific, the Kansas Pacific, and the Santa Fe—was rebuffed by the first two, and didn't believe the figures he got from the Santa Fe. With a lot of detective work, he produced his own. The hunters themselves, who had a great fiduciary interest in the species' survival, were the last to appreciate how efficient they had been. In the fall of 1883, hundreds, if not thousands, set out again, for the second or third year in a row, from Miles City, Montana, the nexus of the northern killing range, provisioned with hundreds of thousands of dollars' worth of horses, mules, food, blankets, tents, and ammunition. Refusing to believe that nothing remained of the herds—there were no longer millions, no longer thousands, hardly even hundreds—they pressed on until many were exhausted, broke, or nearly starved. Later that season, a Minneapolis buyer who sent his agents all over Montana had enough hides to fill one Northern Pacific rail car. For a few more years, the whole mid-continent was blanketed with evidence of the annihilation, but decent money could be made collecting bison bones, which were shipped back east to make fertilizer and glue. (A lot of pioneer families paid part of their mortgages this way.) By the early 1880s, before the bison range filled up with homesteads, the western plains were silent, empty, and cleaned.

Because we live in an age when an owl can stop forests from being felled, and a small, snail-eating fish can almost stop a hundred-million-dollar dam, and the most relentless phenomenon in recent history—California real estate—can be stopped dead (at least for a while) by an endangered mouse, it is hard to make sense of what our forebears did. They were northern Europeans and Christians, for the most part, people who could recite the Book of Genesis, people possessed by a stolid materialism that, even to us today, seems almost pathological. Few had ever known wilderness (there wasn't much left in Europe after the 1700s), and the typical pioneer's goals—to acquire a big piece of land and become a grandee—almost demanded that wilderness be swept out of the way. After you have read a couple of dozen diaries written by emigrants pushing across the frontier, you come to the somewhat desolate conclusion that most pioneers remained indifferent to what they saw, except to the degree that they could make money from it. Not many were driven to rapture by this virgin continent, full of plant and animal life that was wonderfully strange and new. Only a scant few—Francis Parkman, Hamlin Garland, Edwin Bryant (San Francisco's first mayor), artists and naturalists like Audubon and Muir and George Catlin—glorified wilderness; most seemed preoccupied with crushing it. When they saw a herd of two hundred thousand bison, they saw proof that cattle could thrive. (Why the wild bison herds were never regarded as an immense free resource, rather than as competitors of genetically enfeebled and neurotic cows, is really quite baffling.) Valleys filled with antelope were future valleys filled with sheep. As their wagons inched across spectacular landscapes their descendants were to protect within national parks, pioneers dismissed the terrain as "awful" or "appalling" and looked for signs of mineral wealth.

We call this outlook utilitarian. Actually, there was nothing utilitarian about the way in which the settlers wasted game; it was "useful" waste only in that it deprived the Indians of a food source. Later on, during droughts and freezing winters, when pioneer families on the plains nearly starved, they could have subsisted on wildlife, had there been any left. In fact, if there was something perfectly *non*utilitarian, something extravagantly and savagely indulgent about our pioneer forebears, it was their compulsion to kill any wild animal they saw.

Why?

The native Americans, the Indians, are usually portrayed as arch-conservationists, never wasting a scrap of hide or a morsel of flesh from the animals they killed. Like any romantic image, it is somewhat over-blown; the Crow and Blackfeet drove bison by the hundreds off cliffs, and the tribes of the Northwest beached more seventy-pound salmon than they could ever eat. But the Indians, as far as we know, could visualize no species as a mere pest. And they rarely killed animals for "sport"; excessive food-gathering seems to have been as far as they went. Perhaps the whole riddle comes down to this: Indians, unlike nearly all the colonial whites, had always been free to indulge that second most atavistic impulse of mankind (or is it only of males?): to hunt. In the Europe of colonial times—the Europe our forebears were determined to escape—all the remaining wildlife belonged, under the law, to a handful of royals, who, along with their private armies, were also the only people permitted to bear arms. To a starving European peon, who was shot on sight if he entered the duke's wildlife preserve, a game law was simply another instrument of oppression. (And a game warden, who was just a loyal, hired peon with a gun, was the most contemptible figure on earth.) That is an important reason the colonies and nineteenth-century states waited until deer and bears and passenger pigeons were almost gone—or, in some cases, gone—before they brought themselves to protect them. In a nation of immigrants just liberated from landlessness and crowdedness and monarchy, game laws, like forestry laws and zoning laws and gun-control laws, were resisted with a singular passion. The yeoman American citizen, intoxicated by his right to bear arms, made giddy by the omnipresent wildlife he could hunt at will, could not recalibrate his values as the game ran out, could not constrain his impulse (always described as a God-given right) to hunt. Accounts of nineteenth-century hunting expeditions almost always reveal a wantonness among the participants—a need to kill that would not quit. Whatever their proclaimed or subconscious motives, the pioneers were awesomely efficient exterminators. Europe, at the dawn of the twentieth century, after thousands of years of human settlement and several centuries of serious population density, still had pockets of wolves and bears and a fair number of deer, while the United States—depopulate, barely gone from wilderness, and twice as large—had cleaned them out from almost all of their original habitat. Politically speaking, we had stability. Environmentally speaking, we had anarchy. In Europe it was more or less the reverse.

The pioneer mentality dies hard, even in a culture that now enshrines the spotted owl and the harvest mouse. We are the last industrial society with memories of a frontier; we are a culture where, in thousands of rural towns and grimy smokestack cities, your most important rite of passage, if you are a young male, is to kill something large and hot-blooded, to feel a deer's life spill into your hands. There are millions of young men in America who are bored to death with their lives and who sense an erotic adventure in killing and who have been taught that the woods and hunting are the cradle of the American soul, the last domain where all is pure and free. What seems like a full and flowering conservation ethic still has fragile roots. Meanwhile, in countries whose surplus populations the United States and Canada now absorb—Taiwan, Hong Kong, Korea, Thailand, one could probably include Japan—conservation, in principle and in practice, remains a curiosity; that and overpopulation are the reasons their wildlife has all but disappeared. But these same cultures value wildlife a great deal, as long as it is dead. Koreans will pay five thousand dollars a kilogram for powdered bear gallbladders, which, in much of Asia, are prized as a thaumaturgical cure-all. Asians in California have been apprehended again and again with illegal bear galls, illegal deer and elk antlers (which are also used in folk medicine), illegal fish caught in illegal waters with illegal nets, hapless ducks poached in city parks, even dogs stolen off the streets. (In some Asian countries, notably China, dogs, particularly black dogs, are a gastronomical delicacy, as the brains of a monkey eaten before the monkey has died are a potion favored by rich Malaysian businessmen.)

North America, unlike much of the rest of the world, has preserved some of its wildlife and habitat, and for that it is now paying a price. But the fact is we *have* preserved some of it, by accident or by design. On no other continent do predators as large as mountain lions prowl the periphery of urban regions where millions of people live. In 1990, there were five thousand mountain lions in California—there were fewer than six hundred a generation earlier—and the public has insisted that hunting them should be outlawed, so they will multiply. There may be more deer in Westchester County than one would have found two hundred years ago, because they are hardly hunted there and broken woodlots and savory gardens make for ideal deer habitat. Black bears, which were nearly extinct in the East at the turn of the century, are now quite common again. In states such as Pennsylvania and Vermont, which were mostly deforested in the eighteenth and nineteenth centuries, the hardscrabble farms have gone fallow and the maturing third-growth hardwoods are producing lots of bear food—acorns, beech nuts, hickory nuts, cambium, termites, and ants. There are bears in Fairfield County, bears around Camp David, bears denning in New Jersey woods a hundred feet from streets with names like East Spur Court. (New Jersey's bears are, for the most part, weaker competitors chased out of Pennsylvania by more dominant bears; they have ended up sharing habitat with less dominant humans chased out of Saddle River and Tenafly by inflated real estate.)

In the East, wild turkeys, which, like black bears, were once threatened if not nearly extinct, have come back to most of the states where they were originally found; they have also been transplanted to western states where they are not native, and have done well—in Texas, for example, and California. Gray wolves, which were gone from every state but Minnesota a few years ago, have recently drifted into Montana from Alberta, into Washington from British Columbia, into New Mexico from Mexico, perhaps into Oregon from Washington. There are plans to reintroduce them into Yellowstone National Park, despite howls from neighboring ranchers. Elephant seals have rebounded from near-extinction. Sea otters. Pelicans. Ibises. Egrets. Antelope, which used to graze what is now Los Angeles. Gray whales, which San Francisco's grizzly bears ate in the 1840s when they marooned themselves on beaches. Tule elk, all of which are descended from a few surviving pairs protected by a California rancher in the 1870s. Roosevelt elk. Bald eagles. Osprey. Bighorn sheep.

I once asked Dave Hall, "Do you not call this success?"

He said, "To some degree, yes. But as far as I'm concerned, almost all of it is nullified by what's happening to southern Louisiana."

Conservationists, whether they are game wardens or members of the Sierra Club, tend to feel like born losers, even if certain things are going their way. Dave Hall's sense of gloom is so overwhelming, however, that in the five years I spent with him off and on I always struggled to locate its source. After my seventh or eighth trip to Louisiana, I finally realized that it was all around me. It is where he lives. His sullenness, his sense of outrage, his demonic dedication to his work are all rooted in a historic unfolding loss that he sees or hears about almost every day. It is not like the disappearance of wild California, a loss that most people know about and a loss that probably couldn't be helped. California was doomed from the moment it was settled because it is such a desirable place to live. Southern Louisiana is one of the least desirable places on earth for humans to live, and, except for New Orleans, hardly anyone lives there. But natural forces set loose by human energies are causing its downfall—its disappearance right off the face of the earth. And even though many conservationists devoutly pray for nature to strike us back in revenge, in this particular case nature is cannibalizing itself, eating up what was once the most productive wildlife habitat in North America, if not on earth.

And most people have no idea it is going on.

It is a loss that has diseased Dave Hall's mind; at times, one thinks it has driven him mad.

"You got to write about it," he told me. "Even though it's probably too late to do anything about it."

We were driving at the time into Saint Bernard Parish, what is left of it, a reach of Louisiana east of New Orleans that is mainly marsh. The name of the easternmost town is Alluvial City. It sits on a rise of plant detritus and shell middens inches higher than Chandeleur Sound, which was somewhere beyond us, lost in the vague horizon. We were looking for one of Dave Hall's patent-office reformed outlaws, a trapper and waterfowler and shrimper named Dennis Treitler, one of many Spanish Cajuns evolved from Canary Island stock. (His German name is an accident of procreation.) Dennis, said Dave Hall, was forty-five years old and had earned his living from the Louisiana marshes all his life, a lot of it illegally. Since he was a teenager, he had shot probably thousands of ducks. In the parishes around New Orleans, illegal wild ducks used to be easy to sell. Dave Hall uses Treitler—who talks about his outlaw career in a video he made—partly to prove his conviction (which not all, and perhaps not even most, game wardens share) that poaching is a threat to waterfowl nearly as serious as habitat loss. "Take professional hunters like Dennis—basically, he was a modern market hunter—and throw in the ordinary overlimiters who take fifty or a hundred more ducks than they're allowed every season, and you've got a real problem. We've got lots and lots of overlimiters in Louisiana, and probably more guys like Dennis I haven't caught yet and made to go straight."

In Dave Hall's video and on the lecture circuit, Treitler preaches conservation and hunter restraint, but his passion overflows when he speaks of habitat loss. The doomed habitat he preaches about is, in part, the same gigantic marsh we were driving through in Saint Bernard Parish, the marsh Dave Hall insisted we were "losing." To me, it looked quite healthy. There were lots of dead trees and bright green vegetation standing in lots of shallow water, which, I thought, is how a marsh is supposed to look.

"Healthy, my ass!" snorted Dave Hall. "Those dead trees are *cypress* trees. Cypress like to stand in water. They *have* to stand in water some of the time. None of them should be dead. Most of the plant life you see there is saltwater cordgrass. It's replaced American three-square, which is a superb duck, goose, and muskrat food. Cordgrass is about useless for waterfowl. And *it* won't last. The sea's gonna eat it up just like it ate up the freshwater marsh. In the sixties, you had to go twenty more miles toward Chandeleur Sound to taste salt in marsh water. The Sound is miles closer to here than it was then. There's brackish water almost to New Orleans now. *We're losing it.* This is the worst god-damned natural disaster going on in this country today, and hardly anyone knows about it outside of the state. Only it's not a natural disaster cause we caused it. It's a pure man-made fuckup. Ultimately, we're gonna pay a terrible price, but right now it's the wildlife that's paying, and the people who depend on it. Everything's going downhill—oysters, crabs, shrimp. The worst of it is what's happening to waterfowl. This was *the* most excellent winter habitat for waterfowl in the world until the salt intrusion started. When you think about what we're gonna lose here, the habitat, and what we're losing everywhere else, it's just mind-boggling. I don't care what-all else you write about in your book, but you got to say something about this. You got to *promise* me you're gonna say something about this."

So I will.

"Any person who is not blind or idiotic can see that in the old Delitic Silurian period, just a million years ago next November, the lower Mississippi River was upward of 1,300 miles long, and stuck out over the Gulf of Mexico like a fishing rod. And any person can see that 742 years from now the lower Mississippi will be only a mile and three quarters long, and Cairo and New Orleans will have joined their streets together, and be plodding along comfortably under a single mayor and a mutual board of aldermen."

A former riverboat pilot named Sam Clemens wrote that passage in 1883, and it's become more than a fanciful excursion into hydrology—or at least Mississippi River hydrology, which is a peculiar thing. That river, on which Clemens learned his piloting, his hydrology, and his early despair, drains the third-largest watershed on planet Earth. At any given moment, on the Mississippi, you are riding runoff from Tucumcari, New Mexico, and from Shelby, Montana, and Jamestown, New York, and Marion, Virginia, and Caesar's Head, South Carolina. Below Natchez, after all the major tributaries have come in, you are on a river with twice the average flow of the continent's next-largest river. But any river pilot knew that was not nearly enough runoff in relation to the accompanying burden of silt.

From afar, the steamboats going up and down the river in Mark Twain's day were a picture of serenity—the ship plowing gracefully through bow waves, diners silently gorging themselves on banquets of game—until you looked more carefully and saw frenzied pilots madly plumbing river depths, the captain on the bridge in a frothing, desperate state, and the boat now and then veering madly to avoid a submerged mudbank. They formed constantly, everywhere; without warning, overnight. Few boats ever ran from Saint Louis to New Orleans at normal water without running aground. The pilots shrieked their soundings—

"Quarter less twain!" "M-a-r-k three! Half twain! Mark twain!"—as the captain whipsawed the vessel through deeper channels with just enough clearance to avoid simple humiliation or, perhaps, a planted log through the bow and a boatload of drowned passengers on his conscience.

It was a capricious river—more so than most—and such an immense river that its capriciousness could have extraordinary consequences. In the fall, when the Rocky Mountain snowpack was long gone and placid weather had reigned for weeks over most of the watershed, the flow at Natchez could drop below fifty thousand cubic feet per second—just some connected puddles in a riverbed a mile or more wide. But in May or June, when the western snowpack was melting down the Missouri and spring rains had sent the Ohio and Tennessee and Arkansas and Red rivers over their banks, the Mississippi seemed capable of covering the South. Hernando de Soto, the first European who went through Louisiana, arrived in the spring of 1543, which must have been a wet year, because the river was sixty miles wide and all the Indians had moved into the trees, where they were fishing for gar with pieces of drowned animals as bait. That particular flood may best explain Spain's decision to colonize Florida instead, eventually selling the Louisiana territory to France for what amounted to bus money.

But that flood and hundreds of others over the past few thousand years are also the reason southern Louisiana exists at all. Running high—say at a million six hundred thousand cubic feet per second— the Mississippi wasn't half mud, but it was close. The flaked-off skin of the continent, the topsoil of twenty-odd states, came down with every flood, millennium after millennium, and with no real confinement below Baton Rouge the Mississippi spread and spread, its rate of flow diminishing, the sediments settling, making new land. Carrying three hundred ten thousand truckloads of sediment, on average, every day—two and a half tons per truck—the river not only expanded its delta but raised its bed at some imperceptible rate, until a course change occurred. Throughout its history, the lower Mississippi slowly slithered east and west like a huge, languorous, satiated snake. Within the past nine thousand years, it dramatically changed course at least five times. In 7000 B.C., the mouth was closer to Texas than to New Orleans. Then it migrated on over to Mississippi. At about the time of the Battle of Hastings, it worked its way into the Plaquemines delta, its current course, where it ought to remain for a few more years.

Although each was in the making for hundreds or thousands of years, such a channel shift was, in the context of geologic time, an instantaneous event, something like the sudden appearance of a volcanic cone in the Cascades. The errant river took out anything solid in its path, creating a battering ram at the head of a miles-wide flood that could have relocated Detroit. (When whites first arrived in Louisiana, they found at the head of the Atchafalaya a thirty-mile debris dam which, for a long while, was southern Louisiana's principal roadway.) Thousands of acres of bottomland forest went under; square miles of wetlands were suddenly fathoms deep. The Gulf of Mexico became a vast, spinning eddy of smashed trees and dislodged swamp mats, which washed up on beaches from Texas to the Yucatán. Then, for the next few hundred years, the new delta would build at the old delta's expense; the river sediments would lay land twenty or thirty miles into the Gulf while the old delta was slowly eaten up by wave action, salt, and hurricanes.

On balance, though—and despite a steady ocean rise since the last ice sheets melted away—Louisiana grew. In its limited sphere of influence, the Mississippi River overmatched the rising Gulf. It planted eighteen billion truckloads of silt at the ocean's door in the time the Gulf rose a foot. Land versus sea. Ephemeral land subsides under its own weight. Sea pushes forward. Future land comes down the spreading river and settles over drowning land. Land rises up. Sea moves back. Land wins. In Sumerian times, the Gulf of Mexico may have been as far north as Baton Rouge, which is now seventy miles inland. When Rome was founded, somewhere just south of New Orleans. In the past nine thousand years Louisiana has gained nineteen thousand square miles of land—*net*. Half of Kentucky. Nowhere on the continent has anything like this been going on in recent geologic time. The rivers of the southeast coast—the Savannah, the Neuse, the Black—have also been building delta land, but not nearly at the rate the Mississippi has; the southeastern coastal plain has been steadily eaten up by the ocean's recent millimeter-by-millimeter rise. (That's why there are barrier islands.) Southern Louisiana has been both the most geographically dynamic and the most rapidly accreting part of North America since the last Ice Age.

Barely qualifying as land, southern Louisiana has also represented, acre for acre, the apogee of nature's productive capability. Its wetlands can grow ten times more biomass than an Illinois farm—spartina grasses in the brackish zones; then miles and miles of floating vegetation, highly unstable but solid enough to repel the sea; then the semi-submerged hardwood forests of the upland marshes. With its bottomless black topsoil, riotous vegetation, and year-round warmth, the Mississippi-Atchafalaya delta has nourished so much sensate life over the millennia that an appreciable portion of southern Louisiana is made of animal remains. A wintering population of one hundred million migratory waterfowl at the dawn of European settlement is a fairly conservative guess. (There are about half that many on the entire continent today.) Bears were thick as flies. There were cougars, jaguars, wolves. About 80 percent of the marine life in the Gulf of Mexico depends on wetlands—the juvenile forms live there, and the adults return to spawn—and the Louisiana delta has long been the wellspring of most life in the northern Gulf. In New Orleans when the oldest living person was born, you went into a bar, ordered a beer, and got a plate of oysters, free. Gulf shrimp were a dime a pound; blue crabs, a penny each. Crawfish were a dollar for a twenty-pound bag. Speckled sea trout could be scooped up by hand when they ran, and were often given away. It was the richest, fattest smorgasbord in the world, supporting tens of thousands of those people—Indians and Cajuns—who finally figured out how to live in it, feeding millions of people elsewhere.

When New Orleans was about to be founded in 1718 by Iberville and Bienville Le Moyne, they decided to build it as close as possible to the Gulf, on a rise of land eighteen feet above sea level. Their engineer, Le Blond de la Tour, said it was a bad idea. He was overruled. Up above Natchez, there were flood lines painted forty feet above mean water, but the river's topographic confinement ended there, and the founders were certain that there could be no serious flood rise as far south as where they wanted the city to be. They were fools. The city was flooded in the first year of its existence. Le Blond de la Tour was put to work building levees—a word not yet coined. By the mid-1700s, the levee system stretched thirty miles from New Orleans in both directions. The ancestral levees, built mainly by slaves, were made of logs and river muck, and constantly breached—crevassed. But the state of the art of levee construction gradually advanced, especially after steam dredges were invented, and a more durable system of parallel levees had been built nearly to the mouth of the Arkansas River by the advent of the Civil War. The river knew how to keep up with state-of-the-art. Because the levees confined it, it decided to rise more, and faster, overtopping each superior confinement the engineers threw up. During the war, the levees, which were unmaintained, trampled by troops, and battered by cannonballs, also began to deteriorate. They were breached. In 1874, a flood inundated all river settlements south of Natchez. In 1879, there was created a Mississippi River Commission, an appendage of the U.S. Army Corps of Engineers, assigned to plan the prevention of future floods. Without federal funds—the use of which was still barred by Congress—the idea of containing the larger Mississippi floods was comical. Much of its watershed was by then deforested, and the increasingly confined and increasingly engorged Mississippi was rising higher and faster during every new flood. (Deforestation was not yet recognized as a cause of floods.) In 1880, the river overtopped the levees and widened by a couple of dozen miles during what might have been a run-of-the-mill flood. In 1890, some use of federal funds for levee reconstruction was finally permitted, though the money was not enough to permit the Corps to wage anything more than a quixotic battle against the river that had become its obsession and nemesis.

The era of the modern Mississippi probably began during the First World War, a conflict whose sheer magnitude turned the Corps, nominally a modest construction branch of the Army, into a bureaucratic leviathan, an ant army erecting the infrastructure of global conflict. The end of the war left the Corps with a huge staff of civilian engineers and not nearly enough peacetime work to keep them all occupied. Making the Mississippi Valley safe for posterity, and keeping the channel deep enough for ships, was a job that could fill the hiatus between several world wars. If not then, the era of the modern Mississippi certainly began in 1927, when the river played into the Corps's hands by raising the most destructive flood in North American history. Greenwood, Mississippi, normally forty miles east, was at flood's edge. Twenty-six thousand square miles of the South were submerged. The next year, Congress passed what amounted to revolutionary legislation, making levees and channel improvements a wholly nonreimbursable federal expense—meaning the nation's taxpayers, not the beneficiaries, paid for them. It also instructed the Corps to study the possibility that reservoir construction on the tributaries might help in controlling floods. Prior to 1928, the Corps had generally dismissed reservoirs as a means of controlling floods—it had decided on levees as the answer, and when the Corps has an answer, by God, it sticks to it. Eight years later, however, it was building the largest dam in the world (the largest *structure* in the world after the Mississippi levees and the Great Wall) on the upper Missouri River, in the semiarid heart of Montana. Later, downriver from that dam—which is called Fort Peck—it built Oahe Dam (now the tenth largest in the world), and Garrison Dam (now the nineteenth largest), and Gavins Point Dam and Fort Randall Dam and Big Bend Dam. By now it has built probably a hundred and fifty large dams on other Mississippi tributaries, but those hardly count; the Missouri, a psychotically flood-prone river draining sparsely vegetated terrain, has always been the biggest source of Mississippi River silt. Most of it is now coming to a dead halt behind six monstrous dams, forgetting about all the other rivers and their dams and their silt, and the modern Mississippi's total volume of suspended solids is just over one-third what it was a hundred years ago. But even these dams, the planet's greatest network of silt traps (their inevitable filling-in will be a problem for our descendants to solve), do not yet figure prominently in the Mississippi delta's demise—although eventually they will. The levees work well enough.

As an engineering achievement, the Mississippi River levee system exudes none of the glamour of a dam, even if, by weight and volume, it makes the sum total of Corps of Engineers dams seem picayune. After a century of more or less constant work, the river has been straitjacketed on both sides by levees that almost qualify as hills. Fourteen hundred miles of levees, levees high enough for hang gliders to practice takeoffs, an inch of levee outweighs two elephants, levees with thousands of times the mass of the Great Pyramid—the Corps employs people in its three-block-long regional headquarters in uptown New Orleans who are paid to feed tourists such statistical hyperbole. Nothing on earth rivals these levees, not even the Great Wall, and they have worked much better against the Corps's chosen enemy—nature—than the Great Wall worked against the Mongol hordes. The Mississippi escaped briefly from its confinement in 1973, during a very large flood, but has been confined from source to sea, for the most part, since the thirties. Its entire silt load, that which isn't hijacked by the dams on the tributaries, goes straight into the Gulf, much of it dropped off the edge of the continental shelf—a gigantic, growing, useless plateau of suboceanic mud. Only around the mouth of the Atchafalaya is land-building still going on. Almost everywhere else along the Louisiana coast, land has gone into retreat—because of dams, because of levees, and because of oil.

In 1902, a Texas wildcatter named Haywood had a peculiar feeling about a patch of northwest Louisiana prairie as he passed through it on a train. Haywood went back sometime later to drill a well, which, on his first assay, brought up a gusher a hundred and sixty feet high.

The boom pretty much followed a rocket curve until 1982, when oil prices collapsed. Louisiana is not considered an oil state in the sense that Oklahoma and Texas are, but when the most expensive gubernatorial campaign in U.S. history occurs there—as it did when Edwin Edwards ran against David Treen in 1983—then you know that it is not only an oil state, but that oil owns the state. By someone's calculation, enough of the stuff has been pumped from within the state's Bulgaria-size borders to cover the land surface of earth nine inches deep. People tend to believe that most of Louisiana's oil has been found offshore, in the Gulf of Mexico. Much of it has actually come from fields beneath the visible part of the state, especially the Cajun parishes—the part chronically wet. Since 1930, about twelve billion barrels of oil, and perhaps a hundred trillion cubic feet of natural gas, have come out of Louisiana wetlands, forgetting the uplands and the Gulf. In Louisiana, where there are marshes, there is often oil. Or, perhaps better stated, where there was oil, there were marshes. In West Texas, after a company drills a producing well in some desolate badlands of mesquite and prickly pear, it simply lays down a gravel road to move people and equipment in. In the Gulf, oil fields are accessible by mobile platform, helicopter, and ship. But a marsh is a tough place to get around in. The animal perfectly adapted to it is the alligator, which has a low center of gravity, excellent weight distribution, and can swim or scuttle or slither as the occasion demands. In a marsh, in order to go an absurdly short distance—say a stone's throw—you might have to do all three. The earliest Cajun hunters recognized the usefulness of a light, low-draft boat—the pirogue—but a pirogue was useless when a marsh went dry. The more enterprising among them dug tranasses, little channels that were always filled by seepage and were just wide enough for a pirogue. (Using a man's tranass was like stealing his water out West; it was a hellish effort to keep one weedless and cleared of silt.) Digging a tiny channel from a pirogue, using a fat-bladed hand shovel, a Cajun hunter couldn't take much of a bite out of a marsh, and his unmaintained channels were soon history. But the agricultural industry, seeing the efficacy of this approach, decided to improve on it for drainage, and the oil industry decided to improve on it some more. It dug channels for exploration and access to wells that were wide enough to move outsize equipment in, and even when a spent well was capped and abandoned, sportsmen and fishermen found the canals convenient for their own purposes. Unlike tranasses, oil company canals never resilted and revegetated. In fact, with boats constantly going through, churning up the bottom and broadcasting waves, they grew wider, year by year, as the marshes alongside were progressively eaten up.

That word, fragile, is the most leaden cliché in the environmentalists' repertoire. But a marsh is almost always fragile, a freshwater marsh is more fragile than one filled by brackish water, and Louisiana freshwater marshes are more fragile than most. Southeast and southwest of New Orleans, there are hundreds of thousands of acres of unforested marshes, flat and expansive as calm green seas, where everything sort of floats. Plants grow hydroponically there, taking their nutrients from ambient water or sending down thin roots like spider filament. During great hurricanes, thousands of acres of such marshland may temporarily disappear. They are simply blown and washed off the map. Constant boat traffic, with its wave action, can have the same effect, only more permanently. Floating marshes are not adapted to waves at all—no more than any freshwater marsh is tolerant of salt water, which now washes in from the Gulf through the widening canals. A cypress tree, anchored by thick bumpy knees and a fluted lower trunk, will remain standing in almost any storm. But increase the concentration of salt in the ambient water by a thousand percent and its capillary transpiration system goes into osmotic shock. There are now some ten thousand miles of canals cutting through the marshlands of southern Louisiana.

A hundred thirty-seven years ago there were perhaps six million three hundred thousand acres of Louisiana coastal wetlands—a great, fluid, macrodynamic standoff between water and land, between fresh water and salt water. It had been one of the most rapidly changing ecological systems on earth, with river shifts and great Gulf-spawned storms stealing tens of thousands of acres and the rivers' silt building them slowly back—but it was fundamentally stable. Land—or marshland—won. By now, more than one million acres, a sixth of Louisiana's coastal marsh and almost one-tenth of the remaining coastal marshland in the United States, has vanished, mostly since the time of Huey Long. Between 1956 and 1978, Saint Bernard Parish shrank by thirty-one thousand acres; it is losing eighteen hundred acres every year. Lafourche Parish lost sixty-four thousand acres during those twenty-two years. Terrebonne Parish lost one hundred twenty-four thousand acres. Plaquemines Parish, the fiefdom of the Leander Perezes, lost one hundred and seventy-six thousand acres, a tract of land inside which the five boroughs of New York would fit comfortably. It is now sea.

The creation of the marshes was infinitesimally slow and steady. Their degradation goes exponentially. In 1913, the state of Louisiana was losing, on balance, just under seven square miles of wetlands every year. In 1946, almost sixteen square miles. In 1967, twenty-eight square miles. The official figure today is thirty-nine point four square miles of land loss per year—the city of Buffalo—but these numbers are out of date as soon as they appear. Fifty square miles of coastal Louisiana are apt to be lost in 1991. By the end of the century, sixty square miles may be disappearing each year. In the year 2035, the last acre of Plaquemines Parish is scheduled to vanish under water, unless a two-hundred-mile-per-hour hurricane goes through between now and then and puts the place out of its misery.

"What's unforgivable," says Dave Hall, "is how long it took the state to acknowledge that any of this was going on. The trappers and fishermen were the first ones to notice it. They'd go out to what was a marsh island at the Mississippi mouth the year before and it was gone. They'd go back again and again to make sure they weren't just imagining. They'd tell us game wardens about it. We were the next ones to notice, because we spend a lot of time out there. You could see the barrier islands shrinking in the 1950s and 1960s—I mean, it was *obvious*. Woody Gagliano at Louisiana State was already publishing reports about coastal land loss about 1970. He and I had a little road show going where we'd give talks to sportsmen's groups. I talked to the press about it—there were plenty of articles by the mid-1970s. The political interests came down hard on me, boy. 'Who is this upstart *game warden?* What does *he* know?' The Fish and Wildlife Service published high-altitude photos of the Mississippi Delta where it was plain as day. That duck's-foot Delta you see on maps doesn't even exist anymore—there's just a few little islands left out there. About 1980, the state finally started talking about land loss like it was a serious problem. But they didn't start talking *solutions* until two or three years later. The Corps of Engineers wasn't admitting land loss until even later. They're the ones who started causing the problem in the last *century*. I don't think the oil and gas companies have admitted yet that their canals have a lot to do with it. Their lawyers have probably got em all muzzled, because everyone is scared to death of potential liability. What do they owe us for destroying the most productive wildlife habitat in the world? Who's gonna pay to save it, if we can?"

Aside from Dave Hall, the three people who have yelled the loudest and most persistently about coastal land loss are Dr. Sherwood Gagliano, Dave Hall's former Cassandra-in-arms, who is now a consulting hydrologist; Oliver Houck, a Tulane environmental law professor and one of the most prominent conservationists in the South; and Dr. Rafael Kazmann, one of the foremost hydrologists in the world, now professor emeritus at Louisiana State.

Kazmann is the gloomiest of the three—which may be noteworthy, since he probably understands Mississippi Delta hydrology better than anyone alive. "We have utterly, utterly transformed a huge, formerly stable ecosystem," he says. "I'm less concerned about the saltwater intrusion than some others. The main problem is we've stopped the silt. The Mississippi has forty percent of its original silt load-*max*. Even if we breached the levees, land loss would go on. The only permanent solution I see is to take down the dams, which we'll never do. And even if we did, it would take a long time for the silt the dams have trapped to make its way down to the river's mouth. I just don't see an answer. If you're under forty, you may live long enough to watch the Gulf of Mexico make its way to New Orleans. Let's say we have forty more years of land loss, and then a Category Four or Five hurricane. Between the storm surge and the rain and runoff, you could have seventeen feet of water at New Orleans City Hall.

"On the other hand, a big earthquake along the New Madrid Fault could get us first. I don't think the levees could survive one. This is a very uncertain part of the world."

Both Houck and Gagliano are more convinced that coastal land loss can be slowed, perhaps even slowed dramatically, but it will require a drastic undoing of a century's worth of mistakes. One partial solution (and nothing is more than a partial solution) would be to let much more of the Mississippi's flow bypass New Orleans and run down the Atchafalaya channel instead. The Atchafalaya, the river's traditional overflow basin, takes a straighter and steeper course to the sea, and the Corps of Engineers, after committing itself to maintaining the main Mississippi as the country's principal land navigation route, has been nothing less than fanatical about routing the river through and beyond New Orleans rather than let it exercise its own will. In the 1950s and 1960s, it built giant control weirs at the Atchafalaya outlet, a couple of dozen miles above Baton Rouge, which—presuming they work, and presuming they are not washed away the next time the Mississippi rises thirty feet—have transformed that channel into a kind of now-and-then escape valve. Normally, about 450,000 cubic feet of flow per second go down the Mississippi; another 150,000 second-feet or so are diverted into the Atchafalaya. Because the mouth of the Atchafalaya isn't leveed at all, and the upper reaches are in fairly loose confinement, the debouch of that river is the only portion of the Louisiana coast where land- and marsh-building are still going on. Running more water down the Atchafalaya would accelerate that process, and it could be done, according to Houck, with a fairly minimal impact on navigation in the main river. "You're still writing off the rest of the coast," he says. "But at least in this one place where we haven't messed everything up, we would be creating more marsh."

Another idea, which Louisiana and the Corps are taking more seriously, is to build some supersize siphons over the tops of the levees below New Orleans and skim some of the flow into those adjacent marshes that the ocean is now eating up. ("Skim" isn't exactly the right word, since you need to roil the bottom to add as much muck as possible to the water you divert.) The Mississippi's volume is so enormous that you could take out what amounts to a good-size river—the Potomac, say, with the Wabash thrown in for good measure—and lower the crest by only inches.

The Fish and Wildlife Service recommended siphoning water into the surrounding Delta more than thirty years ago. The Corps of Engineers debunked the idea out of hand—it has battalions of civilian scientists and engineers whose duty it is to resist ideas the Corps hasn't thought of first. Lately, however, as the rate of land loss has increased fantastically, both the Corps and the state of Louisiana have endorsed the siphon approach, at least in a limited sense. (A demonstration project was built at Caernevon, a few miles below New Orleans, in the mid-1980s, but it is too soon to determine how well it is working.) One of the reasons the Corps decided siphons are a sound idea is that its own studies have suggested that diverting just eleven thousand cubic feet per second—one-fortieth of the typical Mississippi flow—might ultimately save a hundred thousand acres of otherwise doomed land; the oyster production alone from such a tract of coastal marsh could represent a fifth of the entire annual oyster harvest of the United States.

That figure offers some suggestion of what the preservation of Louisiana's coastal wetlands is worth, in simple dollar terms. "The economic value of what we will lose," says Oliver Houck, "is so unbelievable that no one believes it. People have calculated it—and a lot of it *is* calculable—but politicians look at the figures and say, 'That can't be true.' Then they say, 'And besides, what about transportation? What about oil?' Sure, they're worth more. Not that much more, but more. But how long is oil going to last? Thirty years? Forty years? Then it's gone, and so is the marsh, thanks largely to oil extraction. Transportation is valuable as long as you have a port of New Orleans, and you have a port of New Orleans only as long as you *have* New Orleans. If things keep going the way they are, it's conceivable that we'll lose the city, too. No, it's not. It's predictable."

By weight, Louisiana's annual fish catch is greater than Alaska's. Ten years ago—I am using Houck's figures, which are a decade and a half old—the state's fishery was worth $3.2 billion, annually, after processing. "The overwhelming bulk of the catch is composed of estuarine-dependent species," says Houck. "Menhaden, Atlantic croaker, sea trout. Spot. Drum. Blue crabs, brown shrimp, white shrimp. Oysters. Where do people think they'll hatch, spawn, and mature if there's no marsh? A lot of people come to visit us because of the wonderful, cheap seafood. What if we lose it? People are always saying how environmental protection costs too much and has all these ripple effects. *Not* protecting the environment can cost a lot and have a hell of a ripple effect. There are fourteen thousand fishery-related jobs in Louisiana."

Furs and hides taken from Louisiana—from the marshes, mainly—in 1976 were worth twenty-four million dollars. Alligators were worth a couple of million, and a lot more are being "harvested" today. (Alligators, unlike crocodiles, do not tolerate salt water at all.) Sport fishing is worth a hundred million or more. Sport hunting is worth half that amount, and the loss of winter habitat in Louisiana means the loss of sport-hunting opportunities—and money—up and down the Mississippi and Central Flyways. "Louisiana's Office of Natural Resources," says Houck, "predicts a loss to the state of fifty-seven thousand dollars a day in revenues and severance from oil and gas as the state's boundaries move northward. More and more of Louisiana is becoming federal jurisdiction, beyond the three-mile limit, as the marshes disappear and the state effectively moves northward. The composite inland shift is now about half a mile a year."

By Houck's equation—a potpourri of debits, of declining fisheries and wildlife, of diminishing zones of enhancement and taxable domain, of deteriorating flood protection—Louisiana's coastal wetlands are worth ten and a half billion dollars a year, in 1978 dollars, a figure you can now inflate by at least half. "To protect some small communities east of Morgan City and the Atchafalaya outlet from the advancing Gulf, the Corps of Engineers has proposed building ring levees and extended river bulwarks costing more than a billion dollars. That, in effect, is the value of the marshes as flood protection, as storm buffer. For a few little coastal communities that are imminently threatened. What's it going to cost to build ring levees around New Orleans sometime in the next century? You have no idea what the storm surge of a Category Four hurricane could do if the marshes weren't out there as a buffer."

Dave Hall says, "In a way I'm grateful that we made a mistake that's so big we can't ignore it. It's got to be some kind of lesson to us about thinking we can dump on Mother Nature and get away with it. But what's the value of that lesson compared to the potential loss of forty percent of the coastal wetlands in the United States?"

We were, by then, out at road's end in Saint Bernard Parish, standing at the outermost wharf, watching through binoculars as a big freighter came plowing through the marsh a few miles to the north. In the convection of rising heat, the ship danced and twitched as if it had a case of the heebie-jeebies. Dave Hall saw that I was dumbstruck at the sight of a freighter steaming right through shallow marsh. "It's in the Mississippi—Gulf Outlet Canal," he said. "Mister Go. That's the number-one cause of this marsh's decline. They dredged that sucker sixty feet deep. The ocean comes in like a river in reverse. That ship is putting out a bow wave and a wake that's four feet high. It slops salt water into the marshes, and they start to die. The waves break up the floating mats and they go out, chunk by chunk. The canal's already three times wider than when they built it, in places. All them dead cypress trees we passed, that's all cause of Mister Go. Once you let the ocean in, it can't be stopped. It's like designing a dam with a big leak—sooner or later the water rushing out is gonna erode that sucker away. They're puttin barge-loads of rocks along the canal now just to keep it, it's eroding so bad. Meanwhile it's brought salt water all the way into the Industrial Canal at New Orleans. What that thing did to this parish, to a whole way of life here . . . it's just a *catastrophe* . . . for the little bit of economic benefit it provides."

When we finally found Dennis Treitler—we ended up camping on his lawn until he had docked his crab boat and come home—he offered us some shrimp, some crabs he had just caught, some raccoon and nutria steaks, and a quart bottle of Pepsi—for each of us—to wash it all down with. Then we started right in again on Mister Go. Anywhere you are in Saint Bernard Parish, all conversation leads to that huge, widening, diabolical, marsh-eating canal.

"You can't plug it up," said Treitler, who is a big and hearty and somewhat hyperkinetic man with a curiously high-pitched, nasal voice. "You can't blow it up. You can't even sue it. Some of us have put into a kitty to bring some kind of legal action, but no one can figure out who to sue. The shippers say it ain't *their* canal. The state wanted it built, hell yes, but now they say it's not *their* canal. The Corps of Engineers built it, but they say Congress told them to do it. Goddamn it, no one wants to take responsibility for *nothing* any more."

Treitler said there were hundreds of people earning a living from the Saint Bernard marshes a couple of decades earlier. Now there were only dozens who did, or tried. But the crabs and oysters and marsh mammals were still declining faster than the people who fished and hunted them, so people were now stealing and wrecking each other's traps, raiding each other's trap lines, even sabotaging boats. "It never used to happen. *Never.*" He said the sport fishermen and the commercial fishermen were constantly at war. Speckled sea trout, which spawn in marsh sloughs, had become so scarce that, a few years earlier, the sport fishermen moved to block the commercial season. (Much the same is happening with salmon, also disappearing, in the Northwest.) The commercial fishermen responded by blockading the only road down to the docks. The sheriff refused to come down and break up the blockade. The sport fishermen won, anyway. "They got the lobby and we don't. The politicians and the sports is one and the same." He said his hundred and fifty crab traps used to bring up a thousand pounds overnight. Lately, he had been getting two hundred pounds of crabs to the haul. He said oysters were scarcer, too, and were just recovering from a PCB spill that occurred five years earlier when two ships collided in Mister Go. "They shut down the whole goddamned marsh for months. We couldn't take nothing out of it. They settled with us for twelve hundred dollars a person. Some of these families here, they were starving. I'm a master baker and a decoy carver, I got three and a half years of college, so I can always find some work. But some of these people, living from the marshes is the only living they know. Twelve hundred dollars came around and it looked like an inheritance to them. People jumped at the money. The companies dodged all liability, of course." He said his major source of income these days was trapping—there were still a lot of raccoons left, and he was so proficient at it he could take more than a thousand skins in a season. "We were gettin twelve dollars a pelt, which was good money, but there's a prickly marsh plant that's taking over now, it gets in the coon's belly fur and the buyers pay less for them. We're gettin four dollars today. Whether it's another consequence of the salt coming in, I can't truthfully say."

At the end of a long recitation of loss, Treitler told us what he missed most. Ducks.

"Louisiana was *ducks*. Ducks, ducks, and more ducks. It was like the buffalo on the plains. Only we still had our ducks a century after the buffalo were gone. I killed thousands and I'm ashamed of it. But we had millions and millions and *millions*. What I think now is, no one should be allowed to hunt ducks. The whole season ought to be shut down. You get caught with a few ducks, you go to the penitentiary. For *years*. That's what a former outlaw believes. But forty years ago, you wouldn't have dreamed you'd ever say some such thing. We had so *many*. They talk about the duck famine in the thirties, all the over-hunting and all, the drought . . . I tell you what: I was old enough to see the tail end of that duck famine, and my daddy was a market hunter, and what we had then compared to now . . . we're talkin about different *planets*."

"How many now compared to forty years ago?"

". . . Ten percent."

"Compared to ten years ago?"

"Half."

"All because the marsh is going?"

"Mainly. I'm sure of that. They're losing habitat in Canada, they're losing habitat up north, maybe there're still some overlimiters—down here, though, the commercial outlawing days are over, that is a *fact*. I was one of the last and guiltiest. No, it's got to be losing these marshes more than anything else."

"Salt water comes in, duck food disappears," said Dave Hall. "They diked a little piece of marsh north of here to keep salt water out and it's full of ducks. All around it there's hardly any. You couldn't ask for a better Exhibit A."

"These marshes have been like a dike against the weather," Treitler said. "Billions and billions of dollars couldn't buy you better protection than we had from thirty or forty miles of marsh out there. The marshes were like a dike that produced food. Now they got to build dikes to protect a few pieces of marsh."

Dave Hall suddenly had a seizure of rage.

"EVERY MOTHERFUCKER WHO HAD ANYTHING TO DO WITH THAT GULF OUT-LET CANAL SHOULD JUST BE LINED UP AND . . ."

I believe he meant it.

Dave Hall slowly changed pigmentation, from maroon back to white—he is out-of-doors a lot, but is tanned only from his elbows to his knuckles—and then went to sleep. He awoke at intervals, barely managing to pry open an eyelid, as Treitler and I kept talking. After about an hour, Treitler wanted us to stay and eat "a real supper" with him. He is a lonely man—his wife and children left him because he refuses to do something else for a living. Because he refuses, as he put it with acid disdain, to move "up the road" toward New Orleans. But Dave Hall said he had to go back to his office and then get up early to drive most of the way across the state.

In the car, on our way back to what may be the first great coastal city doomed to disappear, he said something like this:

"Our problem in this modern world is total estrangement from nature. In them urban ghettos, where some people don't even know what a tree looks like . . . how could you expect that there wouldn't be killings and looting and drugs? These Cajun people have some of the best character in the world because they live right with Mother Nature. Where the hell do people think Cajun culture came from? It didn't grow up on Bourbon Street. You take away nature, you lose the culture. It's the same all over the world. The indigenous cultures we got left can't survive without nature and wildlife. Cajun culture is about the only one we got in this country, other than the Indians and Eskimos, and they're hurtin bad, I don't know how long those cultures can survive all the goddamned insidiousness that our culture does to them. We've got to preserve the resource that the culture's based on. Otherwise we lose both. That's true here as much as it is in the Amazon basin. What does this country lose when a man like Dennis Treitler has to move up the road and bake doughnuts for a living? What do all those people crammed along the Eastern Seaboard lose when the waterfowl habitat's all gone and they can't sit on their lawn at night and listen to them honkers go overhead? Those ducks and geese mean there's some wilderness left *some*where. There's a little piece of the planet left that we haven't messed up. Man, people try to put a dollar sign on it all. 'Well, this marsh produces so and so many ducks, and that means so and so much from license fees, and it means so and so many hunters stop and buy gas and coffee and doughnuts. . . . It's all true, but those arguments are *bullshit*. It's like a disease. We got so little left. We should save it *all*. All this calculatin and figurin and this-is-worth-what-compared-to-that . . . Goddammit. God-damn it. . . .

"Poor old Dennis. He's a stubborn cuss. His wife left him because he wouldn't leave his marsh. I can understand how he feels. A lot of us game wardens have run into the same trouble with our wives. They call themselves game warden widows and say we got to choose between them or the job. We've lost some dedicated agents that way. They might not have left, but they weren't as dedicated as they used to be. I wish our women would *appreciate* what we do a little more. All they think of is home and hearth. Meanwhile we're bustin our ass just to make a little dent in the problem. Man, I'm glad Sarah never said anything like that to me. On the whole, she's been pretty understanding. If it had ever come down to 'me or the job,' I don't know what I would have done. I might have told her to hit the road."

Dave Hall dropped me at a shopping center up by Chalmette, where I had left my car. I told him that this had probably been my last trip to Louisiana. "Well, I hope you got what you need," he said. He seemed so far away by then that somehow it didn't seem quite proper to shake hands. The world stood between us. He drove off without either one of us having said goodbye.